MW00559834

Praise for Ca
Incense: Crafting & Use of Magickal Scents

"Anyone who enjoys incense will appreciate the dozens of recipes for creating blends for every occasion."

—MidwestBookReview.com

"As an herbalist, craftsperson, and teacher myself, I find this book essential... The incense recipes are fantastic... They also are imbued with a sense of enlightenment not found in ordinary, factory-made blends. I highly recommend the book and will sell it at my own store."

—*New Age Retailer*

"Mr. Neal might be considered a gourmet incense maker... I recommend this book."

—Anna M. Helvie, priestess and minister,
Eternal Harvest Church and Tradition of Wicca

"Impressive... This book has the 'smell' of a how-to classic."

—*The Cauldron:* A Pagan Forum, eCauldron.com

"The most detailed, helpful, and clearly written guide to making and using incense I have ever encountered. It's sure to be the classic textbook!"

—PaganInstitute.org

"The author speaks directly to the reader... leading you on a path of discovery with incense that you'll never forget."

—*New Moon Newsletter,* United Kingdom

"An excellent book for those with an [interest] in incense making... It's a breath of fresh air."

—SpiralNature.com

"Every page of this book is filled with great information ... Mr. Neal has written an easy-to-follow instruction book that inspired me to gather my supplies up and start making my own incense!"

—*Elements Magazine*

"I cannot imagine anything about the making or use of incense in a magickal capacity that is not covered in these pages ... 5 pentacles out of 5."

—TheDivaDigest.com

"An extraordinarily lovely book to have on your shelf. A must-have for those with an interest in scent and spell crafting through the element of air ... [and] for any crafty Paganite."

—SpiritQuill.com

Incense Magick

About the Author

Carl Neal has been a student of incense since 1977. In 1995 he became a professional incense maker and has avidly researched incense ever since. He eventually set aside his retail incense business and focused on bringing an expanded awareness of incense to everyone who would read or listen. Networking with incense makers and users from around the world has given him a very different view of incense. Carl is a self-professed incense fanatic who has been lucky enough to learn from a variety of incense makers from North and South America, Asia, and Europe. He has traveled across America to lead incense making workshops and discussions and has been a frequent guest at Pagan festivals and gatherings, where he spreads his enthusiasm for incense with vigor. Carl holds bachelor degrees in History and Sociology.

To Write to the Author

If you wish to contact the author or would like more information about this book, please write to the author in care of Llewellyn Worldwide, and we will forward your request. Both the author and publisher appreciate hearing from you and learning of your enjoyment of this book and how it has helped you. Llewellyn Worldwide cannot guarantee that every letter written to the author can be answered, but all will be forwarded. Please write to:

Carl F. Neal
℅ Llewellyn Worldwide
2143 Wooddale Drive
Woodbury, MN 55125-2989

Please enclose a self-addressed stamped envelope for reply,
or $1.00 to cover costs. If outside the USA, enclose
an international postal reply coupon.

Many of Llewellyn's authors have websites with additional information and resources. For more information, please visit our website at http://www.llewellyn.com.

Incense Magick

Create Inspiring Aromatic Experiences for Your Craft

Carl F. Neal

Llewellyn Publications
Woodbury, Minnesota

FIRST EDITION
Third Printing, 2021

Book design by Bob Gaul
Cover art © Pinci/Shutterstock Images
Cover design by Adrienne Zimiga
Editing by Nicole Edman
Interior illustrations by Wen Hsu

Llewellyn is a registered trademark of Llewellyn Worldwide Ltd.

Library of Congress Cataloging-in-Publication Data
Neal, Carl F., 1965–
  Incense magick: create inspiring aromatic experiences for your craft/Carl F. Neal.—1st ed.
      p. cm.
  Includes bibliographical references and index.
  ISBN 978-0-7387-1974-0
  1. Magic. 2. Incense. I. Title.
  BF1623.I52N44 2012
  133.4'4—dc23
                              2011034471

Llewellyn Publications
A Division of Llewellyn Worldwide Ltd.
2143 Wooddale Drive
Woodbury, MN 55125-2989
www.llewellyn.com

Printed in the United States of America

For Michelle Lee—
This book would not exist without you.
Nor would I.

Contents

Acknowledgments

There are a lot of people who deserve great thanks for the completion of this book. First and foremost is my best friend, Michelle Hawkins. If it weren't for her constant reminders, verification that I'd been writing, and her basic drive and energy, this book would never have been finished. I also want to thank Paul Orion Crews, Phillip Crews, Charles Rackley, Cara White, and Kevin Stucker for tolerating the ups and downs of living with a writer at some point during a four-year project.

I also want to extend my thanks to Annette Hinshaw for helping me find my feet on my Pagan path many years ago. She may be on the other side of the Veil, but she is never far from my mind. I likewise want to thank her son, Mike Hinshaw, for walking along that path with me for these past decades as well as sharing his wisdom about ambergris. My deep thanks to Michelle Mays for her beautiful songs and her support as my friend. Her music has soothed me and opened my mind to inspiration throughout the writing process. Thanks as well to the thousands of people who have attended my incense workshops at Pagan gatherings and meetings around the country. I have learned something new in every workshop!

I want to acknowledge the help of many people in the incense world. People who have challenged me over the years have helped me a great deal by forcing me to re-examine my views and double-check my research. First on that list would be David Oller. I appreciate the year he spent sharing his wisdom and insight about Japanese incense. This truly helped to point me toward natural incense and opened my eyes to a whole new world of aromatics and ingredients, as well as the potential hazards of synthetics. I want to thank Ande Spenser, Mark Ambrose, Chrissie Wildwood, and Katlyn Breene for your knowledge, feedback, ideas, innovations, and unflagging interest. I also want to thank all the members of my online group, "The Incense Exchange" (http://groups.yahoo.com/group/incense_exchange/), for the ideas and knowledge that you so freely share, the great incense swaps, and the support when things weren't going so well.

Likewise I want to extend my deepest thanks to everyone at Shoyeido Corporation in general and Randi Smith in particular. You have helped me to learn and grow even further in my knowledge of Japanese incense and I honestly don't know that I would have been able to write this book without my massive supply of White Cloud incense and scentless charcoal.

Finally I want to thank all of the readers of my first two books who have provided me with feedback and ideas for what they would like to see in a future incense book. I've tried to keep all of your ideas in mind although time and space limitations have kept me from including everything I would have liked. My thanks to you, too, dear reader. Thank you for taking the time to pick up this book. I hope you enjoy reading it as much as I enjoyed writing it.

Introduction

Incense is an amazing experience. Seems like a strange way to think of incense, doesn't it? We most often think of incense as an object that can be held in our hands, but incense can't really be enjoyed in your hands. In order for incense to release its gift of scent, it requires not only the physical incense but also the ephemeral power of fire. The pleasure of incense requires both of those elements plus someone to experience the resulting scent. So perhaps incense isn't merely an object or an item; it's actually a process—an experience. Incense is as ancient as the use of fire. It has long been a part of human culture and should never be seen as insignificant or secondary. It ties us to our ancestors and to the Earth herself.

The Joy of Incense

Properly used, incense truly is a joy. There are many reasons for this, but one of the primary reasons is purely biological. Most of the human senses go through a series of relays that connect the "sensor" (such as your eye) to your brain. Unlike the other four senses, your nose is connected directly to your brain without the delay or interference of these biological "relays." It is believed by many scientists that the sense of smell is the most ancient of all our senses.

As a result, scent is possibly the most powerful sense. Although scent is an often-neglected sense, its impact on humans and most other animals is dramatic. Have you ever walked into a bakery, encountered the overwhelming scent of cinnamon and butter, and been instantly transported back in time to your mother's or grandmother's kitchen? Scent is the strongest sense tied to memory (although not everyone agrees on this point), likely because of this direct connection to the brain. Different incense can transport you to the ocean, the deep forest, Asia, America, Ancient Egypt, or back to your own childhood.

Because of the power of scent, incense is a moving experience. It can deepen meditation or transport you through time and space. I also like to think of incense as a way to redecorate a space with the flick of a match. It isn't practical to change your furniture every few hours or to repaint your room every day, but you can easily make a dramatic change to any room simply by lighting a stick of incense. It's simple, fast, and (in most cases) quite inexpensive.

The Magick of Incense

Beyond the uses I've already discussed, incense is also a powerful tool for self-change and magick. While this doesn't apply to synthetic incense, natural incense is a physical representation of the elements. Natural incense contains a variety of materials grown from the earth. It requires the power of air and water to grow and gain power. The power of fire comes into materials through many days of sunshine but deeply impacts incense when it is finally lit; fire then becomes the agent that releases all of the power the materials have accumulated.

Regardless of what type of magick or ritual you practice, incense is a powerful tool. It is used to create an atmosphere that invites specific deities, magickally "marks" an area as sacred space, and can even help to shift your mindset from the mundane world to a magickal one. Above all else, incense releases magickal energy that, when properly aligned, can be a tremendous asset in any magickal working. The biggest key to the use of incense in magick is empowerment. *Empowerment* is a bit of a confusing word because it can mean several different things. It can refer to actually adding energy to incense through physical contact and visualization. You want to "align" your own energy to your goals for the incense and then transfer that energy into your incense. This is a basic power-working exercise, but it can provide amazing results. Your frame of mind alone can be all it takes to align your energy. Then use visualization and see that energy move from you into your incense. Likewise you can raise energy (in a magick circle or otherwise), align it, and move it into your incense.

Your incense also has its own energy. The other part of the empowerment equation is aligning with the energies native to your incense. This can also be accomplished through visualization. See the energy in the incense and then focus upon what results you hope to achieve through the use of that incense. Although the process is simple to explain, it can take a lot of practice to be completely effective. Incense that someone else makes can be fully empowered and aligned. Of course, you can empower incense even more effectively if you make the incense yourself. The more personally involved you are with the creation of the incense, the more effective your empowerment will be. Keep your mind focused on the goal you hope to accomplish throughout the incense making process. You can then completely align the natural energies of the botanicals with your own needs and goals.

About the Author

My interest in incense began as a child. Into early adulthood I remained a curious user of incense. In 1995 I opened a small shop and began to sell incense. I was really price-driven in those early days. I searched for the cheapest incense I could find so that I could undercut the prices of my competition. I quickly learned that this type of incense was cheap for a reason: much of it smelled like low-quality soap and was laden with synthetic oils and extenders. I found some incense that was so low quality I was ashamed to sell it to my customers. I decided that making my own incense would be a better route to my goals of profit and pride.

All I really knew about incense making was that it involved scented oils. After searching I discovered an incense wholesale supplier who also sold incense making materials. "Blank" incense and synthetic oils were combined to make my own somewhat-better but still-synthetic incense. This incense was an instant hit with my customers when they discovered that I had made it. I began to pursue books on the topic of incense making only to discover they were very rare. I found a few books with some very limited—and confusing—incense making instructions. After waiting a long time I was finally able to purchase a copy of *Wylundt's Book of Incense* (Weiser, 1996), a book I'd heard about but been unable to find. This book introduced me to making natural incense. I found this very appealing since I'd been walking a Pagan path for many years by then.

Not long after being introduced to making natural incense, a friend told me about an online discussion group all about Japanese incense. I've always loved discussion groups, and the thought of joining a group that focused on a topic I knew so little about was very appealing. My role (by this time) as not only maker of synthetic incense but wholesaler of synthetic supplies put me in a tough position with this group. It took several hours of phone discussion to even be granted permission to join, but eventually the permission was given. I am grateful to this group (Alice's

Restaurant) and its founder (David Oller) for dragging me—sometimes kicking and screaming—into the world of purely natural incense and the beautiful incense traditions of Asia. After months of discussions with the kind people on that list, I decided to stop selling synthetic incense and the materials to make it. It was a tough decision that required me to sacrifice one of the most successful parts of my business, but to this day I feel it was the right move. I would like to extend my thanks to all the members of the list back in those days. Sometimes with charm, and sometimes with brute force, they opened my eyes to whole new realms of incense and incense use.

During this time I also launched my own discussion group that now includes more than five hundred incense makers from all around the world (The Incense Exchange). They continue to educate and intrigue me with new information about incense, its use, and its creation. Incense makers from around the United States and Europe have found the Internet to be a great way to learn from and share with incense makers in India, China, Nepal, Thailand, and Japan. No matter how much I study the topic, there is so much knowledge to share that I am always amazed by what these other incense makers and users teach me.

By this point in my life, I had transitioned my business and I was selling more natural incense, making natural incense to sell, and selling natural ingredients. I had written a small booklet about incense making ("Roll Your Own: Incense Making for Beginners") that introduced the ideas of natural incense making but really focused on synthetic incense. After I moved away from synthetics, I replaced that booklet with a new one ("Incense Making 101"), which focused on natural incense. The success of those booklets and the encouragement of aromatherapy author Chrissie Wildwood led me to publish my first book. Released in the fall of 2003, *Incense: Crafting & Use of Magick Scents* was published by Llewellyn and introduced many of the basic concepts of incense making. I have lectured and given workshops all around the country on incense making during the last fifteen years and have been fortunate enough to meet lots of incense lovers.

One thing that the people at my workshops consistently told me was that while they love making incense, they were more interested in the uses, both mundane and magickal, for the many types of incense that can be purchased. That is how this book came to be. Although my second book, *The Magick Toolbox* (Red Wheel/Weiser, 2004), had a short section on purchasing and using incense, I wanted to create a more comprehensive guide to the world of incense use. A book filled with traditional and novel ways to use incense was my ultimate goal. I hope that I have accomplished that and that you enjoy reading this book as much as I have enjoyed writing it.

As in my other books, the rituals and spells in this book are created in a general form. They can certainly be used exactly as written, but I have omitted as much tradition-specific information as possible. Before using these rituals, I would urge you to personalize them. Add elements that make the ritual part of your path, such as deity names, your own name and the names of those you love, incense that identifies strongly with your path (like myrrh if Isis is your patron goddess), or specific language or terms that you normally use in your rituals. I have also tried to include rituals that are easily adapted for those of us who follow a non-Wiccan path. Wicca is a wonderful religion in its own right and is growing rapidly in the twenty-first century, but I wanted to include the large number of non-Wiccan Pagans who are equal members of the Pagan/Heathen community. I hope that these rituals demonstrate just how similar we are.

If you have questions or comments, you are welcome to visit my website: www.incensebooks.com.

Part One

All About Incense

1

Background

The original users of incense are lost in the mists of time, but it is safe to assume that ancient humans knew about the power and joy of incense. Excavations of ancient settlements of many cultures show evidence of incense burning, including some incredible censers. The use of incense likely dates back to shortly after humans learned to make fire. From the most practical to the most sacred of applications, incense has long been a tool for mankind.

Cultural Adaptations of Incense

There have been a wide variety of uses for incense in different places and different times, but they fit into four basic categories. The needs, both sociological and physiological, of cultures along with the materials available to them often determine what form of incense was used and the purposes behind it. Incense "technology" in different cultures also influences that society's incense use.

Fumigation: This is possibly the oldest use of incense. At various points in history, unpleasant smells have been associated with evil spirits, disease, and other maladies. Beyond that are the unpleasant odors in civilizations that don't embrace or enjoy sanitation technology. Imagine a city where the time between bathing was measured in months or a society that believed bathing was unhealthy. Then imagine having a large meeting of the people in a small area. The smells of body odor combined with living more closely with animals and a lack of sewers would make for abundant foul odors.

Incense was an early form of fumigation. Large bundles of herbs could be used as extra-large smudge bundles. Undesired smells—and thus the ills associated with them—could be swept away in a cloud of incense. While you can protect the air going into your nose with a scented handkerchief, burning incense can banish undesired smells from an entire room. It is easy to imagine using incense for this purpose at religious ceremonies and other large gatherings.

Aromatics were used in a variety of ways to eliminate foul odors, which were often associated with illness. Herbs were strewn on floors, dried herb bundles were hung in homes, and aromatics were burned. The idea that bad smells are a source of illness remains popular today in parts of Europe. Fire was also a moderately effective way to destroy (or at least relocate) insects. Few insects will tolerate any kind of smoke and some herbs (such as pennyroyal) are particularly suited to that role.

Sacrifice: In some cultures today, animal sacrifice is a part of society. Such practices were even more widespread in the ancient world. For those who made burnt animal offerings, the benefits of incense were very practical. Many ancient cultures added fragrant materials to their sacrificial fires to help with an often overwhelming smell of burnt flesh. Keep in mind that burning animal sacrifices is not like grilling meat in your back yard; hot fires and whole animals make for an overwhelming stench.

Incense itself can also be a sacrifice. Procurement of aromatic materials and then simply burning them to ashes is a gift in its own right. The combination of the initial sacrifice with the addition of incense increases the level of sacrifice and the power of the offering. This eventually led to the burning of incense alone, which is arguably a more pleasant offer to make.

Cleansing or Purifying: Much as with fumigation, magickal "cleansing" is intended to drive away undesired energies. Smoke penetrates even the tiniest openings and can displace the undesired energies that reside within. Many ritual implements are purified in fragrant smoke before being used. This process can also energize tools or be used to cleanse spaces. Many traditions instruct followers to cleanse ritual spaces before a magickal invocation, and incense is a favored tool for the job.

The smoke of incense has also long been associated with speaking to the greater powers of the universe. This could be in the form of a prayer, an incantation, or even a wish. Smoke is believed to carry our words back into the universe. Much like a magick candle, incense can be magickally aligned to your intentions and lit, and then your intentions will continue to flow into the universe until the incense is exhausted. In Asia, some Buddhist temples sell massive incense coils that are hoisted with ropes, lit with a blow torch, and burn for an entire month. For every second the coil is burning, the prayer offered (for the benefactor who purchased the coil) continues to flow out into the ether.

Divination: Divination is the art of seeing the unseen and catching a glimpse of what could be. While tarot is one of the most popular forms of divination in modern Paganry, incense divination is as ancient as any other incense use. Incan priests used incense mixed with their own blood to seek divine guidance. Taking precious materials, including your own blood, and sacrificing them by burning brought forth smoke that would dance and reveal what should be done.

Pleasure: At some point, the pure pleasure of incense became a motivation to use it. Ours is not the first culture to understand the joy of incense purely for itself. Considering the quantity of frankincense consumed in ancient Rome, it is easy to imagine ancient aficionados showing off their latest incense purchase to their friends. In fact, the use of incense in some societies was also a demonstration of wealth.

Europe

In modern times, we don't think of Europe as producing incense-loving cultures, but this was not always the case. The incense traditions of Europe are often forgotten, since Europe faced a change that did not come to Asia, which essentially removed incense from large sectors of the populous. Nonetheless, Europe's incense-loving roots are there if you know where to look.

Rome

Perhaps the culture that consumed more incense per capita than any other, ancient Rome was a hub of Western civilization for many generations. And it was a city fueled by incense. Incense—primarily frankincense but others as well—burned night and day in many places in the Roman Empire. Rome's massive drive to acquire more and more incense fueled a whole new sector of the economy and subsidized other empires.

The Roman economy was massive. Goods flowed into Rome from all corners of the known world and back out to every corner of the far-flung empire. In the city of Rome itself, incense was burned in prodigious amounts at temples, shops, and homes. This deep association between

Rome's polytheistic history and incense would later come back to haunt Europe and ultimately derail incense evolution in the West.

Christian Europe

When the Pagan Roman Empire converted to Christianity, the association between incense and non-Christian religion led to the steady decline of incense use in Europe. Christian tradition maintains that one way in which early Christians were persecuted in the Roman Empire was by forcing Christians to offer incense to the Roman gods. Any who refused were put to death. As a result, many branches of Christianity later turned their backs on this seeming-Pagan tool of worship.

Eventually only the Roman Catholic and Eastern Orthodox Christian churches kept a few incense traditions alive with the use of thuribles and the burning of frankincense and holy blends. The Roman Catholic Church in particular spurred a reintroduction of incense into various cultures as it spread around the world. Use of incense in those churches continues today. In an ironic twist, some branches of the Christian church ended up being the keepers of Pagan Roman incense use they tried to abolish. Ancient Jewish incense rituals still exist in modern times as well, although they are not widely known.

Africa

While Africa isn't commonly associated with incense in the modern world, it continues to play an important role in the incense trade. In ancient times Africa was at the heart of the incense trade. Empires whose names have passed from the collective memories of the West once grew fat on their profits from the incense trade.

Egypt

Egypt was both a producer and consumer of incense. Egypt is the home to a great mystery of the incense world: kyphi. Kyphi is one of the most ancient incense formulas we now possess. The only problem is that we can't read it. Well, it *can* be read, but there is a great deal of controversy about which plants are referred to in the recipe. You will find a number of incense merchants selling "authentic" kyphi incense, but in truth nobody is certain what ingredients belonged in the ancient version. The great thing is that all of the various "authentic" kyphi incense on the market that I have tried have a nice scent.

Egyptian incense traditions were extensive. Gum mastic, labdanum, benzoin, and many other ingredients were combined with priestly ritual. Much as it would centuries later in Japan, incense making grew to become a great, and competitive, art form in Egypt. The best incense makers were held in very high esteem.

Many incense making materials served multiple purposes in ancient Egypt. Many of the same resins used in incense were used in the mummification process. As a result, these materials were held in the highest reverence and commanded high prices. Egypt was another major source of the revenue from the incense trade. Massive quantities of aromatic materials were imported into and exported from ancient Egypt. You can just imagine ancient Egyptian monuments when they were new, standing in a drifting cloud of sweet myrrh.

The Spice-Trading Empires

Many empires in Africa were built on the profits from frankincense, myrrh, acacia, yohimbe, balsams, and other aromatics that traveled north toward Egypt and the Mediterranean for trade. The regions that stood between the aromatics and their ultimate destinations often charged high duties, taxes, and fees to those transporting them. This custom created some kingdoms simply because of geographic convenience.

Many readers will have heard of the Silk Road but it truly could have been called the Incense Road. Huge caravans carried aromatics from the Far East and Africa to the throngs of incense users in the Roman Empire and beyond. Although the charges were excessive to those who took that long trek along the Incense Road, the profits were still tremendous. The merchants were willing to risk taxes, bandits, blazing heat, freezing cold, and hostile governments to deliver their goods so you can imagine how alluring the profits truly had to be.

Those who lived along the road (which was actually a network of roads reaching far beyond the Mediterranean into Asia and Africa) made profit from the merchants. Not only were there fees and taxes, but the merchants needed provisions, equipment, and more on their long journeys, and the locals in the area supplied much of those needs.

Among the great cities in the incense trading empires was Ubar. Located in the southeastern corner of the Arabian Peninsula, Ubar was a city built by incense in the land of Nod. This site has only recently been identified and researched. A most entertaining book entitled *The Road to Ubar* details the discovery of this previously legendary city. Lying along the Incense Road, Ubar was a city built on the riches of incense expeditions. This discovery has led to a renewed interest in the Incense Road and ancient incense practices. Historians have found strong connections between the incense trade and economic conditions in the region, which suggests that incense was a significant source of income.

The Incense Road is also called the Spice Road. Many aromatics were sold for perfuming and as culinary spices. Even today, many of the spices that we enjoy tasting are the same ones we enjoy smelling in the form of incense, perfume, and more. Information about the balance of botanicals carried for culinary purposes versus aromatic purposes is scant at best. Nevertheless, the West seemingly could not get enough of botanicals from distant lands. It also demonstrates that there was wealth enough in the West to afford such luxury items in a time when even salt was a precious commodity.

You will see that I use the term *masala* for incense sticks with a wooden stick in the center to support the incense stick. This is a very common type of incense that is popular in both the East and West. The word *masala* literally means "spice" in the lands of India. The word being used to refer to both incense and spice shows how deeply the two are connected.

Remnants Today

One surprising aspect of the ancient incense empires is that they are still producing incense in the twenty-first century. Modern consumers of natural incense still burn resins imported from the same regions they originated from in ancient times. The aromatics are widely used in the region, but these areas still produce great surpluses. However, the resins that were once so highly valued that entire families and kingdoms thrived on the wealth from exporting them are worth much less today. In the modern world, a pound of high-quality frankincense costs less than most Americans earn in one hour of work.

Still, incense traditions linger in the aromatic-producing areas of Africa. Not only is incense used for its scent, it is still used as a method for keeping time in some parts of Africa. These timekeepers are conceptually the same as Asian incense clocks. While certainly not as accurate as a digital watch, the fact that incense has been used continuously for thousands of years demonstrates its status as a useful tool.

India

One of the most widely used aromatics in the world, sandalwood, was once abundant in India and was one of its most famous exports. Many other important aromatics that are still widely used in incense also emerged from this fragrant land. Benzoin and dammar resins are potent aromatics with scents that are deep and mysterious. Vetiver, patchouli, and dragon's blood all hail from India as well. Even today the marketplaces in India are filled with exotic botanicals that are the stuff of incense makers' dreams. In the modern world we have access to even more aromatics than were available to previous generations, but one could easily spend a lifetime in India learning of new botanicals and new incense making methods.

India is currently a major producer of incense, but sadly the bulk of its market is built on low-quality incense filled with synthetic ingredients. There are still those in India who produce incense in the wonderful traditional fashion, but in an effort to capture uneducated consumers with lower prices, the present incense industry on the whole does not represent the glory of the Indian incense tradition.

Asia

Throughout Asia and the other lands they so strongly influenced, aromatic materials were sought and used in incense. While I can only brush upon a few highlights here, the incense traditions of Asia could be the study of your entire life and you'd never learn it all. Innovation and experimentation with respect for tradition characterizes the various incense cultures of Asia past and present.

Incense Pellet

This ungracious term describes a type of incense rarely seen in America. The incense pellet is in a category that I call "moist incense" and is believed to be an outgrowth of Asian medical practices. We all know that some medications are quite foul tasting, and this was just as true in an Asian medical culture that was steeped in herbal medications. As a result, Asian healers began mixing the distasteful ingredients with honey, jam, fruit, and other foods and spices to disguise the bad taste at some time in the distant past. A mixture was made in the proper proportions and then rolled into pea-sized balls small enough to swallow. Somewhere along the way, this approach was adopted into incense making traditions. Small balls of incense are made using honey or similar materials to help the balls hold their shape. Once cured and added to a hot coal, the incense pellet gives off an intense, mysterious scent that is difficult to achieve with any other form of incense.

Incense Clocks

Numerous cultures have experimented with using incense as timekeeping devices, but nowhere did this process become more sophisticated than in Asia. In the centuries before reliable mechanical clocks, many devices were used to tell time, including candles, water clocks, and incense. This has ranged from the simple process of waiting for an incense stick to completely burn, to incense trails where the scent changed as a form of alarm, to sophisticated clocks that even used bells to mark time audibly. A bell would be tied to the incense stick with a thin thread; when the incense burned through the thread, the bell would drop with a loud clang. This is useful knowledge for those of us who use incense as part of formal spells or rituals, as these setups can allow us to use incense to time particular parts of our rituals—how long to chant, when to move to the next phase, etc. As late as the twentieth century, incense was used to time a visit with a Japanese Geisha. As mentioned earlier, incense is still used as a timekeeping device in parts of Africa.

China

With the creation of the Han Empire around 200 BCE, the modern region we call China was founded (although it took its name from the later Chin dynasty). What grew to be the massive nation of modern China took centuries to unite. It was already a true empire when contact was first made with the West and arguably remains so until this very day. Still, much of the knowledge of Chinese incense making remains a guarded secret. There was a time in Chinese history, during the age of empires, when contact with Westerners was limited to conducting trade and nothing more. While Westerners could enjoy China's amazing scent, the inner secrets of those scents remained hidden. Even after the end of the nineteenth-century Opium War, when greater contact with the West was created through a terrible set of maneuvers by various European powers, incense continued to be a novelty to the Europeans while it was treasured by the Chinese.

While China's exported incense industry has fallen victim to the same forces that drive the modern incense making industry in India, high quality incense is still produced and consumed there. Thanks in great part to Buddhist practices, the art of fine incense making continues throughout China. Alongside greater trade with China has also come greater availability to Chinese botanicals. Even in the twenty-first century there is only limited access to truly high-quality Chinese incense; perhaps one day an enterprising individual will begin importing high-end Chinese incense.

Due to its vast growth throughout history, China had much the same effect on its continent as Rome did in Europe. Disparate peoples eventually became linked by Imperial roads and trade routes. This led to the exchange of many different goods from greatly distant places. One of the keys to the creation of incredible and unique incense is availability to a wide variety of materials, and China has had that type of access for more than a thousand years.

Tibet

The dangerous mountains of Tibet might seem like an unlikely place to find masters of incense making, but from the mountain tops to the valley floors, Tibet has long been known as one of the primary producers of natural incense. Much of the incense of Tibet is characterized by deep, heavy, earthy scents. The richness of Tibetan incense comes from incense often made in small batches by hand in small villages. Projects are underway to use incense to bring a measure of financial assistance to poverty-stricken villages in Tibet. Sadly there are also some low-quality incense mass produced in Tibet, so read labels carefully and use all of the information in this book to help guide you to the best that Tibet has to offer. Costus, galangal, juniper, and many other aromatics blend together to make the unique incense of Tibet worth the effort to locate. The finest frankincense sticks I have ever burned came from this land shrouded in the clouds.

Japan

In the last 750 years Japan has arguably become the center of the incense universe. There was a time when a gentleman in Japan was judged not only by his prowess in the arts of war but also by the arts of flower arranging, poetry, and incense making. Creating personal incense blends was very common in feudal Japan with the intent to create a unique fragrance as a type of olfactory signature.

The art of incense making and incense enjoyment reached its current zenith in the incense world in Japan. The oldest incense making companies in the world are in Japan, with many of them using recipes developed within their companies hundreds of years ago. Several Japanese incense companies are older than the entire United States! The center of the incense making universe is—in my opinion—in Kyoto, Japan.

The kodo ceremony encapsulates the most advanced classification system ever devised for an incense ingredient (aloeswood). Kodo will be discussed further in chapter 9. Incense makers apprentice for decades before being allowed to create their precious blends, attesting to the supremacy of the art of incense found in Japan. Japan is also home to the only major incense producer (that I am aware of) that actually lists ingredients of their incense: Shoyeido. From dissimilar ingredients as star anise, cloves, cinnamon, and kyara, Japanese incense masters create blends that can transport us to worlds never before imagined. It is my life's dream to one day visit Kyoto and experience firsthand the magick created there.

America

When most people think of incense, the New World rarely springs to mind, yet the Americas have valuable incense traditions that are more widely practiced than one might at first think. Remember that Europeans first visited the Americas in part in search for a shorter route to India for its rare spices, fabrics, and other goods for trade. I imagine none of the early explorers paid much attention to the aromatic treasures all around them in the Americas.

North America

North America has its own native incense traditions that, much to our good fortune, were not destroyed by Europeans' attempts to "civilize" the Native Americans through forced cultural changes, theft, disease, deceit, and the offering of "salvation." Wonderful North American aromatics such as sweet grass, white sage, desert sage, piñon, western cedar, and more are still available. The modern Neopagan and New Age cleansing practice of "smudge bundling" is the direct legacy of Native American incense traditions. Any who have performed cleansing with a sage bundle know firsthand the incredible power in that herb and the wisdom of the Native Americans who first put it to use.

Central and South America

The Latinized nations of the Americas also have proud incense traditions whose origins are lost in the mists of time. From Aztecs to Mayans to Olmecs, the pre-Columbian civilizations had powerful incense customs and botanicals. Damiana, copal, tonka beans, palo santo, and more come to use from these regions. Incan priests would mix aromatics with blood, some taken directly from the scrotum, and burn the incense mixture while asking the gods for guidance.

I had the great privilege of touring a pre-Columbian exhibition a few years ago. Although all of the information and artifacts were amazing to view, I was naturally drawn to a display of ritual tools. While the energies of the artifacts made it clear that they were from different origins and separated by many years in their use, the display was still nearly overwhelming. In particular I was drawn to the ancient censers. It was very moving to stand inches from a censer that was once used in rituals that guided an empire. It was begging to be used again, so it was difficult to keep my hands to myself! However, I didn't think the curators would share my enthusiasm to burn some palo santo and copal in their archeological treasure.

————

Clearly this chapter is not intended to be a comprehensive history of incense use in the world—that alone would fill one or more books. Instead I want to introduce the sweeping worldwide inclusion of incense into life. It is easy to look at a single culture as the progenitor of incense, but in reality, incense has been a part of many societies on every settled continent. I hope that reading this information will encourage you to read more about the topic. You will find several interesting books in the bibliography to guide you in this discovery.

Synthetic versus Natural Incense

There is an important distinction between two basic ways of making incense: synthetic and natural. Synthetic incense is made using artificial scents (often petroleum by-products) that are laboratory versions of natural ingredients. On the other hand, we have incense made using only natural products. There are a few brands of commercial incense that are combinations of natural and synthetic, but those are very rare. Although both types of incense have their uses, it is critical to understand the differences between them.

Synthetic Incense

This is by far the most common type of commercial incense sold in the world. Even in Japan—the country best known for high-quality incense—synthetic incense is the type most frequently used. Synthetic incense can come in any form. Cones, sticks, coils, and even loose incense are commonly scented with synthetic fragrance oils.

Most synthetic incense shares certain drawbacks. First, some brands of synthetic incense are simply waste wood powder that is combined with a binder (a type of glue) with the resulting sticks or cones soaked in synthetic fragrance oils. The wood used in the powder might be sawdust from a manufacturing plant—sometimes the wood powder actually comes from the manufacturing of plywood. It could be a waste product from any number of commercial applications. As a result, the wood might have been treated with chemicals or could contain large quantities of powerful glues. I don't want to imply that all synthetic incense uses such low-quality wood powder, but unfortunately there is no way to know simply by looking at an incense package.

The synthetic fragrance oils themselves can also represent some problems. These scents are created in laboratories in an effort to reproduce natural scents at a substantially lower cost than the natural version. This is done through chemical analysis of a natural scent. When natural scents are analyzed, there are many chemical components that might not appear to contribute directly to the scent. Chemical engineers will look at the analysis of the scent and then begin to experiment to see if they can replicate it. They will do so using the simplest chemical method possible. As a result, some components of the scent might be deemed "unnecessary" to the effort to fool the nose. Generally speaking, synthetic fragrances are rarely chemical duplicates of the original. They are "just enough" of the chemical composition to mislead the rather dull human nose. (Well, usually they are just enough—I'm sure we've all encountered incense that was labeled "apple" but actually smelled like a burning house.) The bottom line is that synthetics do not truly represent their natural counterparts. At best they are a simulation of nature. At worst they are a pathetic imitation that smells nothing like the original, natural scent.

Some fragrance oils are not formulated with burning in mind. They might be created to scent soaps, body lotions, or other non-combustible products. As a result their designers never considered the health impacts of burning the chemicals involved, so you truly have no idea what the ultimate result could be.

Furthermore there is the issue of so-called "extenders." An extender is another synthetic oil with little or no scent of its own. Extenders cost far less than scented oils, so many synthetic incense makers use them to "step on" or dilute the more expensive scented oils. This allows incense makers to lower their costs by stretching the scented oils. Without an extender, a pound of scented oil might only make 500 sticks or cones of incense. With the extender, the same amount of oil could make 1,000 or even 1,500 sticks or cones. This does dilute the scent somewhat, but synthetic oils are usually so strong that the incense still has a powerful scent. Aside from the obvious ethical question of diluting oils to lower the cost (although the retail price usually stays the same), there is also a question of safety. The chemicals used as extenders have, to the best of my knowledge, never been tested in any laboratory anywhere for their safety in incense. Most extenders are actually meant to be used in products that are not burned (such as soaps and household cleaners). Dipropylene glycol (also called DPG) is the most commonly used extender.

This is a great point of contention among some incense makers, but both my personal and professional experiences have shown me many shortcomings of extenders. Although I have gotten a few nasty letters from several readers disputing my sentiments on this issue, I stand by my belief that this chemical is dangerous when used in combustible materials. The MSDS (material safety data sheet) for DPG states that it releases poisonous gas when burned! If that doesn't clearly demonstrate its possible hazards, I don't know what would. Some incense makers are so addicted to the extra few cents of profit they get from using these extenders that they resent my mentioning this to customers. I have gotten hate letters demanding that I prove the dangers of DPG in a full-blown university study. My response to this is that the manufacturers themselves do not endorse the use of DPG in incense and the MSDS warns not to burn the material. Therefore a university study would have to be done in order to prove that it does *not* represent any harm. Personally, I can often identify incense with DPG in it because it gives me a headache. If you believe that you are allergic to incense, it could easily be a reaction to the synthetic ingredients in the incense you've tried. In any case follow your doctor's advice on the subject.

Incense labeled "dipped" is generally made with synthetic oils, although there are a few exceptions. "Dipped" means that the incense was formed and dried as an unscented stick or cone. This "blank" incense is then soaked in fragrance oils. Some incense makers use fireworks punks (the long, smoldering sticks used to light the fireworks safely) as their "blank" incense. Aside from the drawbacks of synthetic incense I mentioned earlier, the composition of those blanks is often a cause for concern. Although I imagine there are natural blank producers out there somewhere, most blanks are of unknown composition because the manufacturers aren't required to disclose their materials; to my knowledge, none of them voluntarily provide that information. These blanks can be made from any type of wood, so the base scent is unpredictable. It is of even greater concern that some blanks are made with waste materials from the production of plywood. That type of wood powder can contain many different chemicals including all sorts of glues. The scent is unpredictable but so is the impact of the materials on those who inhale its smoke. Again, I want to make it clear that I'm not making a blanket condemnation of the incense dipping process, but one of the biggest problems with this style of incense is the lack of consumer knowledge about its content.

I know that all of this information seems to make synthetic incense appear to be a worthless product. That isn't true. There is synthetic incense that uses high-quality wood powder and only pure scented oils. It's true that the incense is not natural, but if no extenders are used, if the synthetic oils are pure and appropriate for burning, and if quality wood (or charcoal) powder is used, the incense should be perfectly safe to use. If your desire is to use this incense to cover a bad odor in your house (those of us with cats are very familiar with that problem) or car or other space, I feel it is perfectly fine to use good-quality synthetic incense.

Still, the problem is that synthetic incense is virtually never clearly labeled. I have never seen any synthetic incense that listed the purity of the oils or type of woods used, so it's very difficult for a consumer to know if the quality is high or low. There are some synthetic brands that advertise that they are free of extenders. If you can locate those, they might be your best choice for synthetics. If the incense is made in a local store or by a small company, it's unlikely you'll have access to that type of information. You may want to ask the incense maker directly before purchasing. There are several internationally known brands of synthetic incense that are certainly made of quality materials, but incense from many makers is very difficult to confirm.

Natural Incense

When it comes to the use of incense in magick or ritual, I am a very strong proponent of using natural incense only. The way I see it is that, unless you are trying to invoke the powers of synthetic chemistry, synthetic incense has no place in ritual or on any altar. Understand that the incense used in many religious ceremonies worldwide is cheap synthetic incense because of the lowered cost. It isn't that people intentionally use low-quality incense; it's merely that they haven't been educated about the differences.

My ritual spaces are scented only with natural incense. From a magickal perspective, synthetic incense contains virtually no power. Natural incense contains the energy of months or even years of sunshine, rain, and growth in the earth. Synthetic incense is made from petroleum by-products that are mass produced in giant chemical factories. It is, of course, a matter of personal choice; if a synthetic provides the results that you desire, then you should use it.

If you decide to pursue the path of natural incense, you will have to search a bit harder. There are a handful of natural incense brands distributed internationally. Companies like Shoyeido and Juniper Ridge (to name just a few) are proud of their all-natural incense lines. With a little searching you'll find other national brands and perhaps some regional or local brands as well. There are many budding makers of natural incense around the world. If you can locate one, you might get some truly original, yet natural, incense. You could even make your own incense! If you live in an area that doesn't have shops with a wide selection of incense, you can always turn to the Internet. A great deal of amazing natural incense can be found with just the click of a mouse.

One nice thing about buying natural incense is judging its quality. With synthetic incense, your nose might never be able to detect extenders or the quality of the wood. When you smell natural incense burning, your nose will be better able to determine the quality of the ingredients. The more complex the scent, the more experience is needed to judge the quality by scent alone. Nevertheless, even the most novice incense user can recognize many differences between high- and low-quality incense. Another indicator is price, which I'll discuss in detail later.

If you've never experienced natural incense before, there are some basic recommendations I can offer. Never judge natural incense by its scent in the package. Natural incense can only be judged while it is burning. Unlike scented oils, the oils in natural incense are primarily locked inside the resins, woods, and powders rolled into the stick or cone. Only burning can release those amazing scents. Smelling the package might give you a clue to the incense's aroma but doing so rarely conveys the actual scent.

When purchasing natural incense for the first time, you will find that you have to adjust from the powerful scents of synthetics. Natural incense is usually subtle, although there certainly are exceptions to this general rule. To experience these wonderfully subtle scents, you will need to spend time with them. That doesn't mean you can't enjoy natural incense at any time, but to really appreciate its beauty requires a bit of concentration.

Incense Concerns

Although incense is a wonderful and magickal experience, there are some important things that you need to consider before you jump into this amazing world. In my personal experience, the vast majority of people will never have to worry about any of these concerns. But it is best to think about the following things before you begin widespread incense use in your home.

Smoke

Perhaps the most troublesome part of incense use for some people is the smoke that is generated through burning. Some people have breathing problems that can be exacerbated by the presence of smoke. There are many people who feel that they are allergic to incense, but this is very rarely the case (as mentioned in the discussion of synthetic versus natural incense, these people are usually allergic to synthetic ingredients rather than incense itself). Natural incense generally produces less smoke than synthetic forms and is typically milder. If you find that any incense smoke impacts your breathing, first, stop using that type of incense. Second, you will find that many brands of natural incense are available in low-smoke or even smokeless varieties; try one of those next time you purchase incense. Third, if you use the proper techniques, even incense burned on charcoal will produce little or no smoke; try charcoal burning to enjoy scent without smoke.

Incense makers strive to produce incense that creates as little smoke as possible, since smoke is a by-product of incomplete combustion. The better the formulation of the incense, the less smoke is produced during burning. Incense that produces plumes of smoke is forcing a lot of unburned particles into the air, and those particles can irritate eyes, sinuses, and lung tissues.

The keys to low-smoke incense are moisture content, aromatic choices, and heat. All ingredients must be thoroughly dried. Moisture trapped inside your incense ingredients will produce elevated amounts of smoke, just like wet leaves or logs on a campfire. Your choice of incense ingredients will have a major impact on the amount of smoke the incense produces. Resins tend to produce more smoke than woods or green herbs. You can test potential choices on low-heat charcoal to determine how much smoke they are likely to produce. Finally, you want incense to burn at the lowest possible temperature. The best incense is smoldered rather than burned. With loose incense, this is controlled with your charcoal or incense heater. (You will find detailed information about charcoal burning in chapter 5.) In self-burning incense, the temperature is controlled by the selection of base materials and the ratio of base ingredients to aromatics. Mixing incense that produces little smoke is one of the skills that comes only with years of practice and study.

Another concern about smoke is the physical damage it can do. Using large quantities of very smoky incense can, aside from making you feel ill, also lead to marks and streaks on walls, ceilings, and other indoor surfaces. The best way to avoid this is the most obvious: create less smoke. Use the techniques given in this section to reduce smoke volumes. If for some reason you insist on using significant amounts of smoky incense, you might also want to open a window and even add a fan blowing out to draw the smoke outside the room. Another consideration if you burn smoky incense should be smoke detectors. Incense (and candles) can easily set off smoke detectors, which can be very annoying during a ritual.

Mind-Altering Properties

As you may know, many natural incense ingredients are powerful and can have a significant impact on the brain itself. Burning incense is very similar to smoking the same materials. The incense burns, disperses its scent and smoke into the air, and then you inhale that air in order to smell the incense. As any cigarette smoker can tell you, inhaling smoke can have a dramatic impact on your mind and body. This is true of many botanicals (cannabis and frankincense, for example) and is something of which all incense users should be aware.

In general, this is one of the reasons that people use incense. Incense can deepen meditative states, change moods, and create other physiological changes within the user. However, if you are sober or in recovery, you may want to use care about exposing yourself to particularly powerful incense. A list of such ingredients might include (but would not be limited to) aloeswood, cannabis, coltsfoot, damiana, hops, lion's mantle, mistletoe, mugwort, nightshade, tobacco, white willow bark, and wild lettuce. One of the benefits of incense in magical works is this physiological effect; however, if you work to avoid the ingestion of mind-altering substances, then you shouldn't burn incense with any such ingredients. Naturally, you should also avoid any incense that contains any material to which you are allergic.

Animals

Some animals are very sensitive to smoke and scent, so pet owners need to be aware of this. Perhaps no creatures are more sensitive than birds. Even small amounts of smoke can be dangerous to birds, so I suggest that you keep all indoor birds well out of the area where incense is burned. Of course, you may already have experience with a particular pet and see no problem, but in general birds and smoke should be kept apart.

Other household pets sensitive to scent are dogs and cats. I have not encountered cases where dogs were more than mildly interested in incense, but they are aware of it and you should observe them while burning incense to make certain they are not uncomfortable with the odors. Cats, on the other hand, often love incense. Some incense contains catnip, palo santo, or other ingredients that cats will seek out. As a result, a curious cat might rip open packages, roll on incense sticks and cones, or even eat them! It is a good idea to keep any incense with these types of ingredients well out of the reach of pets. There is evidence that burning lavender can pose a health risk to cats, so be aware of that as well.

Incense is best preserved in a sealed container, but a container that seems well sealed to us might still emit an odor to an animal, so keep any potentially problematic incense well out of reach. Remember that children might also find your incense to be tasty or fun to play with, so keep it out of reach of young kids as well.

Fire

Although it seems obvious to write, incense requires combustion to release its scent and therefore presents a fire hazard. Make certain that you only burn incense in a fire-proof container. It should be large enough and sturdy enough to keep the incense and all its ash inside the container. If for sticks, it should hold the stick firmly with no wobbles. For cones, it should have a wide enough mouth that you can easily place the lighted cone into the censer. As you place the cone inside, your fingers should not touch the sides of the censer. For loose or moist incense, use a censer that is not only large enough but that will be able to take the heat from the charcoal. Although ceramic, metal, and stone all work well, I suggest that you avoid the use of glass censers for charcoal or cones. The prolonged heat can cause glass censers to crack. However, glass is generally fine for stick incense.

Ethical Concerns

Whether you use synthetic or natural incense, both kinds present ethical considerations. I don't include ethical concerns in a book to try and force my opinions on others, but I do hope these comments will cause you to stop and consider the implications of your choices. Act according to your own feelings, but at least take a few moments to ponder your decisions so that you are an informed incense user.

Synthetic incense might contain harmful chemicals and you essentially have no way of knowing what or how much there is. Is that enough reason to avoid using synthetics? That's a choice for you to make. Personally, there are a few brands of synthetic incense that I'm comfortable using. Although I once banned all synthetic incense from my house, I've come to learn that some of them don't offend my nose. I don't use them often, but there are times when synthetic is appropriate for me. It remains important that you understand the risks and some possible underlying causes of people's discomfort with synthetic ingredients (such as the extender DPG).

Natural incense does offer its own ethical considerations. The most notable might be the endangered nature of some incense ingredients. I have watched the ethical arguments on this topic rage in the incense world for years now. Some are convinced that certain incense ingredients have no acceptable substitutes. They argue that, although immediate conservation is needed, the incense industry uses such tiny amounts of these materials that there is no harm in their continued use. Another group argues that we should suspend use of endangered materials completely, regardless of their usefulness in incense. Most incense users, once made aware of the concerns, are somewhere between the two extremes. I think it's important for incense users to remain informed and exercise care in selection of incense or incense ingredients. Luckily, some of these concerns are being addressed by the free market (such as the growing availability of Australian sandalwood).

Another ethical concern of natural incense is the use of animal materials. Once again, my personal position has moderated over the years. For the most part, I prefer not to see animals exploited for their use in incense. I would never support the use of an animal product where the animal's death was required for harvesting. On the other hand, the use of animal products where the animal is unharmed (such as ambergris) seems quite acceptable to me. I have been exposed to forms of magick that include the use of biological products taken from the magician himself. I certainly see nothing unethical about that. Again, this is a matter for self-education.

Perhaps one day the incense-using community will be large enough to support a book that explores these ethical questions in-depth. Until then, research on your own and make informed choices. Search your own feelings and ethics and I know you'll arrive at the right decision for you.

2

Scent

Of the five senses, scent is perhaps the most elusive and least understood. There are legions of artists and others who understand how to pleasure our sight. Armies of musicians will cater to all the desires that your hearing might have. Generations of chefs have built a vast knowledge of pleasing the sense of taste. Of course, satisfying the sense of touch is one of the oldest of all professions. Where are our noses in all of this?

We bombard our sense of smell with overwhelming fragrances on a daily basis, from deodorants and cleaning products to artificial air "fresheners." For the most part, we are stabbing blindly to satisfy our sense of smell. There are historic and cultural reasons for this "scent gap."

The Despised Sense

Once humanity became "civilized," the largest motivators for addressing the sense of smell were negative. The birth of cities meant that people were living in very crowded conditions for the first time. When you combine that with animal smells, a lack of sanitation, and a lack of bathing facilities, you can imagine that many civilizations were primarily concerned with blocking out unpleasant odors rather than creating pleasing ones. While a variety of civilizations overcame many of these problems, the focus of dealing with scent remained for a long time to minimize its offending aspects.

Incense in particular first rose to historical use because of animal sacrifices. It is easy to imagine the stench of rituals where many animals were burned whole. The priestly castes in many cultures learned that the addition of fragrant materials to an animal sacrifice could greatly reduce the negative impact on the sense of smell. Incense and perfumes were then widely used to cover a variety of unpleasant smells.

It seems that in some cultures, especially Western ones, the sense of smell was considered "base" and uncivilized. While the sense of taste was often celebrated, scent was seen as animalistic. It is well known that many animals have a much more sophisticated sense of smell than humans. Perhaps a type of "nose envy" drove some of the common beliefs about the sense of smell being subhuman. It is difficult to pinpoint why some cultures absolutely deplored the sense of smell whereas others celebrated it.

Another obstacle is the difficulty in discussing scent. English and most other European languages lack a sufficient lexicon to allow discussions about the huge variety of scents detectable by even the inferior human nose. Personally, I think this bias is the result of a spiraling combination of many factors. The end result is that the study of the sense of smell lagged far behind that of the other senses in the West.

In some parts of Europe, the sense of smell and the desire to cover unpleasant odors gave birth to the manufacture of perfume. Perfumery has been lifted to a very sophisticated art, but it is generally only practiced by a small group of artisans. Happily there is a growing movement in the United States for the making of perfumes by amateur perfumers and hobbyists. Many of this new generation of home perfumers focus on the use of natural materials. Perfumers do possess a language for discussing scent, but obviously they make up a tiny fraction of the population, so their specialized language is unknown to most of us.

It is also fortunate that this wasn't the philosophy in all parts of the world. In the East, scent enjoyed a far more respectable station. The art of scent grew along with the other arts. As you will see later in this book, the study and pursuit of scent took on no higher elevation than it did in Japan. The finest incense in the world comes from that island nation and is a direct result of hundreds of years of study and experimentation.

Evolutionary Change?

The sense of smell is possibly the most ancient of all of our senses. As you will see a little later in this chapter, the primitive physiology of the sense is one of the reasons for this belief. When complex life forms first began to root around for food in the ancient oceans of Earth, the ability to detect odors provided an evolutionary leap. Smell allowed life forms that used the chemically active sense to prosper by guiding them to ample food supplies. Even today many animals use scent as one of their primary hunting or foraging tools.

Perhaps as humans learned to walk upright and moved further away from nature, the need for sight and hearing was more important to survival than the sense of smell. This is just my own conjecture, of course, but at least one reasonable explanation for our loss of refinement in our sense of smell grew out of our very survival needs and evolutionary path. This might even explain some of the prejudice against scent as being animalistic, since it is associated with our distant evolutionary changes.

The Physiology of Scent

The way that the mind receives messages from the nose is unique among our senses. Scents are transmitted from the nose to the olfactory bulb (directly behind the nose) and onto the olfactory cortex. From there scent information is sent to the area of the brain that controls behaviors and thoughts. Although very little study has been done on the direct physiological impact of incense, existing research does show that incense impacts our scent receptors much the same as an animal steroid or pheromones. If this research stands the test of time, it might explain why incense can have such an impact on our mood, including its ability to reduce depression. The reason for this is that our brains actually process scent through two different organs. In addition to the olfactory bulb and cortex, humans also have a vomeronasal organ. This ancient organ directly processes scents like steroids and pheromones. This certainly implies that incense could easily have impact on the mind in ways that we do not completely understand yet. This organ would not process scent as we normally think of it, and it's completely possible that modern humans wouldn't understand those impulses—our response would be on a purely unconscious level. Research has been done testing the impact of incense on sensuousness and depression, with some positive results. Incense may be helping us in many ways beyond the simple perception of a pleasant smell.

The Language of Scent

While cultures that have placed a high value on incense have developed many descriptive words to describe scents (specifically from incense), that is not something present in most Western languages. Although perfumery has developed its own language, this has not been widely adopted in the incense community nor is it an ideal vocabulary because of notable differences between incense and perfume.

As a result, incense enthusiasts have borrowed words from other disciplines and languages. Cooking, baking, perfumery, and even gardening terms are often applied to incense ("spicy," "sweet," "top note," "bouquet," etc.), but they are used inconsistently from one person to another. Even I am guilty of this, although I have worked hard to ensure consistency in my writing to avoid confusions that are so common in the incense world.

The Psychology of Scent

Scent has an emotional and psychological impact on us that I imagine everyone has experienced. Does the odor of a certain meal make you think of holidays as a child? Does a whiff of a particular perfume remind you of a love long past? The impact of scent on our minds and states of being is dramatic no matter how hard we may want to believe that we are beyond this primitive sense. Not all researchers agree on this point, but I find it to be logical and certainly accurate in my own life.

Smell can have more influence over how we feel about a room than the color or décor. Even a drab room can be warm and inviting when "dressed up" with the proper scent. Our minds easily associate scents with particular places or events. I personally experience this every time I step into an elementary school. That unique combination of scents from crayons, paste, books, and cafeteria food always brings back a flood of memories from my own childhood.

This scent memory not only plays a key role in the magickal use of incense but is also important to our memories of people and places. The fact that a church has a particular scent constantly reminds visitors of where they are and their own particular history in such places. Retailers use various scents to generate calm and happiness, and to create the most relaxing and comfortable environment to help loosen customers' grips on their wallets.

The Magick of Scent

The connection between working magick and the use of incense was revealed long before the advent of written history. Undoubtedly prehistoric shamans of both genders passed the understanding of incense to their protégés thousands of years before such knowledge was ever recorded. Incense touches us in a deep way, and it is easy to see why incense is such a potent magickal tool.

The Power of Botanicals

Botanicals, in the view of the incense user or maker, are any organic materials used in incense. Most natural incense is made using nothing but botanicals and water, but occasionally natural incense includes minerals (like talc or potassium nitrate). Botanicals are the heart of incense's power that touches us on many different levels. They are the reason that I never use synthetic incense in ritual or when doing any magickal work. It is not that synthetic incense will inhibit the process but that synthetic ingredients add nothing to the process. Natural botanicals, on the other hand, bring tremendous energy.

Gifts from the Deities

Botanicals are indeed gifts given to us. Although many different attributes have been ascribed to different botanicals, those attributes are often debatable. While traditional uses for botanicals are often very appropriate, some traditions view the same botanical with different and sometimes opposing sets of attributes. While there might be disagreement about those attributes, there is never any argument about the power contained within.

How to best use that power depends on your traditions, training, and personal discovery. A botanical is often said to "speak" to the user. As a result, different people will use it in different ways, and none of them are incorrect. Whether you view botanicals as a natural result of the evolutionary process or you see them as magick incarnate, the tremendous power of botanicals is easy to experience. I personally find it impossible to deny the Divine after having used natural incense. The divinity of the universe is never clearer to me than when I am sharing a wonderful botanical with someone I care about.

The Power of Nature

One of the sources for the tremendous power of botanicals comes directly from Nature. The various woods, resins, and herbs that comprise natural incense are laden with natural energies. The power of the sun, rain, wind, and moon are all stored within the botanicals, awaiting release. Magick is a symbolic approach to the use of energy, so symbols are very important. Consider, for a moment, the symbology that these botanicals possess. A tree not only grows tall, reaching for the sky (air), but it also sinks its roots deep into Mother Earth (earth). Year after year, the rains (water) fall upon them, and the sun (fire) shines down to bring new growth. Thus, botanicals are the symbolic representation of the four elements.

Beyond symbolism, botanicals are also the physical representation of the elements. Some of the energy that the sun and rain bring is quite literally stored within the botanicals. Nutrition is drawn from the soil and the energy from respiration is required for all organic life. Therefore, botanicals are both the literal and figurative representations of the elements.

Magickal Atmosphere

While natural incense is a powerful way to access or raise energy, it has a much more immediate physical and magickal influence upon us. While discussing the way that botanicals represent the elements is a wonderful, somewhat intellectual, way to discuss their power in magick, the immediate impact of incense on us as animals is another potent part of the magick of incense.

Since scent is quite unlike other senses and the impact of scent upon us is nearly instantaneous, you can observe how your body responds. When you encounter a soothing odor, your shoulders relax, your breathing becomes deeper, and your mood is elevated. Likewise, when you enter a room harboring a foul odor, your body instantly recoils. Your breathing becomes shallow, you avoid inhaling through your nose, and most of us will grow physically tense. A bad smell can certainly affect your mood as well.

This physical response to scent is a powerful tool for magick as well. One element of magick is the mental state of the mage, or magician. A shift from "normal" perception to a magickal frame of mind is one of the important steps to seeing through the Veil and working magick. The physical impact of incense can quickly facilitate the transition to magickal vision. If you use a particular blend of incense exclusively for magickal purposes, you will discover that simply smelling that scent will begin to shift your perspective.

Personally, I use several blends this way. I use one specific blend for cleansing space that I plan to use for magickal work and another any time I call upon my patron deities. Not only does that create a magickal atmosphere for me, it also creates a positively charged environment for the powers I call upon. It is a form of magickal preparation. Just as you would clean your house before guests visit, incense creates a welcoming magickal atmosphere and provides a type of energetic cleaning. In its own way, incense "magickally decorates" the spaces in preparation for a visit from great powers. Not only is it a cleaning process, it also serves as a sort of magickal announcement to the universe. You might think of it as hanging out a "welcome" sign for magickal powers. Incense creates an environment that is easy for those powers to enter and welcomes them into your space. Many mages use specific scents or blends to invite specific powers into their space.

Impact of Scent

It is difficult to overstate the usefulness of scent in magick. This goes well beyond incense, although I have always found incense to be the most powerful implementation of scent power. Aroma lamps, perfumes, and even powdered botanicals placed on clothing or skin all have benefits in magick. Scent can trigger specific states of mind and bring memories to the surface that have been long buried. Who hasn't had the experience of smelling something that reminds us of an old friend or the joys of days long since passed? By bringing that power into your magickal workings, you can accomplish more with less effort. Incense and other scent products are tools that make working magick even more of a joy.

Historic Use of Incense in Magick

As we saw in chapter 1, references to the use of incense in magick or religious work are found all around the world. Historians have no idea when or how incense first came into use, but traditions clearly show that this practice is far older than writing.

It is easy to envision our ancient ancestors discovering the power of heavily scented woods soon after learning how to use fire as a tool. The sense of smell was vital to survival, and after encountering one fragrant wood, it is unlikely that a primitive person would have forgotten that experience. Instead, the energy and power of such woods was used in combination with the power of the fire itself to raise energy. Once this power was understood, it was likely a very short period until these ancient wielders of magickal power began to test other materials to learn the hidden powers within incense. To date, there is very little direct knowledge of the growth of early incense traditions. As cultures shared the knowledge of writing, their incense traditions had already become well established.

Taoists, Buddhists, and even practitioners of Shinto have long used incense. As in many other cultures, one common thread to magick incense use in Asia is the concept that the smoke from the incense carries the wishes or prayers of the users to other planes. As one prays, the words combine with the smoke from the incense to be carried to the gods and goddesses who may be swayed to help a mortal being. Asian tradition is rich with incense magick and lore. One of my very favorite such beliefs regards those who sell incense materials. It is said that unscrupulous merchants who sell incense made with inferior or vulgar ingredients under the guise of being of top-quality materials will spend eternity as "incense demons"—those cursed souls wander the Earth in search of incense smoke to eat, but are denied any pleasure from the wonderful fragrance.

Egypt was one major center of incense use and creation in the ancient world. Perhaps the most famous of all ancient incense blends, called kyphi, was the creation of an ancient Egyptian incense master. The care and attention to detail for the making of kyphi indicates a very sophisticated incense tradition.

Judeo-Christian religions also have a rich incense history, although few of the followers of those religions realize this in modern times. Ancient Hebrews recognized the power of incense and its critical contribution to their spiritual practices. In ancient Judaism there was a special class of priest who created incense. Modern scholars unimaginatively call this the "Incense Cult" of the ancient Israelites. This aspect of incense was so ingrained in their religious practices that being an incense maker was a highly revered position, much as the master incense makers of Asian cultures were revered. Ancient caches of incense mixed for the Hebrew temples have been unearthed in modern times. So powerful was this mixture that even after thousands of years, the fragrance is still distinct and quite potent.

Incense is also quite important to later Christian religions, although in the last few centuries many denominations have lost those practices. In fact, incense played an important role at the very birth of Christianity. Consider that two of the three gifts presented to the Christ child by the three kings were frankincense and myrrh. Some say that the gold discussed in that famous story was actually another fragrant resin that was covered in gold (as is still done with some resins in the twenty-first century). While I cannot offer any facts about that one way or the other, the gifts of frankincense and myrrh were no accident; both were very valuable resins at that time. The resins had to make a journey of thousands of miles up from Africa just to reach the biblical kings. They then carried these precious gifts for their entire journey as the ultimate gifts for the newly born King of the Jews.

The most aged Christian institutions (the Roman Catholic and Eastern Orthodox Christian churches) still use frankincense in their rituals. A large swing censer, sometimes called a thurible, holds burning charcoal onto which is thrown copious amounts of frankincense resin. It is still quite mysterious to me why myrrh has been left out of such rituals, but I am no expert on the inner workings of these religions so perhaps myrrh is still used in less-public rituals. Of course, traditionally, frankincense represents the masculine and myrrh the feminine. Perhaps that has something do with the non-use of myrrh.

Islam also recognizes the value of incense. In fact, the Mideast is one of the largest-consuming regions of fragrant materials. Rare gifts like aloeswood are often burned to display status in social situations. In that region of the world, incense is so popular that cars are frequently equipped with electric incense burners for continuous use.

In both the ancient Pagan world and in the Neopagan movements of today, incense is a part of nearly every ritual. In the ancient world, each Pagan community had access to different fragrant materials. Herbs were one of the most commonly used materials, yet resins and fragrant wood were known all over the ancient world. It is also easy to forget how interconnected the ancient world was. Although many critical resins came from thousands of miles away, our ancient Pagan ancestors in Europe had access to a wide variety of fragrant gifts from Mother Earth.

Twentieth Century

In the modern world of magick, one of the first writers to frequently reference the use of incense was Aleister Crowley. The famous "beast" of the Golden Dawn is, to say the least, a colorful and controversial character from the late nineteenth and early twentieth century. There certainly is not room in a book of this nature to discuss Crowley in detail, but a review of his magickal texts shows numerous references to using incense in ritual magick. Incense was mentioned in many, many of his magickal instructions.

The problem with Crowley's inclusion of incense is the total lack of detail. It appears that he simply went to the Asian district of whatever city he was in and purchased any strong-smelling concoction that was described as "incense." Crowley's instructions on the selection and use of incense are nearly non-existent. Based on his publicly available writings, he had no concept of the composition of incense or knowledge of Asian incense-use traditions. However, he often acknowledged the power of incense to create the requisite magickal atmosphere.

Gerald Gardner, generally recognized as the "father" of the Wiccan religion, was also mostly silent on details about incense use. He did mention its importance in ritual, but Gardner omitted details about the composition of incense and the particular blends that he and others used while working magick. It is important to recognize that both of these magick men often omitted details from their public writings for a variety of reasons. It is entirely possible that both men knew a great deal more about incense than their public writings reflect. Unfortunately, most of us will never be able to answer that question.

In the mid-twentieth century, ritual magick enjoyed a large surge in popularity. Many writers began to apply ancient concepts to modern life and the current Neopagan movement was launched. One of the first popular writers on the subject was Starhawk. Her work tied the women's movement to Paganism in no uncertain terms. She offered many of the first widely available magick instructions to the general public. From simple grounding exercises to instructions for casting and releasing a magick circle, she brought magick to many uninitiated for the first time in her 1979 classic *The Spiral Dance.* Although only scant reference is made to incense, she includes a note that is key to the use of incense in magick: "A Witch depends less on traditional associations of herbs, odors, and colors than on her own intuition" (20th Anniversary Edition, p. 95). That sentence has brought many of us to a new understanding of the power of incense and scent in the pursuit of magick. This idea eventually led me to the practice of "listening" to herbs and incense to let *them* tell *me* how I could best employ their power.

Ten years after *The Spiral Dance,* popular Wiccan author Scott Cunningham brought incense into the forefront of magickal thought when he published *The Complete Book of Incense, Oils & Brews.* This early attempt to teach practitioners not only how to use but actually how to make incense, remains required reading for any user of magickal herbs. Cunningham stresses the importance of natural incense botanicals as well as the historic significance of incense in magick. This book sparked a bit of a revolution in the use of incense in modern magick. Since publishing that classic volume,

Pagans, Wiccans, Druids, Heathens, Witches, and many other Neopagan practitioners began to explore and re-discover what our ancestors knew so well: the power of incense is unrivaled for versatility in not only shaping energy but in raising the energy itself.

Although my name will never be listed among the greats I have discussed here, I hope to shed some tiny ray of light on the subject with this book and my previous book on the topic. Years of study and practice have shown me that I can never learn all there is to know about the power and use of incense. The topic is simply bigger than any one person. I hope that my words will inspire some readers to move the study of incense well beyond the mark any of us have set in the past. There is so much more to learn that I hope you will one day teach me the secrets you have uncovered.

In modern times we are blessed to have access to strange and wonderful incense ingredients from all over the planet. While frankincense of even the lowliest quality was once far too expensive and difficult for some people to enjoy, high-quality incense is only a mouse click and a few dollars away in modern times. Our new international transportation and commerce systems allow us to enjoy incense to a degree that is unrivaled in history. Unfortunately, this same situation has led to some cases where our ease of access might actually lead to the destruction of these precious materials. Aloeswood, rosewood, sandalwood, and others are in danger of extinction in our lifetimes. This topic is explored more in the next chapter, but it is important to understand that the materials that our ancestors so prized—which are now so inexpensive—could disappear before our eyes if we do not exercise caution. Perhaps the materials being very expensive was one of the factors keeping the materials safe from overharvesting or other extreme exploitation.

Personal Incense Associations

The concept of "listening" to incense is more deeply explored later in this book, but I wanted to make note of this important magickal concept early on. It is easy, especially for those new to magick, to pick up a book and use it to determine associations (or links) with specific magickal properties. For example, there are many books for those new to Witchcraft or Paganism (sometimes called "Witchcraft 101" or just "101" books) that will tell you that elm is associated with love and fertility while sandalwood is associated with energy raising. There is nothing wrong with using those associations if you are new to magick or if you feel that those associations are correct. However, I would urge you, my wonderful reader, to never rely upon those books or charts. Such associations can become very personal. You might discover, as I have on more than one occasion, that a particular botanical serves a different purpose for you. You might see dragon's blood as a cleansing scent while nobody else in the world does. Does that make you wrong? Not at all.

Herbs, woods, resins, and other botanicals are individuals, just as you and I are. They might tell secrets to you that they will not tell to me. They may have uses that only a few individuals can comprehend or properly utilize. Never depend solely on someone else's view of the proper use of a botanical. Their opinions are a starting place but never an ending. Many of such traditional associations grow from the use of the botanicals for hundreds or thousands of years, so traditional uses are certainly not without merit. Many different practitioners have found a common experience that has become a part of our common lore. Still, that does not mean you can't find a new use for the same botanical or that it can't impart special knowledge to just you. It is even quite possible that your use of the botanical will not work for others; it might be for you alone.

Sadly, there are tons of "experts" out there who will tell you that there is only one way to do things. Do not let anyone tell you that you are using a botanical in the wrong context, e.g., "you can't put vetiver in a love blend!" It might be a good idea to consider their input and question your choice of materials, but if you do so and still feel the use is right for you, then do not be concerned about the opinions of others. They are only opinions. Let the botanicals themselves tell you how best to utilize them, even if your use is contrary to what you have read in a book somewhere (including this one). Your personal magickal associations are the true heart of incense power.

———

Although the use of incense is far older than written history, it is accessible to the twenty-first century world with just as much power as it had in those ancient times. While the detailed history of incense use is sketchy at best, it does not take an anthropological genius to understand the natural progression of incense use in magick and spirituality. History gives us perspective and understanding of a time long gone, but the botanicals still speak to us today. That gives us the chance to not only utilize the ancient secrets of incense but to find new approaches and uses in the coming centuries.

3

Incense Ingredients

Many books will give you a more in-depth look at the huge variety of aromatics that are used in incense making. The listing that follows isn't intended to be comprehensive or detailed but rather just an introduction to the wide world of incense. Check the bibliography of this book for some good ideas on where to go with your research. Remember that any associations that might be mentioned in the descriptions here should not be taken as a rigid fact. Spend time with the aromatics and they will speak to you and guide you in their use. For those who purchase incense, find an incense maker who will disclose the ingredients or create custom incense for your needs if you want specific blends. If all else fails, you can buy single-aromatic incense and use the air-mixing technique described in chapter 6.

Aromatics

Acacia (*Acacia senegal*): Also known as "gum Arabic," it has a somewhat astringent scent, almost like a mint. The scent is quite mild, and acacia is primarily used in incense for its magickal properties or as an incense binder.

Aloeswood (*Lignum aquilariae*): Aloeswood is normally graded into one of six different types (kyara, rakoku, manaka, manaban, sumotara, and sasora) based on the place of origin. This is the most highly regarded aromatic in Japanese incense (and the foundation for the kodo ceremony) and is treasured across the world. Also known as iron wood, agarwood, and eaglewood, aloeswood is endangered in the wild.

Amber: Amber is preserved tree resin and comes from a wide variety of trees. I always try to introduce people to the incredible power within incense itself, so consider this: for any resin to be classified as "amber," the resin must be at least 100,000 years old. Just imagine an aromatic that has spent its first phase of life growing within a massive, prehistoric tree, reaching into the sky and feeding on sunshine and rain. The material was then forced out of the tree and into the ground for thousands or even millions of years. Think about how much energy such a resin would contain. That is why I've always treated amber as a resin associated with earth powers. Some amber was buried under the surface for 200 million years. Interestingly, I've never encountered an amber that is appropriate for both making jewelry and making incense. For some reason, the most beautiful amber I've ever seen smelled quite awful when burned.

Benzoin (*Styrax tonkinensis* or *S. benzoin*): Benzoin is graded into either benzoin Sumatra or benzoin Siam, based on its origin. The two types create significantly different scents, but both are widely used in incense making and perfumery as a fixative.

Camphor (*Cinnamomum camphora*, et.al.): To me, camphor has one of the cleanest scents of any aromatic. I'm always reminded of a clean room when I smell camphor. The incense community has long debated the difference in scent between natural and synthetically produced camphor, but I think the jury is still out on that one.

Cedar (*Cedrus* spp.): Cedar is found in many different parts of the world. Different species have their own unique properties but cedarwood has been used in incense throughout written history, and we can safely assume it was used long before then. Most evergreen trees produce resins and woods that make wonderful additions to incense.

Cinnamon/Cassia (*Cinnamomum zeylanicum* or *C. cassia*): It surprises most Americans to know that the majority of the "cinnamon" they've eaten in their lives was actually cassia. While both are considered "cinnamon" by the USDA, they are distinct plants that have very similar scents. Incense is made from the bark of both of these botanicals, but cassia generally produces better results in incense. Cinnamon and cassia are "hot" aromatics that can lead to nose and throat irritation if used in a high ratio in incense. In small amounts, this is an amazing aromatic.

Clove (*Syzygium aromaticum* or *Caryophyllus aromaticus*): This humble herb is actually the unopened flower bud of an evergreen tree. Clove not only has a wonderful scent (it is often at the heart of incense named "spice") but it also is a tool for incense makers to create incense that burns hotter. A higher burn temperature can help to burn aromatics in the mixture that won't otherwise burn in self-combustible incense.

Copal (*Bureseru microphylla*): True copal resin comes from one particular evergreen tree and a few of its cousins. While the trees do grow on other continents, true copal comes only from Latin America. It is available in many different grades and colors depending on the particular species of tree, its age, and how it is harvested. In the current marketplace you can find virtually any resin labeled as "copal." Purchase from a reputable seller who can verify the origin of the copal for sale to ensure you are getting the proper resin. I have rarely found a well-cured resin with a scent that was unappealing, so no matter what resin you buy, the odds are good that you'll enjoy it. I think that consumers should know what they are paying for, and it is up to the seller to make that clear.

Dragon's Blood (*Calamus draco* or *Daemonorops draco*): Without a doubt, this is one of my favorite resins, maybe even my favorite out of all aromatics. Dragon's blood is a dark, dense resin. It gets its name from its thick liquid nature and dark red color. It is a heavy, dominating scent that is excellent alone but should be used sparingly in blends of incense to avoid overpowering the other scents.

Frankincense (*Boswellia* spp.): Frankincense resin is also called olibanum or boswellia. Olibanum actually refers to frankincense from a particular region, but this name is commonly used to describe all frankincense. Frankincense is likely the most famous of all aromatics in the West. Popular since ancient times, some cultures have used frankincense in unfathomable quantities. Its importance in ancient Western history is truly brought home when one considers that it was one of the three aromatics that the Eastern kings, or wise men, brought to the infant Jesus.

Juniper (*Juniperus* spp.): Junipers are found in many parts of the world. Not only the foliage of the tree is used but juniper berries are also used in incense making. The strong evergreen scent is matched by the uniquely sharp characteristics of the juniper. Juniper berries are also called sloe berries and are sometimes used to flavor gin. Juniper has long been considered a sacred aromatic.

Mastic (*Pistacia lenticus*): This gum has a fairly strong, distinct scent and has been used since antiquity. It was even chewed in some cultures to freshen breath. Incense makers often seek Greek mastic, but it is not produced only there. As one of the softer gums, mastic requires great skill to incorporate it into self-combusting incense.

Myrrh/Sweet Myrrh (*Opoponax*) (*Commiphora myrrah/C. karaf* or *Opoponax chironium*): Myrrh and opponax (also known as sweet myrrh) are often confused in labeling but will never be confused in scent. True myrrh has a bitter, earthy, and dark aroma that only works well when skillfully combined with other aromatics. This botanical is interwoven with many ancient tales. Sweet myrrh, or opponax, has an enchanting scent that is a much lighter and, as the name implies, sweeter scent.

Palo Santo (*Bursera graveolens*): This is a sacred wood from the Amazon Rainforest. It has only been available commercially for the last decade or so, but it is a truly amazing addition to the incense world. Its strong scent will often draw the attention of animals, so I usually include it in any animal-focused magick. The wood is so filled with resin that after chipping it, the wood must be allowed to dry before further refining it to powder.

Patchouli (*Pogostemon patchouli*): This famous aromatic is one of the two defining scents of the 1960s counterculture. Patchouli has a distinctive scent that (in my experience) people either love or hate. I am one of the few who has moved from the ranks of the haters to the lovers. Patchouli is a unique aromatic because of the way it is processed.

Unprocessed patchouli has an ordinary "green herb" scent. Once it is properly aged and fermented, however, it takes on its classic scent. It is an excellent aromatic for incense making once it is properly prepared. If you've ever tried to use patchouli grown at home and been disappointed by the scent, this is the probable reason.

Pine (*Pinus* spp.): This very common wood makes an excellent base material for incense. It burns hot, it's inexpensive, and it's easily acquired. I was surprised to see a discussion in a recent incense-making book about using bases like pine with the advice that using a base is optional and, if used, it won't alter the energy of your incense blend. That's just not true. The addition of any materials to your incense can alter both the scent and the energy of any blend. In addition to the wood, pine resin and needles can be used as aromatics. Although needles can be used as a base material, I don't recommend it because they tend to produce more smoke than does the wood.

Piñon Pine (*Pinus edulis*): This pine of the southwestern United States produces an amazing resin. I have had the great joy of harvesting piñon, which is quite easy, as piñon generously leaves large chunks of resin on the ground all around it. If you harvest fresh resins like this, you either need to give them many months to cure or boil the water out of them before they are suitable for powdering. You can use "younger" resins in loose incense blends, but expect large amounts of smoke and occasional crackling from the water still in the resin.

Sage (*Salvia officinalis* or *S. apiana*): *Salvia officinalis* is the common "garden sage" that most of us have in our spice racks. The term "sage" is most commonly associated with white sage (*Salvia apiana*). This classic Native American aromatic is renowned for its cleansing and healing properties. It is not to be confused with "desert" sage (*Artemisia tridentata* or *A. tripartita*), which is a completely different plant.

Sandalwood (*Santalum album*): Here I refer to yellow or white sandal-wood. Although there is another wood named "red sandalwood," the two species are not related. This threatened species of tree is slow-growing and needs to mature to a certain age before it can be harvested. Thus, sandalwood can be expensive.

Storax (*Liquidambar orientalis*): Often found in combination with cala-mus, storax has a sweet scent that can overpower lesser aromatics. This balsam has been used by man for millennia as an intense addition to incense blends. It will enhance your intentions, but beware of over-indulging yourself.

Sweet Grass (*Hierochloe odorata*): This amazing Native American aro-matic still grows and is gathered wild. Traditionally braided into long strands and used as a smudge bundle, sweet grass is not at all a lim-ited botanical. When combined with an appropriate base wood, sweet grass is also an excellent aromatic for use in self-combusting incense. Easily available in North America, the growth in international trade means it can now also be found anywhere in the world.

Vetiver (*Vetiveria zizanioides*): Vetiver, more commonly called khus khus, is a unique aromatic with a distinct scent. Khus khus is generally thought of as an Indian spice rather than an incense ingredient. This is one of the many reasons that a certain form of incense stick has come to be called *masala* ("spice"). Roots of this grass have been used in incense for many generations. This is another strong herb that can overpower more subtle ones. I find it ideal for grounding, be it in a magick ritual or just relaxing after a hard day.

Yohimbe (*Pausinystalia yohimbe*): Not traditionally considered for in-cense, yohimbe root is a very interesting aromatic. While often associ-ated with love (or, more accurately, physical love), it has shown me its ability to aid in visions. This is a case where listening to an herb told me something I would not have otherwise guessed. Though difficult to work with, once you use an incense containing yohimbe, you may never do divination again without it.

Endangered and Rare Ingredients

While some botanicals are abundant and easily located, some are rare and more difficult to find. Sadly, some are endangered and are facing extinction. How we treat Mother Earth and her gifts to us says a great deal about us and our respect for Nature. As incense users (and incense makers) we have legal, moral, and ethical obligations to use Earth's resources wisely.

I want to briefly discuss two primary incense ingredients that are endangered. These botanicals have been in use for thousands of years and are amazing gifts from Nature. The loss of either of these would be far more than a loss to incense users. It would not only deprive future generations from enjoying them in incense, soaps, perfumes, and more—it would also be a tragic loss of biodiversity.

Aloeswood

Aloeswood is one of the most unique aromatics. It is not only taken from a particular species of tree but it also requires some very special circumstances to transform into the aromatic that is so beloved. The resin that we treasure is only formed when the tree itself is under attack, such as from insect infestation (this is likely the evolutionary reason that the resin develops) or a physical wounding from animals. This unique circumstance is why aloeswood is such a rare and precious commodity.

Aloeswood grows in some very poor regions of the world, yet it is more expensive than gold in its highest-quality forms. It should not be surprising, then, that where the trees grow, natives exploit them for profit. Frankly, I feel we have no right to criticize them for their desire to feed and clothe their families. As a result of the profits to be made, the trees have suffered terribly from overharvesting. As if that weren't bad enough, because of the peculiar circumstances required to create commercially useful aloeswood, there are those who will intentionally inflict damage on the trees in an effort to force the development of the precious resin. This results in many trees, including quite young ones, suffering intentionally inflicted wounds in the hopes of harvesting resin. Sadly, many of these trees die without producing any resin, which leads to a smaller and smaller species population every year.

Before we are too critical of the people doing these things, consider their plight. Poverty eats away at the soul, and if someone offered you a relatively large amount of money for something that was growing all around you, wouldn't it be nearly impossible to say no? Your first thought would likely be about feeding your children, not worrying that you are selling precious wood to poachers.

The real source of the problem with poachers lies with the consumers. Consumers must know the source of their endangered materials in order to ensure that they are coming from legal, legitimate sources. Such sources do exist, but only the consumer can take the responsibility for looking into this.

Aloeswood is treasured in many cultures. It is used in perfumes and incense, plus there are those who collect aloeswood with the intent to simply hold it in their collection or resell it to another collector. All of this points to the fact that aloeswood is recognized as a true treasure.

In order to incorporate aloeswood into perfume, the resin's essential oils have to be extracted. This process requires large quantities of wood. The quality of the oil depends on the quality of the resin as well as the skill of the person distilling the oil. That means that extracting oils (which are used in some incense as well) has the potential to destroy a great deal of aloeswood for a very small return.

In incense, the wood itself is most often used. Even low-quality aloeswood has an amazing scent, and incense makers generally add the wood to their blends. In Japanese kodo (a formal Japanese ritual akin to the famous Japanese Tea Ceremony), tiny splinters of aloeswood are enjoyed slowly and individually. As far as environmental impact goes, incense making can be far less destructive than perfumery, but that does not relieve us of our duty to ensure we aren't hastening the destruction of this amazing aromatic species.

The clear danger here is that our love of aloeswood could eventually lead to its demise. Overharvesting could lead to extinction by destroying the old-growth trees as well as the destruction of the habitat in the process. The other major danger is one that I have already mentioned: poachers. This is one of the primary ways that we as consumers can help to protect all of the vital resources on Earth, including aloeswood: knowing the source of your materials is key. Purchasing from established, reputable vendors is a great way to protect these resources.

Making your best effort is the only good approach, apart from simply never using any endangered materials. There are two drawbacks to avoiding the use of these materials: The first is that you deny yourself and others from enjoying these amazing aromatics. I admit, that is a bit self-serving, but it needs to be included in your thinking. The second reason is less obvious. The money spent buying these aromatics from legal, legitimate sources helps to support the efforts to conserve and protect these resources.

This all sounds a bit depressing, but there is hope on the horizon. In recent years sustainable, managed aloeswood has come onto the market. While still lacking some of the depth that much older trees can produce, I can't begin to thank enough those who have worked to make these projects come to life. Without them, it is doubtful if future generations would get to enjoy the wonder of aloeswood.

The first hope is the Agarwood Project. The Agarwood Project is sponsored by the Rainforest Project (TRP) and is intended to preserve aloeswood while providing economic support for communities as well. One key aspect of the project is planting and harvesting sustainable aloeswood populations. There is a pilot project in Vietnam right now that is already producing commercial aloeswood. While the quality of this farmed aloeswood has not reached the level of the wild harvested wood, the aloeswood coming out is very nice and improving in quality every year. This is the kind of project that all incense users should support. The future of other aromatics might hinge on the success of projects like this one. The Agarwood Project has been ongoing for some years now, which is why we are able to buy products resulting from it, and it demonstrates the foresight that is needed to save our precious natural resources. I am deeply grateful to everyone involved in this project and hope that it serves as a model for future economically aware conservation efforts.

In 2007 the second agarwood conference was held in Thailand. This was a gathering of specialist from around the world whose goal was to save this species of tree while keeping the needs of native populations, governments, and ecological realities in mind. The conference discussed a wide variety of topics including legislation, nurseries, genetics, sustainability, and more. Visitors heard lectures, attended discussions, and spent time in the field as well. Again, I hope that this is a model for future conservation.

Sandalwood

There is perhaps no more universally used aromatic than sandalwood. While there are several varieties of yellow or white sandalwood and scents can vary widely within those species, they are all, in a word, awesome. Sandalwood is another unusual plant that is actually quasi-symbiotic. As a result, it only grows and produces its distinctive scent in the perfect environment. Yellow sandalwood is one of the most amazing aromatics I have used. Its scent is strong, ranging from dark and woody to light and sweet. It mixes well with virtually any other aromatic. And not only does it have remarkable olfactory qualities, it also has excellent burning and magickal properties.

I should point out that, although red sandalwood is in even more danger than white or yellow sandalwood, this discussion is specifically aimed at the white/yellow variety. I haven't purchased red sandalwood in several years and may not purchase any again until I see improvements in the longevity of the red sandalwood species.

Sandalwood is used as a ritual aromatic in many cultures and serves as a holy substance as well. Nowhere is this truer than in India. In this distant land, sandalwood is much more than a nice-smelling wood; it is sacred and serves in many different revered roles. As a result, it has a place in many different phases of life. From birth to death, sandalwood accompanies people at critical moments of life. Traditional funerals in India have often included the burning of huge quantities of sandalwood. When you consider the size of the population of India and the ever-shrinking supplies of sandalwood, it is easy to see the problem. The rituals of death are so important in most cultures, that we cannot overstate the importance of this issue to many in India.

Once you learn to recognize the scent of sandalwood, you will be amazed at how often you smell it. Many perfumes contain sandalwood, as do other scented products. These oils are often synthetic, but not always. The perfume industry is just as enamored with sandalwood as the incense industry. When you consider that many fragrance products (soaps, air fresheners, deodorants, etc.) look to the perfume industry for inspiration and methods, the impact of the perfume industry is significant.

It is hard to imagine the incense world without sandalwood. Its amazing variety of scents, subtle variations, and the depth of its sweetness all make it a nearly perfect aromatic wood. It is used in construction, religious rituals, manufacturing, and more, but to me it will always be a gift for the incense user. Sandalwood has been used in incense since prehistory and its qualities make it clear why. I would weep should we ever lose sandalwood as an incense material. To think that future generations will not get to enjoy its magick is beyond horror for me.

The problems of endangered botanicals have not escaped the attention of governments and other organizations. The government of India has made some attempts at conservation, including the limitation of sandalwood exports from their country, but the success of these efforts is virtually impossible to measure. The level of information about the sandalwood trade in India is limited and poaching is rampant. While I advise people to know the origin of their incense materials, the issue with Indian yellow sandalwood is nearly impossible to overcome. (There is a solution for incense makers that I will discuss shortly.)

There are many dangers in this situation. First there is the financial impact. The destruction of India's sandalwood would destroy many businesses. All aspects of India's fragrance industry would be impacted (including the incense industry). There is also the impact on tradition. India's traditions associated with sandalwood are deep and ancient. The loss of sandalwood would have significant social impacts in India and other cultures. Finally, and honestly less important, would be the impact to incense makers and users around the globe.

I did mention that there is hope for white sandalwood: Australia. In Australia, the sandalwood population was nearly wiped out in the mid-twentieth century. Australia is home to several different species of white/yellow sandalwood and provides some ideal environments for growing sandalwood. Excellent management and cultivation have seen the Australians burst into the incense world in recent years with their own yellow/white sandalwood. This well-managed population is entering the commercial markets and will likely become the dominant source for sandalwood in the coming decade.

The government of Australia is firmly behind the sandalwood industry, and I salute everyone involved for their foresight. Sandalwood could have easily vanished from Australia or been completely marginalized. Instead, people recognized the danger that was looming ahead, even if it was decades away. Years were invested into research and the establishment of commercial production, and people are now marketing these new sandalwood products. This was a case of people looking beyond their own lives and worrying about future generations. We are fortunate enough to be here while the products are coming on to the market.

I don't want to leave anyone with the impression that all yellow sandalwood comes from India or Australia. Sandalwood is found in many parts of the world and is an important aspect of many economies. However, the supply level from other countries is small and the dangers of extinction are ever-present. I know incense aficionados who collect sandalwood from around the world and enjoy nearly endless combinations of scent all composed of sandalwood. I think there's no harm in buying small amounts of sandalwood from nearly anywhere (with the obvious exception of India), but if you make bulk purchases, I would urge you to buy from Australia. Not only are there no concerns about wiping out an endangered population of sandalwood, you are supporting the efforts of people who have created far-sighted policies intended to benefit the world. As consumers, we vote with our money; I urge you to vote for the nations that have taken responsibility for conservation and preservation.

CITES Treaty

The Convention on International Trade in Endangered Species is another important step that may help us save many valuable species, and this is not limited to the incense world. The current CITES treaty does not address white/yellow sandalwood, but it does address both aloeswood/agarwood and red sandalwood. This treaty defines how the trade of these endangered species should be conducted and the limitations of the trade.

Sadly, poachers don't respect this treaty, as is seen by many nations that are forced to hire police to protect these gifts of nature. This is a strain on smaller nations, but I think it's important to recognize these efforts and salute those who dedicate their lives to protecting natural diversity. The problems of poaching continue to haunt the world, as those who are more interested in money than their children's legacy will stop at nothing to add a few more dollars to their pockets.

Ambergris

This aromatic is rare because it is so unlikely that it will ever be created and when it is, it is rare that any is found by humans for their use. Ambergris is an excretion from sperm whales. It is believed that they expel this material as self-preservation to protect their intestines from bones or the sharp beaks of squid they consume. When first expelled from the whale, it truly isn't usable as an aromatic. Thankfully, this means no poachers will go out to kill sperm whales in order to steal their ambergris.

For ambergris to be a genuinely useful aromatic, it needs to spend time curing in salt water. Most ambergris is collected from beaches, although it is occasionally found floating in the ocean. You can imagine how rare this substance is. The description makes it sound very unappealing, but once it is properly cured and aged, the scent is enchanting. You can also imagine that although poachers can't supply anyone with ambergris, there are those who will adulterate other aromatics and try to pass them off as ambergris. Once again, find a supplier you can trust with a proven track record to ensure that you are buying real ambergris if you choose to use this aromatic.

Saffron

Saffron is a tiny part (the stigma) of a particular crocus (*Sativus linnaeus*). Saffron is rare and expensive simply because it is so difficult to harvest. Not only do these particular crocuses have to be grown, but the tiny little stigma must be picked by hand, and each flower only provides the tiniest amount of saffron. You can imagine how long it takes to collect an ounce of saffron. This also explains why it is so very expensive. There are no massive saffron farms, no saffron-collecting machines, and it can only be produced through the ancient technique of very hard work.

———

As you can see, there is a huge variety of botanicals that range from common plants found in most grocery stores to rare treasures. You can see from this chapter why I so love to harvest my own incense materials whenever possible. That way I know exactly where it came from and how it was handled; I understand the energies to which my materials have been subjected. That's clearly not an option in most cases, but the use of locally harvested materials, or at the least personally harvested even if not from your local area, gives you greater knowledge and control over the energies of your ingredients.

4

Selecting Incense

After reading all of this information about incense, how to use it, and the creative ways in which it can be employed, I hope that you are excited! It's likely that this book will introduce you to styles of incense, burning techniques, and aromatics to which you have never before been exposed. If you are like me, reading all of this has you ready to go out and begin acquiring all sorts of tools for your new obsession. But hold on a minute! Before you rush to the Internet to order rare aloeswood and sandalwood, I think it would be great to determine exactly what you *need* for your uses. Not everyone needs to buy $100-per-ounce incense from Japan or the rarest woods and herbs in order to enjoy this art form.

Quality

Quality is the first consideration when looking for any type of incense, paraphernalia, supplies, or aromatics. So before making any incense purchase, ask yourself where and how you plan to use this material. If your desire is to create the perfect atmosphere for your personal meditation, you would look to a different quality of materials than you would for, say, incense that will cover up the smell of a musty house. Materials for your rituals will have different requirements than those for unwinding after a long day at work. Once you know the quality of incense that will best fit your needs, you can start to look at other aspects as well.

I hope you will notice in the information in this chapter that I distinguish between rolled and dipped incense and natural and synthetic incense. I know that I, like many other incense fans, have sometimes made the mistake of assuming that all dipped incense is synthetic and all rolled incense is natural. Many of us have also been guilty of considering all natural incense to be safe and superior and all synthetic incense to be useless, inferior, and possibly even dangerous. I don't want you to fall into that same trap.

I do feel that, in general terms, natural incense is preferable to synthetic. Yes, there are concerns about untested chemicals, inappropriate extenders, and poor quality "blank" incense that are often used in the creation of synthetic incense. However, these concerns do not apply to all synthetic incense. Likewise, "natural" is not *always* a marker of safety or superior quality. I will discuss these aspects in more detail in the following paragraphs, but I would ask that you keep this information in mind as you read the remainder of this chapter.

Finally, I wanted to say a word about extruded incense. Extruded incense is neither hand rolled nor dipped. It is made by blending the ingredients, aging the blend (in many cases but not all), and then forcing the incense dough through a die to create incense sticks. This is how virtually all joss sticks and Asian incense is made. There are exceptions (for example, I know that Shoyeido offers a line of incense cones that are not extruded), but most Asian incense falls into the category of extruded. The reason that I have not given extruded incense its own section in this chapter is that it generally follows the same guidelines as rolled incense. Although extruded incense is made with the help of machines, it begins as a blend made by hand. It may be synthetic or natural, but to the best of my knowledge, all of the major manufacturers of extruded incense begin by hand mixing the ingredients.

Dipped

Dipped incense is often made with low-quality synthetic oils, inappropriate extenders, poor drying techniques, and blank sticks and cones that contain questionable ingredients. That is not to say that all dipped incense falls into that low-quality category. I know there are incense makers out there trying to create dipped incense that addresses each of these concerns. So I ask that you keep this fact in mind when shopping for incense. Ask questions, look for key indicators of quality, and consider dipped incense for your needs.

With that disclaimer, I admit that I rarely use dipped incense. I have experimented with making my own incense blanks and dipping them in essential oils to achieve truly natural dipped incense. While I wish only the best for those incense manufacturers who try to do the same, I have not found it to be cost effective (not even remotely) to make incense this way. It's a case of something that appears great in theory but fails in practice. It seems to me that dipped incense is, for the most part, created to be very inexpensive and aimed at incense purchasers who are not aware of other alternatives. I'm certain there are exceptions to this, but most incense fans quickly lose interest in over-scented, dipped incense that is still dripping with oil when it is removed from its package. Does this mean that you should never buy or use dipped incense? Definitely not!

I think it is safe to assume that the majority of incense fans in the West began their love affair with dipped incense. I like to think of it as "gateway incense" that can bridge the gap to better incense experiences. Dipped incense also has practical uses. Why would you want to spend $40 for ten sticks of incense to dispel ordinary household odors? I think most incense fans still use incense as a way to overwhelm a less desirable scent from time to time. Dipped incense is certainly one of the most affordable types you can buy and is often quite strongly scented.

Dipped incense is also a gateway incense for budding incense makers. I myself began as a reseller of other people's incense, moved into making my own dipped sticks and cones, and then eventually on to make natural incense. Had I never put my toe in the water through incense dipping, I doubt that I would have ever become a roller of incense, nor would I have ever published any books on the topic.

Dipped incense certainly has its place in the pantheon of products available to us as consumers. For the majority of people in the West, it is the only kind of incense they will ever know. For the lucky few who learn about the myriad of other options, dipped incense is still a common starting place. Dipped incense might be the perfect fit for your needs and budget. You can still use dipped incense for making incense chains, scenting large areas, or banishing unwanted smells. Although I rarely use it, it might be the perfect solution for your needs.

Rolled

As I explained in the introduction to this chapter, it is easy to be misled by the label "rolled incense" or even "hand rolled." Just because incense is rolled by hand does not mean that it uses high-quality ingredients or that it is natural. I know the first time I looked carefully at a stick of incense (I will not mention the brand, but it is widely available in the United States) and noticed a fingerprint formed on the surface of the stick I was thrilled. Here was proof that the incense was hand rolled, and that became a selling point to my customers. Well, for a while anyway, until I became a more educated incense user.

Further experimentation with this brand of incense led me to believe, as I still do, that it contains strong synthetic oils and possibly DPG (dipropylene glycol). Yes, it is rolled by hand, but out of inferior materials. How can the fact that incense is rolled by hand offset the fact that it is unpleasantly strong, could cause harm because of its components, and frankly doesn't smell all that good to a practiced palette? Simply put, it can't.

The majority of the hand rolled incense I have encountered does not fit the description I have just given. Most of it is made from wonderful materials by loving hands dedicated to incense. Hand rolled incense may be made in small batches, which is something I look upon favorably. This is not universally true, and it certainly isn't true in the case of the hand rolled synthetic incense I mentioned previously. Small batches mean, to me, that there is care put into each piece of incense. Small batches could also mean bigger variations from one batch to another, so be aware of that.

Hand rolled incense can also fall victim to more manufacturing problems than dipped. Dipped incense, for the most part, is foolproof when it comes to burning. Incense blanks have rarely failed me when it comes to the burn test. Hand rolled incense, on the other hand, requires a great deal of skill in the creation of the recipe, the selection of ingredients, the storage of those ingredients, and the skillful hand of the roller. With so many more factors impacting it, it's hardly surprising that you are more likely to encounter problems with burning when using rolled incense.

What is the most appropriate use for rolled incense? It's great for virtually any use where self-combusting incense is called for. There are no hard and fast rules about how and where you use rolled incense. It is almost always more expensive than dipped incense, but that is clearly influenced by the greater amounts of time needed to create it. The only inexpensive rolled incense I have encountered was from parts of the world where labor costs are still intensely low. Those types of incense usually contain synthetic or low-quality materials. Rolled incense is not a guarantee of higher quality, but it certainly is a factor that should be considered.

Synthetic

From whence came these synthetic oils, and how did they invade our precious heritage of natural incense? From the Age of Enlightenment and the desire to please humans *and* their budgets, of course! Okay, all kidding aside, synthetic incense is the unnatural outgrowth of the perfume industry. I would call it the "fragrance industry," since many scented products aside from perfume also fall under this umbrella, but I consider incense to be a part of that industry as well and I don't want to confuse incense with other fragrance pursuits.

Perfume is to the West what incense is to the East. The two traditions grew up far apart culturally, but both serve many of the same purposes. The primary purpose of both is to change odors into scents, to turn the ordinary to the fantastic, and to transform the world into what we wished it were rather than what it was when we found it.

Given so much connected history and similar paths, it seems inevitable that the two professions would have an interchange of knowledge. When America experienced a sudden surge in the interest and use of incense in the 1960s and 1970s, movement into new markets caused a new synthesis between perfume and incense.

Competitive business, according to some economic models, drives innovation and results in a lower-cost product for customers. In this case, the innovation was combining oils used in the perfume industry with traditional incense making. The perfume industry had developed long before the "chemical age," but before the incense industry could borrow from it, the perfumers had looked for alternatives to the rare materials from which they extracted the valuable oils. The synthetic chemical industry began the process of synthesizing fragrances and flavors.

A synthetic scent is often developed something like this: A designer or industrial customer wants a scent. The request could also be from within the synthesizing company itself. Let's take, for example, sage. A chemist will examine the chemical structure of the aromatic components of the essential oil. Then the trick is to duplicate the structure of the oil artificially. One of the steps to accomplish this, with a much lower cost than the natural alternative, is to only duplicate the chemical parts of the essential oil that are detected by the human nose, leaving the undetected parts out.

The result of such experimentation has added a whole new aspect to the incense industry. Asia manufactures its own synthetic scent oils and they are regularly added to inexpensive incense. A few years ago a study was released that raised concern in the incense community. The initial data released from the research was sketchy and met with many questions. As further research developed, the general consensus among the researchers was that exposure to particulate matter on a regular basis, over a period of many years and in areas with poor ventilation, is unhealthy and ill-advised. Cancer is one of many risks that are associated with exposure to small particles, such as the ones incorporated into smoke of any kind. The research did not address the issue of the type of incense used by the participants, but I think it is good advice to have proper ventilation any time you are burning incense, candles, or charcoal. The research doesn't prove that incense causes cancer, but it certainly should serve to increase our awareness if the health risks from smoke of all sorts.

How I have seen the debates rage over the use of synthetic chemicals in incense! My basic approach is to avoid synthetics in most instances because of the unknown factors involved. Some synthetic oils were not manufactured with the intention of having them burned, many contain questionable chemical ingredients, and some are of dubious quality overall.

Most synthetic incense is quite strong, making it a good choice for covering up undesirable odors, which is one of the few reasons I ever use synthetic incense. Another benefit to synthetic incense is that you can incorporate scents that would be difficult if not impossible to access in any other way. I personally have ethical problems with most aromatics that come from animals. This is especially true of musk. So how do you incorporate that type of scent without causing harm to the animals in question? Synthetics, of course. Synthetics also offer an inexpensive way to utilize scents that would normally be cost prohibitive.

I still hold that synthetic incense should rarely, if ever, be used in ritual or magickal practice. I know of many practitioners who don't agree with me on this point, and I respect their feelings; but I feel that incense is an offering I make to natural forces and I should respect those forces by not using synthetic incense.

Natural

As I'm sure you have realized by now, I am a strong proponent of natural incense. I have never encountered any high-quality incense that obviously had any synthetic ingredients. I say "obviously" because there is no way to determine this with any certainty without a detailed chemical analysis. It is a shame that more incense manufacturers don't include a list of ingredients on their incense. Let me take a moment to offer my sincere appreciation to Shoyeido for putting a list of key ingredients on their incense packages. I hope that other companies will follow suit for several reasons: to ensure that customers know what they are getting, that there are no synthetic ingredients included, and most importantly so that people with allergies to certain aromatics can use incense safely.

Is natural incense the best choice for you? Again, the question comes back to what you plan to do with the incense. If you are simply scenting a room, then any incense that doesn't put off annoying amounts of smoke or causes you any physical discomfort will do. The question of natural versus synthetic goes far beyond incense and is an issue that many in our culture are grappling with. Food, cosmetics, and health care are all areas in which we as consumers have to make a choice. The consideration of synthetic materials in our culture is far beyond the scope of an incense book, so I won't try to address all of those factors here, but I do feel confident in saying that if you avoid synthetic hormones in your food and drink or if you choose natural products over pharmaceuticals, then you will most likely gravitate to natural incense on your own once you are aware that it exists.

I previously mentioned that I prefer to keep my magickal and ritual incense completely natural. While that is a personal choice for me, I also believe that those who follow a nature-based path (as most Neopagans, Wiccans, Witches, Druids, Asatru, and others who are put under the general "Pagan" or "New Age" banners do) should consider this carefully. What does it say to the powers you evoke if your incense offering is composed of low-quality wood saturated with glues, synthetic fragrance oils, and an abundance of saltpeter? I admit that of the things I just listed, saltpeter sometimes does have a legitimate place on your altar, but only if you have incorporated it into the planning for your work. Using it routinely simply because it is in the inexpensive charcoal from the local New Age store is not, to me, a legitimate use.

What qualifies as "natural incense" can be debated. Does this mean only "whole herb" incense, as incense-group founder David Oller has called it, or can it include incense that uses essential oils (which are distilled or otherwise extracted from whole herbs)? Is incense "natural" if it contains a synthetic binder but is 99 percent natural? No government that I am aware of has ever set standards that would define this for us, so it is up to each individual to make that determination. For me, the ultimate test would be if the powers that you evoke were to ask you the same question, could you provide a ready answer? These points are truly rhetorical, and I won't pretend to have the answers. This is a topic that both the Pagan and the incense communities need to continue discussing. Does synthetic incense offer the same energies as natural incense? Does it offer any energy at all?

In the West, especially in the United States, we have few incense traditions to draw upon. In many ways, we are blazing new trails in the incense world in the West, and what we decide now may have a profound impact on future generations. Discuss this with your friends, your fellow incense fans, your coven mates or kindred, and see what this trail has to offer. I expect to see a continuing evolution of knowledge and opinions in the coming decades.

I mentioned this earlier, but I feel it bears repeating. Rolled incense is not necessarily natural, and dipped incense is not necessarily synthetic. I have been guilty of making those mistaken assumptions in years past, and I hope it is something that you can avoid. For the most part, those assumptions are correct, but you should never assume that to be true.

Homemade

I admit that homemade incense has a special place in my heart. If you are interested in exploring this wonderful art, there are several books on the market and a number of online discussion groups that will teach you how to make incense at home. Homemade incense offers some unique benefits that cannot be found elsewhere. It is true that any skilled practitioner can empower or align the energies in any incense, but there is no way to equal the charge you can achieve when you create your own incense. If you choose to use synthetic incense in your practice, you can still accomplish more by making your own than buying off the shelf.

Frankly, you never know what has happened to your incense before you buy it. Even if you purchase only the finest incense from Japan and Nepal, you have no idea how long it has been in transit, how it was stored, how it was handled, etc. If you choose to make your own incense, you at least know how it has been handled, stored, and treated since it was created. You can improve the situation even further if you make incense only from ingredients that you have grown or harvested yourself.

When you start with natural ingredients, carefully prepare and blend them, and align the power within them at every step, you create incense that is not only very potent for magickal work but also replete with your energy and your intent. Will and thought are the heart of magick. If you keep your mind focused on the purpose of the incense you are making throughout the creation process, the end result will be something unmatched by any incense created by another.

Is homemade incense the right choice for you? The first factor to consider is your own experience. Rolling your own natural incense is remarkably simple once you know a few basics; however, there are those who are simply not destined to be incense makers. There's no crime in that since we all have our own unique set of skills in life. So my first suggestion is that you try incense making and see how well you do and if you enjoy it. Some communities have skilled incense artisans who offer classes in incense making. That is an ideal situation for many people, since it offers you expert guidance and the chance to make incense without having to invest money into tools and ingredients. Reading a good book on the topic is a great foundation for those classes.

If you find that you do not enjoy making incense, you should not force yourself. The negative feelings you have while making the incense will become a part of that incense and will be released when it is burned. I tell my students to never roll incense when they are angry or upset for this very reason.

Assuming that you do enjoy making your own incense, there are still other factors to consider when selecting incense. Do you have the space for making incense and storing the ingredients? Are you able to invest in good quality ingredients? Do you have the time? This is especially important for any self-combusting incense. Incense making is a slow process that requires patience. Blending and rolling your incense is the fast part of the operation and can literally be completed in just a few minutes. Slowly drying the incense requires sufficient storage space and the patience to allow it to dry completely before use.

Do you have access to all of the ingredients you need? I have an extensive collection of aromatics, but there are still ingredients to which I have very limited access or none at all. Large incense companies often have access to materials that most of us don't. They can also purchase them in large quantities to reduce the cost. They can choose from a variety of sources and are not limited to what is for sale in the local herb shop.

Do you have the skill to create the incense you need? Incense making is not hard in general, but some very complex blends can take months or years to perfect. The great incense houses have master incense makers who have decades of experience making incense every day. Most incense does not require that level of knowledge and dedication, but in some instances that expertise is important.

I truly believe that everyone who uses incense should experience the joy of creating incense from raw ingredients. I hope nothing I've said here will discourage you. Although I've been an incense maker for many years, I still have a significant amount of incense that I have purchased commercially or received from my fellow incense enthusiasts. I don't think anyone should be devoted to only making their own incense or only purchasing commercial incense. A combination of the two paths is the most beneficial and practical solution for most of us.

Rare Incense Pleasures

There are some commercial incense made with wonderful ingredients by skilled craftsman that are perfect for certain uses. I have used incense from around the world in my magickal work and have found particular incense that are ideal for certain things I wish to accomplish. Even with more than a decade of incense making experience, I cannot duplicate those specific scents. In fact, I gave up trying to do so long ago.

Some of these blends include rare grades of aloeswood or aromatics from certain botanical cultivars to which I will never have access. Some are so mysterious in their scent that I cannot even begin to assemble a list of ingredients to copy them. If you find commercial incense that works really well for you in a particular role, it would seem folly to me to avoid using it for anything other than economic reasons. Some incense is far more expensive than gold, and whenever I have had the pleasure of experiencing that type of incense, it has been bliss. However, no matter how perfect those blends are for work I may do, I can't invest the money for their regular use although they are rare beauties.

Are these rare treasures the right choice for you? If you can afford them and have used or sampled them in the past to ensure they are right for your needs, then I believe wholeheartedly that you should employ them when possible and appropriate. Just understand that you needn't spend a fortune on incense to get great benefit and pleasure from it.

Price

The price of any consumer good will usually impact our decision to buy or not to buy. This is true of incense as well. Many factors go into the price of incense, but the bottom line is still the same for our budgets. Incense devotees sometimes spend literal fortunes on incense purchases. In some parts of the world, incense purchasing and use is seen as "conspicuous consumption" and is a way for people to demonstrate their wealth. They will purchase rare and expensive aromatics and then burn them. I suppose it is akin to burning money in order to demonstrate that you are so wealthy it doesn't matter to you! I find that sad on several levels, not the least of which is that rare aromatics are being wasted by those who don't care about the scent or the effect on the brain; they are merely trying to impress other people.

For those of us who have to live on a budget, cost is a very important factor when selecting incense. I certainly don't think that price alone should be the deciding factor in your decision, but you have to realistically consider how much you can afford to spend. No incense is worth bankruptcy (although I've encountered some that came close).

As I said, the price of incense is determined by a number of factors, but a dominant one is quality. Never base your opinion of the quality of incense just on price, but be aware that the finer the incense, the higher the cost. Just as with most things in life, the more valuable the materials in incense, the higher the quality and the more it will cost.

Factors beyond quality will impact the price of incense. As in any industry, marketing and packaging have to be added in to the price of incense if the manufacturers are to make a profit and stay in business. There is little advertising for incense in the United States, but there is marketing. The fancy signs, expensive displays, and promotional packages all factor into the price of incense. Likewise the shipping cost to get the product to you is reflected in the price. There is also a question of volume; the more incense a company is able to produce and sell, the lower its costs due to purchasing and producing in bulk.

These factors are certainly at play in the Western incense markets and the results can be strange indeed. Very inexpensive synthetic incense might end up costing a lot more than it should due to elaborate packaging and behind-the-scenes marketing done to retailers. The reverse can be true as well. High-quality incense can come down in price as its popularity increases (more sales = more bulk discounts, etc.). If there is a type or brand of incense that you truly love, please keep buying it. Each sale may make the difference between a price decrease or an increase! Yes, supply and demand are also important, so buying tons of one type of incense could cause a shortage and increasing prices, but take the gamble. Your support of the makers of high-quality incense is critical to future availability.

If you become a true incense fan, as I suspect you will, I would suggest creating an incense budget. See how much you can reasonably spend in a month on incense without straining your budget; now, don't go over that number. I know, this is just basic economics and common sense, but it is easy to get carried away in the heat of the moment and find yourself skipping meals because of some nice sandalwood. One price-conscious tip is to look for variety packs of incense. Many incense companies offer these, and they are a great way to sample a variety of incense for a low price. When you find one scent you love, you can then purchase it alone in larger quantities.

One final note on price ties back to homemade incense. If you have need for incense containing expensive aromatics, it might be more cost effective to make the incense yourself. This is certainly true for non-combustible incense, but even with combustible incense, you may be able to get higher-quality incense on your budget if you focus your money on the ingredients and then use your own labor to avoid ultra-expensive commercial incense.

In-the-Package Scent

Now we come to a factor that many, many people overlook. If you are buying synthetic incense (like the bins you see in stores where incense is sold by the stick for pennies each), it is normal to pick it up and smell it. That is a viable prospect with a lot of synthetic incense, but don't be fooled. Some synthetic incense is made with oils that were never intended to be burned. Have you ever brought home incense that smelled wonderful in the store but smelled like a house fire when you got it home? An oil that was meant for sniffing, not burning, is a likely cause.

This is even more important to consider when buying natural incense. Whether hand rolled, extruded, or dipped in natural oils, most natural incense has a significantly different smell when it burns. Many "whole herb" incense products have no scent at all until burned. It is very similar to purchasing wine. You have to rely far more on the package description and the help of your retailer to pick the scent you want. Just smelling the package will tell you very little or—worse yet—mislead you about the true scent.

———

Selecting incense is both fun and exciting. It seems like there are so many factors to balance when selecting incense, it is almost overwhelming, but it doesn't need to be a difficult task. If you are an educated consumer who knows what she wants, then the choices narrow themselves down quickly. For magickal purposes, incense doesn't have to smell like perfume. In fact, the most appropriate incense in some magickal work may not have a pleasing fragrance at all, so don't let your nose alone decide. Do some shopping, do some experimenting, and enjoy the journey. Incense is relaxing and enjoyable, so don't let the process of choosing it ruin the other aspects.

5

Censers and Holders

The incense censer (burner) is a versatile tool that is a vital part of incense use. Sticks, cones, powder, coils, and charcoal-fired incense can all work well in a properly prepared censer. Although there are specialized censers or burners designed for specific types of incense, one carefully selected censer can serve virtually all of your incense needs.

The first factor you should consider is how you are going to use your censer. Will it be used strictly indoors resting on an end table, or will you bring it to outdoor rituals where it will be carried and handled by a variety of people? Knowing your censer's purpose will help you decide what material it should be crafted of as well as the form or shape that would be most appropriate.

Another important consideration is the type of incense that you burn. Most stick incense, especially masala-style, needs nothing more than a container that can catch ash. Masala-style incense will not distribute heat to its censer unless incorporated into "incense chaining" (see chapter 12). Joss sticks will burn down to whatever material holds it, so a wooden censer, or one of other combustible material, isn't an ideal choice (although the typical thin joss stick doesn't produce enough heat to be a major concern). When burning cones, cylinders, powder, or charcoal incense, there can be significant amounts of heat transferred to the censer. This has a major impact on safe handling while incense is burning and later as it cools down.

I have personally owned a hundred or more censers over the years and still haven't tried a fraction of the wonderful censers I've seen. One of my incense making students once did me the great honor of gifting to me a censer he had made of copper—a material I had never even considered for a censer —and I've found it useful in many unintended ways, including burning powders and cones. Once you've become an incense addict, it is easy to begin collecting censers, but I think it is important to have one general-purpose censer to begin with. You can then add more esoteric ones as the need or opportunity arrives.

Materials

Incense censers can be found made of nearly any material. Essentially any substance that can be shaped in some fashion and is not flammable can be used to make a censer—even some materials that are flammable are used. Personally, I think that some materials are superior to others, but the reality is that your choice in material can be based on aesthetics or personal taste. For those who make ritual use of incense, the choice of materials can reflect the work you are doing or path that you follow.

Metal

A wide variety of types of metal are used for making censers. Brass is perhaps the most popular choice for censers, but aluminum, pewter, bronze, copper, iron, steel and other metal censers can be located with ease. Aside from the aesthetic aspects, care and durability are things to be considered when purchasing or creating a metal censer. Softer metals (such as copper and pewter) are easier to shape or engrave but obviously also more subject to physical damage. Harder metals such as iron and steel can provide rugged durability but are also significantly harder to modify.

If you intend to use a censer outdoors, especially while camping or attending an outdoor festival, a sturdy iron or steel censer would be a great choice. On the other hand, a large iron censer might not be the best choice for your bedroom end table. If you don't intend to modify the censer (engraving, carving, etc.), you can purchase one made of any type of metal. If you do plan to modify your censer, bear in mind your personal limitations with regard to cutting or engraving the metal you choose.

Another consideration with any censer is how it conducts heat. Generally speaking, metal censers become quite hot with certain types of incense (especially charcoal burning), although one that is large and contains the proper fill material is still safe to handle. Unless you have tested a metal censer to ensure it does not become hot with your incense use, it is always a good idea to place it on a heat-resistant plate or tile to avoid damage to the surface underneath. Metal censers are sometimes designed with handles, chains, or other attachments that allow them to be safely moved even if they do become hot.

Stone

While stone may not jump to the front of your mind when considering censers, it is actually quite a common material. The most popular form of stone censer in the United States right now is soapstone. Soapstone is well-known as an excellent distributor of heat and is sometimes used around fireplaces. As a result, it tends to spread the heat evenly around the censer and will stay warm well after charcoal has been extinguished. Soapstone is easy to work with and can be found in a wide variety of forms, from dish censers to cone "temples" to deep bowls. Soapstone censers are easy to modify because of the softness of the material. Knife blades, sandpaper, and simple metal drill bits can all be used to customize and modify soapstone censers.

Marble is another common stone that is used in censer construction and it handles heat extremely well. Although marble is beautiful and has no problems with heat, it is much more difficult to modify. Lava rock is also used in some censers, along with a variety of other stones.

It is important to note that sedimentary rock, such as sandstone, should be avoided in most cases or at least used with extreme caution. This type of stone can trap water and can actually explode if overheated. I will grant you that I have *never* heard of this happening with a censer, but it is still good to keep this in mind.

Although stone censers are generally heavy and seem quite durable, many stones (especially after having been worked) are brittle. They can shatter if dropped, so handle them with care. Most stones will also retain heat for longer than most other materials.

Ceramic

This is my personal favorite as a material for censer construction. From the simplest hand-formed dish fired in a ceramics class to the most intricate and beautiful Japanese koro, ceramic censers have long served both casual and formal uses of incense. Ceramics handle heat very well, can be formed into virtually any shape or color, and cool faster than most stones. Ceramic censers are typically fragile, so they aren't ideally suited for outdoor use. This isn't to say that they can't be used outdoors, but caution is always called for when used over bare earth, concrete floors, or other areas where they could so easily be destroyed by a simple fall.

Ceramic censers are so flexible in form that nearly any shape is possible. Modifying a ceramic censer is much more difficult than it is with censers made from some other materials. If you have access to the proper materials and equipment to make ceramics, then you could make and form the shape of your censer and use colors of your choice. For the rest of us, it is best to buy a ceramic censer that you don't feel a need to modify. Even paint on a ceramic censer can be difficult to apply and easily worn away.

Wood

Although at first thought you wouldn't see any use for a wooden censer apart from holding masala-style sticks, wooden censers have come in an interesting assortment of forms. In the past, some types of incense clocks actually used wooden censers. One form included the use of wires strung between two sections of wood where a joss stick or cylinder was suspended. The thin wires did not cause enough burn resistance to impact the incense. Simplified versions of this type of censer are still for sale today. When used as a clock, the wires allowed an alarm bell to be attached to the incense.

Wood certainly offers a material that is easily modified. It comes in a variety of shapes and range from very plain, utilitarian forms to elaborately carved censers. It is simple to add your own designs with carving, burning, cutting, painting, and staining. Generally speaking, I think wood is best incorporated into a censer made of a combination of materials, but with proper construction and appropriate fill materials, nearly any type of censer could theoretically be made from wood.

Glass

Glass is often seen as an ideal material for censer construction, but there are important considerations to keep in mind when selecting glass. Because of its flexibility when in its liquid form, you can find glass censers in a wide variety of forms. With an appropriate fill material and when matched to the right style of incense, glass censers can be both beautiful and functional.

Perhaps the most surprising thing about glass censers is the consideration of how they handle heat. It seems natural to think that since glass requires such a high degree of heat to liquefy, it would naturally resist any heat from incense. This is not the case. I have seen more than one improperly used glass censer shatter from heat, so don't assume that a glass censer is heatproof.

Much like ceramics, glass censers come in a huge variety of colors and shapes. Also like ceramics, glass censers are difficult to modify. Glass is easier to modify in at least one regard: it can be etched. Etching is most commonly done by sandblasting or with a chemical etcher, allowing for some customizing not possible with ceramic censers.

Glass etching kits are available at many hobby and craft stores. Chemical etching is quite simple and fun to do. An easy way to accomplish customization with chemical etching is as easy as applying peel-and-stick letters, numbers, or symbols on the glass. The entire area is then "painted" with the etching chemical and allowed to sit for a while. You then wash off the chemical and the stickers. The result is that all the glass that was "painted" is then etched while the areas that were protected by the stick-and-peel material are left untouched. In minutes you can modify many types of glass censers using this method.

Combinations

Some of the most beautiful censers I've seen were made from several different types of materials. Brass censers with wooden handles, wooden censers that hold a stone dish for burning, and pewter censers mounted on a marble base are all examples of what can be done using a combination of materials. Combinations of materials can allow you to take an essentially un-modifiable censer and customize it to suit your needs. Add your own wooden base or holder to an otherwise difficult-to-customize stone dish and you suddenly have something personal and very unique.

Size

The size of your censer depends primarily on how you plan to use it. If you need a censer that you can easily handle during a ritual for one, a small censer would likely be better. Conversely, if you plan to use one to scent a three-hundred-square-foot room, you would need quite a large censer (or numerous small ones). There are a few important factors to remember in regard to size when considering censers.

One important consideration is the height of the censer. Height essentially impacts your decision in two ways: First, height determines how much ash, or how large a piece of charcoal or incense, the censer can hold. If you plan to experiment with Asian-style incense burning, you will need a deeper censer to allow you to bury the charcoal. If you are burning small cones or incense trails, you could use a censer that is very shallow.

Width also impacts a choice in censers. I am an advocate of censers that are easy to use, and a deep and narrow censer is very difficult to use. Therefore I prefer the bulk of my censers to have a mouth double the height of the censer. A 1-inch-tall censer should be at least 2 inches wide. Obviously when you get to larger censers (any censer more than 4 inches wide), this concern drops away. When it comes to smaller censers, wider is better.

There is a very specific aspect of the use of your censer that width impacts. Although you can put incense into a censer and then light it, with many censers this can be very difficult. In the case of charcoal, it is very ineffective. In general, I prefer to light my incense or charcoal and then place it in my censer. In order to do that, it has to have a mouth wide enough to accommodate your fingers and the burning incense. I can't count the number of times I used to burn myself because I was trying to insert burning incense cones into a deep censer with a narrow mouth. If you must use a censer that won't comfortably accommodate your fingers and the incense, consider using tongs or tweezers to move the burning incense.

Styles

Just as censers come made from a wide variety of materials, they also come in a seemingly endless variety of shapes and forms. Clearly the most important consideration of form should be the type of incense you use, but as I mentioned before, it is always a good idea to have one all-purpose censer and then acquire any specialty censers you might want. It is certainly true that virtually anything can be transformed into a censer, but tools designed for a specific purpose, following a long-standing tradition, are often more useful than those that tinkerers like myself create based on a whim.

Censers for Charcoal Incense

If you use incense that is not self-burning, your censer is perhaps a more important consideration than for other forms. This type of censer needs to be able to withstand the heat from charcoal tablets. If you use the "self-lighting" style of charcoal, it burns very hot indeed and requires a censer that won't break or crack from the heat. I talk more about the material used to fill such a censer later in this chapter, but I do want to mention that some fill materials transmit heat more than others, so take that into consideration as well.

Typically, any censer that can be used to burn incense on charcoal will also work for all of the self-combusting varieties of incense. There are specific styles listed later in this chapter that will work only with self-combusting styles, but I've always felt that this type of censer offers the most versatility and utility. I've broken these types of censers into three general forms to make them convenient to discuss, although really the variety is endless.

Dishes

This is my least favorite of the all-purpose censers. A dish censer is just what it sounds like: a shallow container, sometimes without a lip, where charcoal or self-combusting incense can sit while burning. Dishes can contain a fill material, but often do not. The lack of fill is one of the reasons I don't care for them. If you select a dish censer, make certain it is of a material that can resist a great deal of heat, and avoid glass dishes. Charcoal tablets placed directly onto glass can easily crack or even shatter the censer. Even for dish censers, I recommend using some type of fill material.

Cups

Cup censers are cylindrical and are sometimes literal drinking cups. I've used coffee mugs in this role many times. With an appropriate fill material, cups and mugs can work quite well. I don't recommend glass for this style of censer either, as cup censers usually have a small diameter and can be subject to a lot of heat.

One particular type of traditional censer is certainly worthy of mention here. The Japanese koro is a type of censer traditionally used in the kodo ceremony. Most traditional koros are quite expensive, although I have seen a few priced under $50 from time to time. You might want to look for censers described as "kodo censer," "kodo cup," or similar names. The name doesn't matter, only the size and shape. When used with low-heat charcoal, koro-type censers can be easily handled or passed. See chapter 9 for more details on this, but the koro is a perfect example of a cup-style censer. Cup censers don't have to be small, either. I own one that is 6 inches in diameter and because of its size, it functions more like a bowl censer than a cup.

Bowls

In my opinion, this is the most versatile of all censer shapes. Unlike cup censers, bowls are narrowest at the bottom and are wider nearer the top. Bowl censers are often much larger than their cup counterparts, although small bowl censer are sometimes used as well. Large bowls that aren't terribly deep (for example 10 inches in diameter and 4 inches tall) have served as my primary censers for years. You can purchase ornate censers in virtually any form, but the most useful censer I own is a thick ceramic bowl of those dimensions. I purchased it for a very low price at a local discount store, and it has served me extremely well for many years. The real advantage of the bowl style is its width at the opening. The wide aperture allows for easier access to the incense and the fill material. This is especially important when burning incense trails, but it is helpful with any form of incense.

———

In all fairness, there are some censers that don't fit neatly into these categories. Another Japanese form is a bowl that tapers at the top. Is it a bowl that tapers or a cup that is distended in the middle? I don't want to slice my definitions up that finely, so suffice it to say you can always find censers that won't fit into these convenient categories, nor is it a critical consideration.

These categories are merely intended to give you ideas about the censer that you need to find for your own incense magick.

Incense Boats

Sadly, this is one of the most familiar styles of incense burners in America. Perhaps *sadly* is overstating it a bit, but the incense boat is such a specialized form that it shows how little exposure the general public has had to the incredible variety of incense forms. The incense boat is a long, narrow (relative to the length) censer designed primarily for masala-style sticks of incense. Available in glass, metal, and other materials, it is often made of wood. This style of censer is often seen in supermarkets or discount stores. My only real dislike of this style of censer is its the lack of versatility. Wooden incense boats aren't particularly safe for anything aside from masala sticks. This isn't to say that incense boats pose a safety hazard (although as with any censers, it might), but using cones or even joss sticks in a wooden incense boat could cause damage as burning incense comes into contact with the boat itself. There are incense boats made of metal or stone that are much more versatile. A metal or stone incense boat can handle the heat from cones, coils, cylinders, and—with some designs— even charcoal.

The incense boat has risen to higher levels of sophistication in design. Covered incense boats (sometimes called "incense coffins") can easily conceal and contain ash and often come with storage compartments in the bottom. Some of those made of stone could serve as a primary censer. There are designs that are ventilated well enough to burn with the lid closed. They present an almost mystical visage as they exude smoke from multiple openings. They are also a good way to conceal the glowing of burning incense if you are trying to control every aspect of light in a ritual.

Tibetan Burner

Although this type of incense burner has become popular in modern times with censers exported from Tibet, they are actually a common style throughout Asia. Unlike an incense boat, the Tibetan burner allows the incense stick or cylinder to lay flat while burning. They use a series of wires or rods, widely spaced, to support the incense. One advantage to this style of censer is cleanliness. As the incense burns, the ash falls through the gaps into the compartment below the wires. If the ash doesn't all fall through, a gentle tap usually pushes the remainder inside. This style of censer is also a good base unit to use if you wish to construct your own "incense alarm clock." Usually made from wood, they are sometimes constructed from stone or metal as well.

Cone Burners

The dedicated cone censer is generally too small to serve as an all-purpose censer, although there are exceptions to this. Cone burners are most commonly found in the small brass design we see in many shops and even some grocery stores. This is far from the extent of their design and size. In shops that carry a wider range of incense paraphernalia, you can choose from much larger brass, copper, pewter, or stone cone censers. These types of censers are generally a small dish censer on a raised base, usually with a lid. Large cone censers will work as well as any dish censer, but it is unusual to find one of sufficient size. By nature, these censers are generally too small for use with charcoal, coils, or powder. Many cone censers can accommodate stick incense as well.

There are certainly stylistic and aesthetic reasons to use dedicated cone censers. Like most styles of censer, they come in a huge variety of colors, materials, and designs. From the simplest brass censer to elaborate censers made of stone, the cone censer can have great visual appeal. Personally, I find the common small cone censers to be of minimal functionality. They are great for looks and the purpose to which they are dedicated, but only the larger versions have any versatility.

There is a special adaptation of the cone censer that takes on a special role in more than one religion. Often called a thurible, some censers are suspended by a chain and can be easily carried or swung to disperse incense smoke over a wide area. The categories that I used to describe different censer designs are not all-encompassing in their definitions. Whether to consider the hanging incense censer to be a large cone censer or a raised bowl censer is an example of that. No matter how you view it, the hanging censer is a specialized censer that is familiar to many people. In the West we most closely associate the hanging censer with Christian practice, but it serves other religions as well. Certainly in magickal practice and especially in outdoor magick, the hanging censer offers options that are difficult to duplicate in any other way. A large hanging censer can contain large pieces of charcoal or even fire embers for burning loose incense. Powders, herbs, resins, and woods can all be placed inside the censer. While swinging a lit censer seems like it would result in ash or embers flying all around, the force of the swinging is usually enough to keep everything inside the censer.

Obviously there are some safety concerns with all censers, but this is especially true with a swinging censer. If you choose to swing a hanging censer, keep some common sense guidelines in mind. Test the chain or cord that holds the censer. A damaged chain could break while the censer is swinging and the result could be fire, injury, or at the very least a really big mess. Hanging censers usually have a lid. I'll talk more about lids shortly, but for a censer that will be swung, I think a lid is a really good idea. A swinging censer also needs to be well-balanced. Test it before buying, if possible. You can swing an empty censer and see if it would be safe for use in your space.

Space is another safety concern. When swinging a censer, check out the space where you will use it *in advance*. The worst way to find out there isn't room to swing your censer is when it's full of burning materials. Obstacles of any type, including the human variety, need to be avoided. Banging someone in the head with a burning censer is clearly something to be avoided. The space you have to work within should also help determine the level of energy you should use when swinging your censer. Smaller spaces require less swinging. If you use the censer outdoors, you can usually swing with as much enthusiasm as you like, but remember that you are wielding a fire hazard; try to keep yourself in check no matter how much fun you are having!

Bottles

This is a newer trend in censer design, but it certainly has its place in the pantheon of censers. Bottle censers are dedicated stick burners, although most can accommodate joss or masala-style sticks. They are ventilated bottles, often with colorful designs painted on them, that completely contain the ash of the sticks. If you are concerned about messy ash escaping your censer, bottle censers might be the best choice for you. There are other variations on this concept as well. I have a covered wooden censer from Brazil that is a large wooden cylinder snuggly fitted into a wooden base. Air flow is provided through a series of vent holes along the cylinder. This censer provides a nice visual effect and it holds all the ash. It's wonderful for outdoor burning if there is too strong a wind for other types of censers.

Novelty Burners

Okay, I admit it. I couldn't think of a nifty name for this category of censers, but I still felt they are worth mentioning. Incense burners are made from a huge variety of materials in a staggering array of designs. Many of these incense burners are well-crafted and quite functional but with an unusual twist of form. For example, I have a wonderful and quite large incense burner in the shape of a multi-headed dragon. It uses cone incense that is placed in a holder in the bottom of the burner. When incense burns inside, air is drawn up through holes near the bottom and smoke pours from the mouth of each dragon head.

I have another unusual burner designed for masala-style incense sticks. Similar to a bottle incense burner, it has a long cylinder that is perforated in strategic locations and a base that holds the incense. The top cylinder slides down over the base and smoke pours from the mouth of an Incan tree spirit carved on the cylinder. This gift was purchased for me in Peru by a friend of mine, which demonstrates that the use of masala-style sticks goes far beyond India and the United States.

These novelty burners come in every imaginable shape and size. From tree frogs to miniature fireplaces to smiling suns, you can find a novelty burner in nearly any form. Have a favorite band or animal? The odds are very good that you can find a novelty burner that will suit your aesthetic style.

In the broadest terms, novelty incense burners can be tricky to use effectively. Air flow is a critical part of the success of a censer or burner, and many novelty burners sacrifice air flow for an entertaining design. Carefully consider the design of any burner before purchasing, but give novelty burners an extra look. If you find very restricted air flow (as demonstrated by a lack of openings to feed oxygen to the incense or many holes at the top of the burner but none at the bottom), consider if you would be willing to buy the censer strictly for decoration. If yes, then at least you didn't waste your money should it have poor performance. Some novelty burners work very well. Some have an open form, like an incense dish, and will always have good air flow.

A few novelty burners that don't perform well can be modified to work much better. You may be able to cut vent holes to improve air flow, raise the burner's cover to add additional air flow, or learn the limits of the type and size of incense that can be used with that burner. The Incan incense burner I mentioned earlier had very poor performance until I realized that the incense, once placed in the base, stood taller than the highest vent hole in the cover. I tried breaking the wooden part of my masala incense off about 1 inch from when the incense coating began. That shortened the sticks so they no longer extended above the top vent hole, and the burner now works perfectly.

Hanging

Often called thuribles, hanging burners come in a huge variety of sizes but often follow very similar design styles. I discussed these a bit earlier in this chapter but want to bring a few points to your attention. The majority of hanging burners are essentially cup-style cone burners with cords or chains attached from which they hang. Hanging burners (especially those that can also sit safely on a flat surface) have enhanced versatility, since they can be used in places where there are no flat or level surfaces. They can be hung from tree branches or plant hooks. The length of the chain can be altered to allow an incense burner to hang at a precisely determined level. This concept can be incorporated into rituals or used in large spaces to focus the scent so that it impacts people in a particular location. A burner hung a few inches above head height can scent parts of a room that no burner set upon a table or the floor can reach.

Hanging burners are also a very safe choice for a burner that will be moved with burning incense or charcoal inside. There are a few burners out there with handles that will allow them to be safely moved, but the thurible has been a traditional choice for this purpose for hundreds, if not thousands, of years. Not only can the burner be moved while in use, it can be swung to distribute scent more widely. This is still a common practice in many Christian denominations. The burning of frankincense in a thurible is a magickal experience when a cloud of smoke wafts over your entire body or scent unexpectedly falls from above.

Some thuribles have decorations that hang from the bottom of the burner. Others might have a rounded bottom. These types of designs are a bit more difficult to use and aren't as functional as those that will sit or stand without their chains. The burner needs to be level as you prepare and light it, so if your thurible can't sit level, you will have to accommodate this. Loading a thurible that can't stand on its own either requires the building of a stand, the assistance of another person, or some true talent and tolerance to burns. You can load one while suspended from its chains, but that is a trickier proposition than a nice stable burner.

Lids

This is a topic that I have seen widely and hotly debated (pun intended) among incense enthusiasts. When and how to use a lid on a censer or a burner? For the most part, I am a very big supporter of lids on burners. How you use them is the most critical part. Most of the lidded incense burners I have seen, used, or owned will not burn well with the lid in place. There are certainly numerous exceptions, but lids are generally best employed when the censer is not in use. Lids add a decorative element to most censers and unless you clean your censer completely after each use, a lid serves to keep the ash in your censer. Even a slight breeze can stir the ash from incense, so a lid will help you to maintain a cleaner environment.

For censers that do work successfully with the lid in place, the lid can add a whole new dimension to the visual aspect of your incense. Different lids will yield very different smoke patterns—the way the smoke curls and spreads. Some lids are deeply perforated with many tiny holes, which produces a much wider stream of smoke. Some are perforated in only a few specific locations to guide the smoke in a certain direction. Some censers are not perforated at all and serve to force the smoke to leave the censer via a different path (such as through holes in the sides).

If you choose to use a lid over burning incense, remember a few key things. First, your incense can never come into direct contact with the lid. If it does, the incense will not burn properly. It is best to keep burning incense at least 1 inch below the level of any lid. Next, you will have to perform more maintenance to keep your burner working at peak efficiency. Resins and other materials will collect on the inside of the lid. On lids with small perforations, this residue could plug up the openings and disrupt the air flow. Incense residue can be easily removed with a high-proof alcohol or any one of several adhesive removers available commercially. One nice trick for cleaning lids was given to me by David Oller, who suggests cleaning your lid with the moist leaves from a recently brewed cup of tea. Not only are you finding a new use for something normally discarded, but it is also an effective and natural way to easily remove resins.

Another option is to leave the resins in place. As long as they are not impeding the incense burn, you can allow the resins to build up, giving your censer a unique scent of its own. Every time you burn incense with that lid in place, it will accumulate more resins and release its unique, and generally subtle, scent. Even as it releases its characteristic scent, the scent or your censer is being altered by the new incense being burned. The scent of the lid of your favorite censer will be ever-changing yet always familiar.

Fill Material

Not all censers require a fill material—sand, gravel, salt, or ash used to provide a "bed" for burning incense—but many styles of censer will benefit from being filled. For some types of censers, fill is mandatory. The primary determining factor in the decision to use a fill material is the type of incense you plan to use in that censer. Obviously an incense boat used only for burning stick incense will not need a fill material. On the other hand, a cup-style censer used to burn sticks usually will need a filler.

Fill materials serve several purposes. First, they protect your censer. Some styles of incense, and definitely charcoal, get very hot. A fill material can insulate your censer from that heat. Although a glass bowl censer seems like a very heat-resistant censer, one large incense cone or charcoal brick can generate enough heat on the bare glass to cause it to shatter. That same censer with an appropriate fill will safely handle several cones burning at once without fear of damage. *Don't assume that using a fill material will keep your censer cool enough to handle while in use.* Some censers, such as a Japanese koro, can be easily handled even with a charcoal brick burning inside when properly filled. Many censers will still pick up enough heat to give you a nasty burn from a single cone. Protecting the censer from heat is not the same as protecting your fingers from it!

Another purpose of a fill material is to give a level, secure area to insert incense. Virtually any filled censer will allow you to insert masala or joss sticks safely. A fill material can level out a bumpy or convex-bottomed censer to allow you to lay sticks flat or burn charcoal, cones, or cylinders more evenly. Fill materials also serve a decorative purpose. Using colored sand in a censer adds to its beauty. From a magickal perspective, fill materials allow you to employ color magick or even sand art into your censer. Finally, fill material is critical if you plan to experiment with kodo-style techniques (see chapter 9).

Sand

One of the most common fill materials, sand is readily available and can be purchased in a wide variety of colors. From fine sand to coarse, this is a good fill for inserting sticks or to protect many censers from excessive heat. Different-colored sands can be combined for interesting effects or for sand "painting" symbols or words. That not only enhances the beauty of the censer but also provides another tool for incorporating your censer into your ritual work.

Personally, I am not a fan of sand as a fill material. The magickal applications I suggested above are valid reasons to use sand, and it is appropriate for some types of censers, but sand does not enhance the burning of your incense. Many people believe that a bed of sand in the bottom of a censer will help cones burn completely to where the base of the cone meets the sand. In actuality, the reverse is true. Sand blocks the flow of air under the incense and may cause the bottom layer of incense to remain unburned. This is true with some types of charcoal as well. Sand does have the advantage of being heavy, so it is less likely to be blown out of your censer than ash or fine salt, but it is not my first choice for an all-purpose censer.

Gravel

Gravel is sand's big sister. Gravel can also be found in different colors (visit an aquarium or art supply store for colored gravel) and different levels of coarseness. It has basically the same properties as sand but, because the grains are much larger, it will not form as smooth a surface as sand. However, the gaps between grains do provide for better airflow under the base of the incense than does sand.

Salt

Salt is a popular choice among the magickal community. Not only is salt a symbol of earth and used in many rituals, it is also found in most homes. Salt can also be found from very fine to coarse, just as sand or gravel. While salt certainly does add its own flair to your censer (you will be hard-pressed to find sand as white as salt) and it can be used in combination with sand, I consider it an even poorer choice for any incense or charcoal burned directly on its surface. Salt itself can scorch or even burn under the heat of incense or charcoal. Scorched salt will add its own scent to your incense, so keep that in mind as well. If your only need is to insert masala sticks into the salt, then it is an excellent fill material; if any burning incense or charcoal will come into contact with the surface of your fill material, I would not recommend salt. Salt can be dyed to be almost any color you'd like. With such a pure white base, salt crystals absorb food coloring easily.

Ash

Ash is, in my opinion, the most beneficial and versatile of all the fill materials. Ash offers many of the advantages of the other fill materials while overcoming many of their drawbacks. Best of all, the level of ash in your censer will grow over time. The more incense you burn, the more ash you have! Although you can do limited drawing in sand or salt, ash offers a unique medium for writing or drawing in your censer. Ash can be drawn upon with anything from a writing quill to a toothpick. Symbols, words, and geometric designs can be prepared on the surface of the ash. If you wish, you can then fill those impressions with powder incense and burn it as an incense trail (see chapter 11). You can create detailed and controlled incense trails in ash unlike any other fill. Ash will yield to your touch but hold the sharp edges of your design.

The true gift of ash as a fill material is the way it traps air. As with most fillers, you can insert incense sticks into the ash. Cones and cylinders will often burn completely in an ash bed, without a leftover "nub" of unburned incense. Incense will even burn below the surface of the ash. All of this is possible because the ash traps air.

Ash does require maintenance for the best performance. You will need to periodically stir the ash to "fluff" it into a more workable medium and replenish the air within it. You should also screen your ash occasionally (frequently if you burn a lot of joss sticks) to remove any bits of unburned incense or charcoal. I just use an inexpensive mesh strainer that has been retired from kitchen use. This sifting will reduce unexpected scents from the ash.

When ash has been used extensively, unburned oils and resins can seep down into the ash. Eventually those oils and resins will cause the ash to generate its own scent. That is usually not desirable, but you could view it like leaving resins on the lid of a censer. However, the scent of well-used ash is rarely as pleasant to my nose as the subtle scent from a censer lid. If your ash begins to take on a scent you don't like, sift and spread the ash on an old cookie sheet. Bake in a low oven for an hour and then allow it to cool. Stir the ash and check it for scent. You may have to repeat that step several times if your ash is heavily used.

I can almost hear you asking, "But how do I get enough ash to fill a censer?" That's a great question. The surprising answer is that you can buy it. Usually called white ash, this is used in Asian incense burning and can be found from most retailers who carry high-quality Asian incense. The ash does become gray over time (quite quickly if you use "hidden trails" as discussed in chapter 11), but when purchased it is white and scentless and ready to be added to your censer.

————

I have seen and experimented with other fill materials, as I know many incense users have. Soil is a good choice for certain types of ritual work, especially soil from a sacred place or a place related to the magick work at hand. Sea shells, marbles, chocolate candy (I do NOT recommend using chocolate as a fill material), and more have been used in censers. As long as you take care not to use any flammable material (which would disqualify chocolate from the list) you can be very creative with fill materials. For an all-purpose censer or one that is frequently used, ash or sand is probably going to be your best choice.

Heat Source

Non-combustible incense requires an external heat source. Heat for incense comes from a variety of sources, but for the most part needs to be compact, easy to use, and safe. Incense cannot live without the element of fire, and the power of fire should always be respected. In the twenty-first century we still tend to use ancient techniques to heat non-combustible incense even though a modern alternative is available.

Embers

The most traditional of all heat sources, hot coals or embers from a fire can be used in a censer. If pre-cut wood chips are placed on the outside edge of a fire, they can be easily removed once they are glowing. That's a nice way to be certain you will have an ember that will fit in your censer. Keep a close eye on the wood! Wood chips small enough to fit into an average censer burn quickly. You will need to add several of them to get one that glows properly before it is burned away. You also need to watch the chips in the fire because they can vanish very quickly once touched by the flames.

Self-Lighting Charcoal

This is the type of charcoal often found in New Age and magick shops. Charcoal becomes "self-lighting" when it is impregnated with saltpeter (potassium nitrate or sodium nitrate) during the manufacturing process. While it isn't truly self-lighting, it is very easy to light. Holding a charcoal brick with tongs over a candle flame will cause it to quickly spark to life. You will see tiny explosions across the surface of the charcoal as the saltpeter helps the charcoal to ignite.

This type of charcoal is ready for use faster than other charcoals. Other than that, self-lighting charcoal is a method of last resort for me. The addition of the saltpeter has two significant drawbacks. First, it burns far too hot. Incense should be smoldered, not burnt to a crisp. You can take a lovely tear of frankincense and drop it onto self-lighting charcoal and have a disgusting smell within moments. At first you smell the wonderful aroma of frankincense, but it is then followed by the lingering odor of its burnt remains. Very well-made loose incense can burn up in seconds with this type of charcoal. For this reason, the only practical use I've found for self-lighting charcoal is for incense burning in windy conditions. In a well-made censer with a proper lid, self-lighting charcoal can remain functional in weather conditions that would disable any other type of charcoal.

The second drawback to this type of charcoal is the smell. If you use a self-burning charcoal brick, you may want to allow it to fully ignite, then move it to a fresh censer and carry it into another room (this completely isolates the smell of the charcoal from any of the tools or other incense). You will be amazed at how foul the smell is from self-lighting charcoal. Saltpeter is one component of that smell, although I have never found any charcoal of this type that was made of high-quality wood either. So it is likely not the saltpeter alone causing that unpleasant scent.

Scentless Charcoal

The next choice for a heat source may be a little more difficult to locate, but it is certainly worth the effort. Scentless charcoal is very nearly that—scentless. I would classify all of the "scentless" charcoals that I have used to be "very little scent" instead. When compared to self-lighting charcoal, scentless is a real blessing. Scentless charcoal is generally nothing more than powdered charcoal and a binder. It does not contain saltpeter or other such oxidizers. Not only does that reduce the odor dramatically, it also means that this type of charcoal burns at a significantly lower temperature than self-lighting. The result is that incense burned on this type of charcoal gives a truer scent and smolders for a much longer time. Your incense lasts longer and smells better. Those two things alone make it worth the search.

Look for "low scent," "scentless," or "bamboo" charcoal if you want to get the best results. Be sure to read the package carefully, but certainly any charcoal from a respected name in incense (such as Shoyeido or Baieido) will give you results that exceed self-lighting charcoal. It does take a few minutes longer to get the scentless brick to fully ignite, but I have found that a small, scentless brick burns as long as or longer than a much larger self-lighting brick. A nice surprise is that, brick-for-brick, scentless charcoal is usually no more expensive than self-lighting.

Aroma Lamps

An aroma lamp is a great alternative to charcoal that is often overlooked. They come in a huge assortment of shapes and sizes, but a typical aroma lamp will be similar in its functional aspects to all other aroma lamps. There is usually a small bowl that rests or is suspended above a small candle. Tealight candles are usually placed underneath to provide heat to the bowl that is partially filled with water. Once the water is warm from the candle, drops of essential oil are added to the water and the gentle heat slowly releases the scent into the room. You can accomplish the same kind of gentle heating with the use of an aroma lamp in place of charcoal.

Most aroma lamps are adjustable after a fashion. You can vary the heat by moving the candle up or down below the bowl. When selecting an aroma lamp, I prefer to have the candle rest several inches below the bottom of the bowl. Although being so far separated from the bowl would cause the candle to heat the bowl very slowly, this gives you the range to adjust it. I usually place coins under the candle if I want to increase the heat. Each coin placed beneath the candle will raise it a fraction of an inch. Tiny changes in the proximity of the candle can have a noticeable difference in burning time and the scent of your incense.

To modify an aroma lamp for use with incense, I have never found that I need to do more than place a little aluminum foil or a small ceramic tile in the bottom of the bowl before use. That prevents any residue from remaining in the lamp and you can easily clean it. It also allows you to continue using it as an aroma lamp rather than dedicate it to incense only. You will have to experiment with each aroma lamp you acquire, but I typically keep the candle flame from making too much direct contact with the bowl. One inch below the dish's bottom is a good starting place. This approach to incense, when used at the lowest practical heat level, allows your non-combustible incense to burn virtually smokeless.

Electric Incense Warmers

Another option now available to us is electric incense warmers. Available from both Asia and the Middle East, these popular items are often adjustable. They use a small electric heating element to gently heat your incense. A friend of mine sent me one that I enjoyed for many years until it wore out. That particular warmer was not adjustable and tended to be too hot, so she also included a plug-in lamp dimmer to allow me to adjust the temperature. I admit that this type of burner is the height of luxury. To have such control, to not need to wait for charcoal to ignite, or aroma lamps to warm up, and so on is wonderful. Electric heaters offer nearly instantaneous satisfaction.

Although electric incense warmers are versatile and utilitarian, I have never found a way to comfortably fit them into any spell work. If you just want to have a "background" scent throughout your work, then you could place an electric burner just outside your working area. I would never string an electric cord into an area where I was doing spellwork, but that's just me. I'm sure there are many readers out there who feel differently, and those people may find some very creative ways to incorporate an electric warmer into their magickal work.

Preparing a Charcoal Censer

These instructions assume that you are using your censer for non-combustible incense and charcoal. Censers for combustible incense only require special preparation if they are used for incense trails (chapter 11) or chains (chapter 12). The careful preparation of your censer can have a huge impact on success with any particular incense experience. For instructions on preparing a censer for kodo-style incense burning, check out chapter 9.

The first step is to determine if you will use a fill material and, if so, which material you will use. For any type of non-combustible incense, I suggest using a good fill material if you are using any kind of charcoal. If you are using new fill material, you can pour it into your censer. If your censer has a lid, be certain to leave enough space between the lip of the censer and the top of your fill material. In most cases I do not fill censers past the halfway mark. This is not a hard and fast rule, but it is a good place to start when working with a new censer.

You can level out the top of your fill material by setting your censer on a sturdy, level surface and sliding it back and forth gently. You can also very lightly tap the bottom of the censer. Take care with the tapping approach, as it will also compact your fill material slightly. This is particularly important when working with ash.

Next you need to light the charcoal. Regardless of the type of charcoal you are using, it is best to hold it with tongs or pliers so that you can handle it easily and safely. Hold one edge of your charcoal brick directly in the flame of a candle. You can use a lighter for this process, but it will get very hot before your charcoal is ready for use. A candle is a steady source of flame that won't burn your thumb. Slowly rotate the charcoal in the flame. You want to see every edge of the charcoal glowing before putting the charcoal down.

Once the edges of the charcoal are glowing, let it rest for a few minutes. For formal uses, you can place the charcoal into one censer to ignite, then move it to the censer in which it will be used when it is ready. You need to allow the charcoal to rest until the entire brick is glowing. In bright light the brick will appear to be covered in a thin gray ash, but in dimmed light you will clearly see it glowing. This is the sign that the charcoal is ready to be placed in your working censer and put to use.

If you want to lower the heat from your charcoal, you can use a small ceramic square on top of the ignited incense brick. I have some 1-inch-square ceramic tiles that I use for this purpose. Placing one atop your charcoal and then putting your incense on the tile will reduce the heat, lengthen the burn time of the incense, and also make for simple cleanup afterwards. Placing incense directly onto charcoal requires that you periodically scrape the ash from atop the charcoal brick. If you use a ceramic tile, you can simply change the tiles. Always use tongs or pliers to handle hot tiles, and place them into a safe container, such as a ceramic bowl on a heat-proof surface. Those little tiles can get deceptively hot!

Selecting the right censer for you might look like a daunting task, but it shouldn't be. Incense is supposed to be relaxing and a tool for peace and introspection, which is the same attitude you should adopt any time you are shopping for incense or paraphernalia. Look for a censer that speaks to you or your task, and then use the information in this chapter to see if it will meet your needs. One carefully selected censer will last you a lifetime. As you might imagine, I do own and have owned a great variety of censers during my thirty-five-year romance with incense. Still, I use the same censer 90 percent of the time. I have owned that censer for well over a decade and will likely continue to use it for much longer. There is great joy in setting out to find a censer like that for yourself. If you can't find a censer that speaks to you, then consider making one yourself. Or you can do as so many of us have and acquire a collection of different censers. In the end you'll discover which of them best fits your needs; the others can still be used when the occasion calls for it.

6

Other Techniques

There are a few other aspects of incense use that didn't seem to fit anywhere else, and I didn't want to leave them out, so they are gathered here for you. I'd like to be able to tell all of my readers that this book is completely comprehensive and contains every approach and technique ever created for the use of incense. It isn't. Ancient approaches keep coming to light, new techniques and approaches are being developed by enthusiasts every year, and by the time this book is printed, someone will probably have shown me an approach I've never thought of before. I hope that you will continue to learn about incense long after you have finished reading this book. Perhaps one day you can teach me your latest technique!

Incense Sweeping

This is a technique that I have mentioned in passing already, but I'll go into more detail now. This is the process of using incense to "sweep" over your body to cleanse, purify, and prepare it to enter a sacred space. Some practitioners use this technique daily or before every magickal working; others use it only in preparation for rituals.

There are several ways to approach sweeping. Often times in group rituals or ceremonies, someone will walk among the gathered attendees before the ritual begins. A smudge bundle or other form of incense is offered to each person so they can use their hands to "sweep" the smoke onto various parts of the body. While sweeping can involve any or all parts of the body, sweeping the head, face, and chest are the most common. A thorough practitioner may sweep her entire body with smoke.

A complete sweeping of the body is most easily accomplished with the help of another person. The person being swept can pull smoke down the front of her body and over her head easily. The person holding the incense can then move smoke down across her back. Or, as I discussed earlier, you can sweep yourself without help if you sweep the front of your body and then place the censer on the ground and carefully step over it to allow the smoke to travel up your back.

Air Mixing

This is a great technique that I truly love, although I have never thought of any mundane uses for it. The concept behind air mixing is that incense is often composed of several different aromatics that, when blended together, create a unique new scent. So what would happen if you mixed those same aromatics *after* they have been burned? This idea was the birth of air mixing.

I first used this technique by accident. In fact I imagine anyone who has burned two different scents simultaneously in the same room has noticed the effect. I had cast my circle with censers at all four quarters. As I called each quarter, I lit a stick of single aromatic incense. I had used a representative herb in each quarter, so I had four different scents burning together by the time the circle was cast. As I walked around my altar several times, the smoke from the four censers was pulled into my wake. Soon the four independent scents had become a single new scent. Several of the rituals in this book are based around that experience.

Air mixing is an interesting effect. It happens slowly and requires that you stir the air in a specific way to get the full intensity. The only effective way I've found is to walk in a circle between the censers. I can't imagine that you could easily duplicate this effect outdoors, but in a reasonably draft-free room it is easily accomplished. It truly is a magickal experience and it can symbolize many things to many people, e.g., "From the many, one" (*e pluribus unum*). Air mixing is unity, it is change, and it can be quite moving. Best of all, it is easy to do.

I suggest that you avoid using "complex" incense for this method. Simpler is better in this case. Using multiple incense with many ingredients in each can easily turn into a cloud of overwhelming scent. The odds that all of those aromatics would be compatible in scent are quite low. By using single-aromatic incense (like sage, frankincense, or sandalwood) you can select a few that blend well without fear of scent incompatibility. The technique will work for all forms of incense, although using multiple censers with non-combustible incense might be challenging. You could even use different forms of incense in each censer. If you choose to analyze the symbology of this process deeply enough, you can make every aspect different for every quarter. You can use censers of different shapes, colors, and materials. You can use a different form of incense for each quarter (sticks at one quarter, loose incense at another, powder incense at another, etc.), use a different aromatic, draw a different symbol in the ash, and on and on.

I enjoy contemplation of the elements (as my rituals clearly reflect) and how they interact with each other, but I'm certain this concept could be applied for totally different reasons. You certainly aren't limited to four censers. You could use two or ten as you had need. If nothing else, air mixing is fun. Light different scents at your quarters and then spiral dance in the circle. The energy of the different incense will blend with the energy of the dancers and the energy that they raise.

Outdoor Incense Use

This is another unexpected facet of incense use. Who thinks of using incense outdoors? Pagans do, among others. A bale fire is an amazing tool for incense burning. Outdoor incense requires a different approach, but the basic mindset is still the same. It is simply a matter of scale.

While you might be blessed to live somewhere with days of no breeze, the wind is blowing, at least a little, in most places at any given moment, and the winds outdoors are not like a blowing fan in a room. Let's face it, the outdoor world is vast. It's also where we can most easily commune with the elements. There are no walls to confine tiny streams of smoke, so you have to think bigger. One ramification to this is that your incense will scent a huge swath and could impact people at quite a distance. Keep this in mind and be polite to those who haven't asked to participate in your plans; try not to "smoke out" anyone unexpectedly.

Thinking bigger also means preparing a lot more incense with greater heat sources. You can burn self-combustible incense outdoors, but because of the scale, you will either need a huge quantity or some up-scaled sticks and cones. I definitely don't recommend the use of self-combustible powder outdoors. Large quantities of burning incense powder could actually pose a fire hazard. If there's one thing I've figured out when it comes to worshiping nature, it is to never burn down the forest where you are holding your ritual.

I have seen some very large cones and cylinders that could be employed outside, and I have made incense cones with a stick pushing out of the bottom. I could insert the stick into the ground and not have to worry about the cone blowing over. You can certainly make large-scale versions of sticks or cylinders that would work for outdoor burning. In some Buddhist temples, huge incense coils are hung from the rafters. They are incredibly expensive and hang down from the ceiling to just above the floor. At 1 inch or more in diameter, these coils have to be ignited with a blow torch and will burn for a month. How I would love to use a few of those for an outdoor ritual! Sorry. I got a little carried away at the thought. The point is that even self-combustible incense can be up-scaled for outdoor use.

However, the better outdoor solution is loose incense. Pure resins, woods, and herbaceous materials properly heated can quickly scent a large area with little danger. The effect is also wonderful. I did this at a Samhain ritual some years ago where there was little wind and the moon was very bright. When I added the first batch of incense to the heat, a column of pale smoke rose, illuminated by the shining moon, into the universe. The scent was amazing and the sight was surprising.

The process for outdoor loose incense use is simple. You don't need censers or special charcoal, and it's a natural addition to camping. Begin with a campfire. If you are in a hurry, you can use a bag of charcoal instead. I can't imagine that I need to remind you, but please take care to use a safe fire pit or grill to contain the fire. Let the fire burn down to embers and develop a light coating of ash. Sprinkle a small amount of incense onto the coals and watch it burn. I like to use a resin, like a tear of frankincense, and then I observe how quickly the resin burns. If it melts quickly or burns in under thirty seconds, then the coals are a little too hot. If this is the case, you can adjust by placing the incense around the edges of the coals rather than in the center.

I will usually apply a handful of incense at a time. Remember that this is a case where we have to adjust our scale, so I do the same with the incense itself. I prefer coarse blends with whole tears of resin, large splinters of wood, and whole herbs. If your coals are cool enough and you use a coarse incense blend, you may only have to add extra incense every fifteen minutes or so. When the first handful is dropped onto the coals, a cloud of smoke will rise and drift with the wind. Watch the smoke to determine if it might blow into some undesirable location. Don't forget that some people have a true allergic reaction to certain aromatics or to any particulate matter in the air. You don't want to make anyone sick with your excellent incense blend.

Finally, I will mention that it is possible to burn incense on a small scale outdoors. Even a single stick or cone, in an area that is not exposed to the wind or on a day with little wind, can still be enjoyed. It is often difficult to find a good spot but if you do, remember to share the experience with a friend. Incense is not only magickal, it is social as well. Incense can be shared among a large group of people for the same time and expense as for a single person. Share this great gift from Nature.

Part Two

Non-Combustible Incense

7

Using Non-Combustible Incense

Sounds like an oxymoron, doesn't it? A more proper name would be "non-self-combusting" incense, but who would want to have to say that mouthful? This is, simply put, incense that needs an outside heat source. This would include any incense burned over charcoal or on an incense stove or aroma lamp. This type of incense is very commonly used in ritual magick, as it has been since before the beginning of recorded history.

I'm definitely a proponent of using magickal tools that connect me to ancient practitioners. Bale fires, candles, and incense seem to give me that connection better than any other tools I've used. Perhaps it's because

I'm a strong fire sign, but somehow smoke and flame allow me to look deep inside and see shamans, priests, priestesses, and many others looking back at me through their own magick flames. No other form of incense serves this purpose better than that of loose incense smoldered on an ember from a larger fire. The smoke and the warmth are gateways into a new vision.

Types of Non-Combustible Incense

There are essentially three general categories of non-combustible incense. "Loose incense" is usually coarsely ground, although it can range in particle size from as tiny as a grain of sand to as large as 1 inch in diameter (or more). Dried leaves can be gently crushed in the palm of your hand and added to loose blends. Smaller pieces of resin and wood can be used as well as some materials in their whole form (such as lavender and other small flowers). It's easy to see how this type of incense can be assembled very quickly and a different blend used for every occasion.

"Powdered incense" is exactly what it sounds like: incense materials that have been ground or chopped into a fine powder. This style of incense can actually be created to be self-combusting by any practiced incense maker, but many people use it strictly in its non-combustible form. Powdered incense is easy to blend and will smolder much more evenly than loose incense. It is convenient to carry and also simple to blend to suit your tastes and needs.

"Moist incense" is an ancient approach to incense that is seeing resurgence in the early twenty-first century. It goes by many names and has been produced in many lands since ancient times. In some ways, this is an advanced form of powdered incense. To the powdered ingredients are added gums, honey, fruits, and other ingredients to bind the powders together. Those binding agents not only add the convenience of holding the incense together in a more portable form, they also add a whole new dimension to the scent.

Moist incense is known by different names in different cultures. Perhaps the most famous blend of this type is kyphi. A truly ancient incense, kyphi is still a mystery despite having ancient recipes. We can say with confidence that it includes raisins soaked in wine, several identifiable resins, and several hotly debated ingredients. The ancient Greek explanation of the process for making kyphi includes some aromatics that have not been definitely defined. There are different interpretations of the meaning of the ingredient lists, so it's likely that any incense you buy with that name won't be an exact replica of the ancient version. Nevertheless, kyphi blends are time-consuming to create and require patience. I've never found a kyphi blend I didn't like, so don't be afraid to try some if you find it for sale. Japanese nerikoh is perhaps the finest example of moist incense.

Advantages

Obviously, this type of incense offers several advantages. Perhaps the biggest advantage is that it always burns. Sticks, cone, cylinders, and other forms of combustible incense run the risk of going out prematurely or of simply not burning at all. When an outside heat source is used, the incense mixtures always burn (or preferably smolder) completely.

The range of ingredients that can be used in non-combustible incense is far wider than with combustible. The outside heat source means that difficult-to-use botanicals, like parsley, will burn completely. The use of some minerals, sometimes included for magickal purposes, will not negatively impact the burning properties of the incense blend.

Another advantage is ease of creation. This type of incense can be put together in a matter of seconds. This makes it perfect for impromptu use, whether in ritual magick or just to freshen a room. For many who use magick every day, this type of incense makes it simple to create a blend that fits the needs of each day. The incense can be made in just a few moments in the morning and used all day long.

Disadvantages

As with most things in life, non-combustible incense also has some drawbacks. First, it is time-consuming. A censer must be prepared, charcoal burned to the correct point, incense applied in just the right amounts, and more if you want an excellent result. The process itself tends to be messy. Ash, sand, or other fill materials are needed for the censer. The censer itself needs to be a much sturdier variety than what would typically be needed for self-combusting incense. The entire process is far more vulnerable to the effects of wind. Conversely, self-combusting incense is fairly tolerant of wind, often needs no censer at all, and requires no more equipment than a match.

Preparing the Material

As you've seen, non-combustible incense comes in a wide variety of forms that will work in a nearly endless variety of censers. Self-combusting incense is a little more intuitive than its non-combustible cousin, so it does require more finesse than incense that will burn on its own. The effects that can be accomplished with non-combustible incense are different in several ways from those of self-combusting incense.

The primary preparation for self-combusting incense is completed long before the incense is used. Non-combustible incense, on the other hand, can be prepared just moments before use. The way you prepare your non-combustible incense will have an important impact on how and where you use it.

Loose Incense

Although loose incense is the easiest to prepare in some ways, it offers some unique challenges as well. The burning properties of aromatics can be somewhat different in a "large" form as opposed to when they are made into powder. Different materials burn at different rates, and this is accentuated by large particle sizes. Using powder helps to even out the rate at which incense burns, but powders lack many of the aesthetic aspects of loose incense. With loose incense, you can see the colors of the different material and you can usually identify many of the different parts of a blend simply by sight.

Some loose incense are whole herbs. By this I don't so much mean starting the process with whole herbs—which ideally is how all incense should begin life—but I mean using a single aromatic as your loose incense. When using any non-combustible incense, the heat source (usually charcoal) can generally burn anything you place upon it. You could, therefore, place an actual whole herb (a sprig of sage, for example) directly onto your heat source, but doing this won't work as well as if the herb were properly prepared.

Even single aromatics work well as incense. The key is to process the material into the right size of pieces to improve burning properties while delivering the scent appropriately. I will talk about the specifics of how to process the materials a little later in this chapter, but processing materials into a smaller size improves the burning properties of nearly any aromatic.

While whole herbs are a relatively simple idea, loose incense is more often composed of multiple ingredients. That makes a huge change in the preparation and burning properties of your incense. Blends can combine herbs, woods, and resins, all of which have very different burning properties. Blending aromatics will not only allow you to create a unique scent, but it can give you much greater control over how your incense burns as well. Blends of similar materials will have far less impact than blends of different types of material. But even if you use only herbs, your selection of ingredients can still help to improve the burning qualities.

In many cases, loose incense begins as whole aromatics. From wood chips to plant buds to resin tears, the materials will usually have to be processed into smaller pieces. The ratio of your blend will impact scent and burning properties. Generally speaking, the smaller the pieces, the more evenly the incense will burn and the longer it will last on the charcoal. The smaller pieces will also help the scent to blend more completely.

Selecting Botanicals

This is a subject that goes well beyond the scope of this book. You will find many good books on the market that discuss the use of various aromatic blends. One shortcoming you will discover from these books (including those I have written) is that they can't include several key factors. First, they can't allow for your own personal experiences with various aromatics. "Listening" to your incense will tell you more about how and when to use a certain aromatic than all the "experts" can tell you in all the books ever written. Trust what you feel, even if it totally disagrees with what an author has printed in a book.

A second shortcoming is that aromatics can vary widely. The same materials gathered from different parts of the world (for example, lavender grown in Fresno, California, and lavender grown in Leon, France) can have significant differences in oils and oil concentrations. Plants grown during a dry season can be very different from plants grown in a wet season. Even the same cultivar grown in different places or harvested at different times of the year can smell very different. There is no way a book can account for those differences.

Another aspect of aromatics that can affect scent is how materials are harvested, dried, and stored. This is one huge advantage to growing or harvesting your own botanicals: you know how everything was harvested and its source. When you buy aromatics or any botanicals from a store or other supplier, you rarely know these details. There are a few specialty suppliers who can provide you with the harvesting and cultivar information, but even the best suppliers can't give you the same level of information that you have when you grow and harvest botanicals yourself.

Storage is a huge factor in the scent and power of aromatics. If a botanical is harvested, properly dried, and stored in an airtight container, it will retain its essential oils (the heart of scent) far longer than botanicals that are not handled with such care. Although there is an ancient Asian adage that says "no incense materials ever go bad or become too old," I don't strictly agree with that. I do agree that you should never waste a botanical, regardless of how long it has been stored, but you should not expect the same results from fresh botanicals that have been properly harvested and stored as you do from materials that have been neglected. Just looking at how aromatics are packaged and displayed in a store can tell you a lot. Are they in sealed bags out of sunlight, or are they in open containers sitting on a counter? These factors can have a significant impact on scent.

The only way to get consistent results from making your own incense is to use the exact same ingredients, handled correctly from start to finish, every single time. Just as lots of fabric and yarn dye will vary from one lot to another, your incense will vary from batch to batch. Variation is not at all a bad thing unless you are producing your incense professionally. In that situation, proper suppliers and experience at selecting botanicals are the only way to create a consistent product. This is even true when using synthetics. Just because you buy synthetic oil from the same supplier and you select the exact same scent each time does not ensure that you will receive the same product. Some suppliers are notorious for doing this in an effort to keep their own prices low. One supplier I used to use, whose name shall not be printed in this book, does this to customers weekly.

One month you order dragon's blood synthetic oil and you receive oil that is green and smells of sage, while the next month you get one that is red and smells of cinnamon. If you ever find yourself in this situation with any supplier, I would suggest looking elsewhere for materials.

"Sizing" the Ingredients

As I mentioned earlier, size matters when making loose incense. There are some advantages to having larger pieces. I find them more aesthetically pleasing to use. This is true with most materials but especially so with resins. Large pieces of piñon, frankincense, and other resins are very appealing to the eye. Herbs are also appealing in larger pieces, but they are more troublesome that way. Large pieces of green herbs tend to do well when first placed on heat but burn with a large amount of smoke, and then the ash will continue to smolder with a less pleasant scent until removed from the heat. Woods have better burning properties in large pieces than herbs, but they can suffer from some of the same drawbacks.

If you feel a need to use large pieces of herbaceous materials, you might consider using them as smudge bundles instead. If you do wish to use large pieces of green herbs in your loose incense, you might try binding the large pieces of herbs in a miniature version of a smudge bundle. Herbs still on the stem can be tightly bound with thread. If tightly bound, air flow to the herbs is more restricted and they tend to burn more slowly and evenly. You can even add small pieces of resins or woods inside the bundle.

Larger pieces don't tend to burn as evenly or as long as an equal amount of smaller ones. As you will see in the next section, there are several ways to process your materials into smaller pieces. No matter what method you prefer, smaller pieces will usually perform better in your censer. I prefer my loose incense to be about the size of rice grains. I will often process green herbs into pieces a little smaller than that. I like the contrast of the smaller green pieces and translucent pieces of resin with a scattering of wood splinters with a little bit of wood powder. For me, this produces the best combination of burning qualities with visual appeal.

Mixing

Mixing loose incense, although intuitive, does have a few factors to consider. Unlike powders or other finer forms of incense, loose incense has a tendency to "shake out." That is, when stored even for a brief time, the smaller particles tend to settle to the bottom of the container. This is true with heavier ingredients to a certain extent, but it is the smaller particles that can most easily fit through the gaps and end up in the bottom of your container. As a result, you might end up with a less-than-ideal mixture when you put the loose incense onto your charcoal. As you work your way toward the bottom of the container, the mixture will always be different rather than giving you the consistent results most of us prefer.

You can use this apparent weakness to your favor if you'd like. While in most cases, incense users strive for consistency, you can create layered incense with the intent of having a constantly changing scent. Just remember that the finer particles will settle to the bottom—to get the best result, place the coarsest material at the bottom of the container and layer finer and finer particles as you fill the container. Over time those small particles will filter down, so every time you take out a pinch of incense you will get a slightly different blend. You can even use this for a visual effect and create incense that looks like layered soup or pasta mix inside a glass jar.

If you prefer to avoid this kind of inconsistency, you should keep your loose incense thoroughly mixed. The simple way to do this is to either use your loose incense as soon as you make it or to store your incense in a container with a tightly closed lid (always a good idea anyway!) and give it a few firm shakes before each use.

Aging

While you can use virtually any form of non-combustible incense as soon as you make it (moist incense being a notable exception), aging your incense does provide some strong benefits. This is especially true if you use oils (see the end of this section for more information about the use of oils in non-combustible incense), but all incense benefits from proper aging.

I'll discuss the proper storage of your incense at the end of this chapter, but when stored in an air-tight container, blended incense ingredients share their oils. When loose incense, or really any incense, is used immediately after mixing, you can often easily pick out the individual ingredients. There are times when you might want that effect, but most incense users find that the final result of your incense is much nicer when the various ingredients blend and become a single, unique scent. This synthesis can be accomplished by aging your incense.

Assuming that you don't expose your blends to air or sunlight, the longer your incense is aged, the more clearly the unique scent of the blend will come through when burned. Much of the finest incense, regardless of form, is aged like fine wine or liquor before it is sold. Being a huge fan of chili, I like to draw a comparison between incense and chili in this regard. When I make a pot of chili, it tastes good as soon as all of the ingredients are cooked, but it's surprising how much better it tastes the next day. Two days later, it tastes even better—all those herbs, vegetables, and meats blend to create a single, consistent taste. It becomes nearly impossible to pick out the flavor of many of the individual ingredients as time goes by. Luckily, unlike chili, incense won't go bad no matter how long you age it if you use proper storage.

Powdered Incense

Compositionally, powdered incense is essentially the same as loose incense. Any loose incense recipe can be easily modified to work in powdered form. While each form has its own advantages and disadvantages, it's really an easy transition from making and using loose incense to making and using powder.

Although they are virtually identical compositionally, powdered and loose incense do differ in several major ways. Powdered incense tends to burn much more evenly, and it also requires different handling. When the larger materials are broken down into very small pieces, the quicker-burning materials are more evenly balanced with the slower-burning ones. This also means ingredients that are radically different in form or properties (such as a green herb and a soft resin) work in greater harmony. The final incense will typically burn longer because of this consistency.

Powdering results in more consistent burning as well as a superior blending of the scents. Powdered incense is also more controllable. It is easier to make accurate measurements with powdered ingredients and to measure the completed incense. A pinch, or a teaspoon, of powdered incense will be a much more accurate measurement than the same amount of loose incense composed of larger pieces. Powdering makes the large air spaces that exist in loose incense disappear. You also get a more consistent scent. Unlike loose incense that needs to be stirred or shaken before every use, powdered incense won't separate out because all the ingredients are the same powdery size.

The process of powdering does present one of the drawbacks to this form of incense. There are essentially two ways to powder any botanical and both can impact the quality of the botanical and thus the quality of the incense. Some practitioners like to mix the botanicals before powdering them. Powdering them together can force some of the essential oils to the surface, and the oils from different materials will blend during mixing.

Powdering your own incense will help you control the loss of the essential oils from which botanicals derive their scents. I'm a strong advocate of making your own incense so you have control over this aspect of it as well as knowing how all the ingredients were stored before and after powdering. You also have to recognize that some botanicals are very difficult to turn into powder, so you may have to purchase them already in powdered form. While some incense makers freely use their kitchen tools for incense making, I've always kept my incense tools separate from my food tools. I will retire old kitchen tools for use in my incense workshop, but I never bring anything from the workshop back into the kitchen.

Grinding

Grinding is powdering incense by applying a great deal of pressure. Some incense makers use mills that grind two steel or stone plates together. When material is poured into an opening in one of the plates, it is drawn between the two plates and the powdered material falls from the bottom. This is the process used to turn wheat into flour. Some materials, especially harder woods, are nearly impossible to powder any other way.

Another common grinding tool is the mortar and pestle. These come in a variety of forms but work in the same fashion. Material is placed in a special bowl or plate (the mortar) and a grinder (the pestle) that is shaped to fit tightly into it is used. A combination of using the pestle as a hammer to smash larger pieces and pressing the pestle against the mortar with maximum force results in powdered material.

Grinding presses a great deal of the oils from the materials. It is also a hot process because of the friction between the two plates or the pestle on the mortar. This can result in the loss of essential oils. With some materials, it will result in a sticky mess! This would be my last method of choice for powdering resins.

Chopping

This is the preferred method for powdering botanicals. Rather than using the broad pressure of grinding, chopping uses very focused pressure to cut the material into smaller pieces. Coffee grinders and blenders qualify as choppers. (These are not the same as a true coffee mill, which is a grinder as described earlier—many coffee grinders are inappropriately labeled as a mill.) Coffee grinders use blades spinning at high speed to chop the material into smaller and smaller pieces. Since pressure is only applied to a small part of the surface area of the material there is less loss of essential oils. It is also an overall cooler process, but chopping machines can still subject the material to inappropriate levels of heat if used for a prolonged time. Resins should be chopped with care, and the chopper should be pulsed rather than allowed to run.

Scissors and chopping blades also belong in this group. Scissors are very useful tools for the initial stages of chopping. All cooks know that a sharp blade is also very good at chopping, although that is the slowest method.

Chopping may not give you as fine a powder as grinding, but it can produce a nice powder by sifting it before use. A fine meshed sifter will turn chopped incense into superb powder. Some incense makers use more coarsely chopped materials in some forms of incense. Coarsely chopped botanicals can also be used in loose incense blends or moist incense.

Mixing

For optimal mixing, powdered ingredients would be stirred together. However, it is very time-consuming to get an even mixture for any large amounts of powder. Shaking is a better solution for larger quantities of powder. Put all of the powdered ingredients into an airtight container and shake vigorously until the powder is one consistent color. Optionally, you could pour ingredients together. The disadvantage with pouring powders is that you run the risk of losing essential oils if you lose any of the dust from the powder. Pouring is often used for initial mixing and then one of the other techniques is used to produce the finished blend.

Moist Incense

This is incense that is made with honey (or sometimes with jams or jellies) as a binder to keep the mixture together. It is simple to make and has a wonderful perfume quality. Japanese nerikoh is moist incense that is shaped into pea-sized balls. While the incense will cure, it will always retain some moisture if properly stored.

When I first learned to make nerikoh, I had very low expectations. As many of us did, I burned white sugar in science class in elementary school. The result was a chunk of carbon and an awful smell. I foolishly assumed that honey would have the same effect. Instead, I was stunned at the results from my first attempt. The scent was sweet and mellow. I was honored to be gifted with a nerikoh making kit by Shoyeido incense and was even more stunned the first time I made nerikoh with the high-quality ingredients included from one of the world's most famous makers of incense. The kits are not commonly sold in the West, but they might be available through special order.

I strongly recommend that new incense makers begin by making moist incense, like nerikoh (you'll find instructions in chapter 8). You will get outstanding results from a virtually fool-proof incense making process. "Dhoops" would also fit into this category, although their properties are not the same as nerikoh.

Oils

I'm personally concerned about the contents of essential oils that are commercially produced. There are certainly reputable retailers of high-quality essential oils, but it is very difficult to know exactly what you are buying. Labeling variations, undisclosed synthetic ingredients, and deliberate efforts at fraud make it difficult to have confidence in the natural origins of the oils you purchase. Oils are also very powerful and need to be used with reservation in incense. It is easy to create incense where the added oils overwhelm the botanicals in the mixture.

As a result, I'm not a strong advocate of using oils in incense. If you extract your own oil (which seems to be a growing hobby) then you know precisely what has been done with it. If you like working with essential oils, whether in incense or other uses, find a reputable seller who conducts rigorous quality control and publishes periodic results from their reports. Likewise if you aren't concerned with keeping your incense completely natural, you can use any brand of oil as long as it produces the desired scent.

If you choose to use oils in your incense, only add a few drops at a time. Never underestimate the power of essential oils! If you find you have not gotten as strong a result from the oil as you would have liked, then add a bit more the next time you make a batch of the same incense. Only increase the amount of oil by one or two drops until you achieve the desired scent.

Controlling Burn and Heat

As I discussed in chapter 5, one common problem in incense burning is charcoal that is too hot. Using "self-lighting" charcoal and a lack of spacers can cause your incense to burn too hot, resulting in a loss of scent and premature replacement of the incense on the charcoal. Properly prepare your charcoal before you ever add any incense to it.

Loose incense will have to be replaced the most frequently because it burns faster because of the large air spaces in it. Powder incense will usually burn more slowly and evenly, so it won't require as frequent replacement. Nerikoh or other moist incense will usually burn the slowest. *Usually* is a key word here. The composition of moist incense can vary widely, so some burn quite quickly. Typically a pellet of moist incense on properly prepared charcoal will burn longer than any similar amount of other forms of non-combustible incense.

Unless you plan to apply incense to your charcoal one time and then allow it to burn itself out, you will need to clean your charcoal while it is burning. A feather is a good tool (this is a traditional tool for cleaning ash from the lip of a formally prepared censer) but is obviously subject to scorching. A metal tool such as a spoon or a knife will work fine. Even a pair of tongs used to handle burning charcoal can be used to brush burnt material from the surface of the charcoal. Avoid blowing the ash from the charcoal. That will also blow around many fill materials and scatter ash around the room.

The only way to control the temperature of your charcoal (aside from using low-scent charcoal) is, as I mentioned in chapter 5, by placing insulation between the incense and the charcoal. In kodo, a mica plate is used atop the buried charcoal and the temperature is adjusted by raising or lowering the ash mound atop which the plate rests. The mica plate itself acts as insulation and also spreads the heat more evenly.

For some substantial insulation, you can use small ceramic tiles. It is not safe to bury self-lighting charcoal under ash, but it is safe to use a ceramic tile on top of the charcoal. This will lower the heat level, spread out the heat, and allow for quick changes of scent. You can prepare tiles with different incense blends ahead of time. When you are ready to change scents, you simply replace a tile with another one already prepared with the next scent. Glazed tiles are easier to clean, but unglazed tiles may be used.

Although these tiles are insulators, keep in mind that they will still be very hot. Don't attempt to handle with bare hands one that's in use. These types of tiles can be found in many craft stores and in some home improvement stores. I like 1-inch-square tiles, but even large tiles can be used. The thicker the tile, the less the heat will pass from it and the more slowly it will cool.

Extinguishing Charcoal

Ideally, you should allow charcoal to burn completely, but in some situations you may need to extinguish it. Take care when using water to extinguish charcoal. The charcoal doesn't like water (it may even be an offense to the fire element in some traditions) and tends to violently disintegrate. I once dropped a burning charcoal brick into a toilet—it turned the entire toilet bowl black with charcoal as it exploded upon impact with the water. You can also smother charcoal in an airtight container. I only recommend glass or ceramic containers for this process. Plastic containers may melt from the heat and wooden ones could be scorched. Whenever possible, just allow the charcoal to burn out on its own. Clean any burnt incense from the surface and leave it in a safe, observed spot until the censer and ash are completely cool. You can even set the censer in a safe location outside if it needs to be removed from the room.

Storing Non-Combustible Incense and Charcoal

Once incense reaches the proper moisture content, it should be kept in an airtight container. Practically speaking, those who do not make their own incense would want to keep the incense sealed from moisture but without anything that would intentionally create a drier atmosphere. Don't, for example, store incense in a humidor or a box with a desiccant pack (those little silica gel packets that come in all sorts of items these days). This is true for all categories of incense. Once plants have been processed into forms that are suitable for incense, many of the oils have been forced to the surface. That makes the oils far more vulnerable to evaporation. You also want to seal the incense from absorbing additional moisture from humid air. Store your incense out of the light, especially sunlight. I prefer to store incense in glass or plastic containers. These can be tightly sealed and some are made from dark colors that help protect the incense from light exposure. Wooden containers can absorb oils from unwrapped incense, so I recommend that you put your incense into a plastic bag before storing it in a wood or paper container to minimize oil loss.

Charcoal should be stored just as you would store incense. Some charcoal comes in sealed packages and it can be stored that way until the package is opened. An open package of charcoal should be stored in an airtight container. Charcoal is more susceptible to damage from moisture. Charcoal with too much water will not burn properly and may not burn at all. If you suspect that your charcoal has been damaged by humidity, you can bake the water out of it. *Don't try this with self-lighting charcoal, as it could actually ignite itself in the oven.* Bake the charcoal in a 250° F oven for 30 minutes to remove excess moisture.

––––––––

Non-combustible incense is the most ancient form of incense. It is easy to make, although more cumbersome to use than self-combusting incense. It does seem well suited to magickal or ritual uses because it offers the practitioner more involvement with the incense and it adds a touch of pageantry. Non-combustible forms are a good place for novice incense makers to start. These will teach how to combine various ingredients before learning the skills of adding binders and making sticks or cones.

8

Magickal Applications of Non-Combustible Incense

As I have mentioned earlier, incense is often seen as "magickal wallpaper" or an afterthought when it can, in fact, figure prominently in many magickal situations. The energy that incense brings to your work alone is worth the extra consideration and preparation. When you couple that with the incredible scents and visual aspects of incense, it's a huge return for a small investment of time and effort.

Standard for Most Ceremonial Magick

If incense wasn't already an important aspect of ritual and ceremonial magick before Aleister Crowley began publishing rituals, then it certainly became so after him. Even going back to those roots, incense was truly seen as a secondary (if not tertiary) consideration. Perhaps in those early writings the incense was being used solely to create a magickal atmosphere, but further explorations into magick have shown us that incense can contribute so much more.

While there are many in our community who create their own rituals "from scratch," even more people use rituals created by others or modified versions of such rituals. The impact is that when the instructions for a ritual state "light some incense," it certainly gives the reader or student no clue as to how incense form and scent selection can impact the success of your work. In the mundane world, I encourage people to use incense that is pleasing or relaxing to them. However, we in the magickal community know that there are times when the most powerful incense for the situation may not be the most pleasant to smell.

Given that the role of incense is almost always mentioned but rarely elaborated upon, coupled with the natural human desire to be surrounded by pleasing scents, many in our community have been left to make poor choices when it comes to selecting the form and the scent of their ritual incense. Non-combustible incense is commonly used in rituals. This shouldn't be surprising since a great deal of ritual magick is about symbology and pageantry. Adding incense a pinch at a time to charcoal and enjoying the intense but brief puff of smoke seems much more interactive than lighting a stick or a cone. This is not strictly accurate, but it does seem to be the *perception* among some incense users. We certainly see the "flair" of loose incense, but incense chains, seals, and trails (see chapters 11 and 12) are all interactive incense applications as well.

Adding Incense During Rituals

With regards to drama and ritual, the use of charcoal and non-combustible incense is difficult to equal (although I believe that incense trails equal and surpass this grandeur). The sorcerer's face, lit from below by candlelight, glows orange when he leans over his censer. His eyes grow wide as he adds another pinch of a mysterious plant and releases its scent and its power into his magick circle … At least that's an easy image to relate to magick and one that is understandably appealing.

Of course if you are burning your incense at a low enough temperature, even a pinch of resin will last for many minutes, so a properly prepared censer might not give you quite the burst of smoke that this fictional scene offers. Since your charcoal-burning censer is a tool that can easily handle a wide variety of aromatics and incense blends, it can take on the role of the glowing incense burner sending forth fragrant clouds on command.

There are several things to keep in mind if you choose to use non-combustible incense on your altar. The first is the amount of incense to add. This will depend on the work you are doing, the kind of charcoal and incense you use, and the desired duration of burn. For indoor rituals, it is important not to overwhelm your space. You don't want a fog of incense smoke obscuring your vision, nor do you want to set off any smoke detectors! With that in mind, less is often more. Adding smaller amounts of incense more frequently allows you to change scents more effectively than you can with combustible incense, and it gives you the maximum control over all aspects of your incense. If you are doing magickal work that is short in duration, or you are doing multiple spells/work during a single ritual, then small amounts will also work to your advantage because it gives you the freedom to quickly change incense without the longer process of using combustible incense.

If you use "self-lighting" charcoal, you will have to add incense to your censer fairly frequently. The higher burning temperature of this type of charcoal means that it will burn your incense far more quickly (and with a less pleasant scent in most cases) than "low scent" charcoal. The type of incense you use will also have an impact. Herbs tend to burn off very quickly and have to be replenished often. Resins burn slower and need fewer applications. Woods, especially large pieces, tend to burn the slowest and require the least amount of attention.

Finally, you need to decide how long you want the incense to burn. If you have a lot of magickal work to do while the incense burns, then you will want a longer duration between the additions of incense. In that case, you want to keep the heat in your censer as low as practically possible. The use of "low scent" charcoal will help, as will a plate (mica) or a tile (ceramic) placed over the charcoal. Censers prepared in the style of kodo incense (with the charcoal buried beneath the ash) will allow for the longest burn times from a single addition of incense.

Cleaning your charcoal is another consideration. How quickly the material burns on the charcoal and how frequently your work calls for you to use different aromatics will determine how much you need to clean the charcoal while it is in use. Incense scattered on charcoal will generally leave ash on the charcoal. This ash insulates your charcoal (which can be good or bad), but heated ashes of this type often give off an unpleasant and unintended odor. To avoid this situation, you may need to periodically clean your charcoal. This is a simple matter of pushing or scraping the ash from the top of your charcoal to provide clean charcoal for your next addition of incense. Using a tile or a plate over your charcoal will make this an easier job. Plan ahead for this need and have a tool available in your circle for scraping the charcoal. This is not something you want to do with a bare hand! If you are using plates or tiles, have tongs or something similar to remove the plate from the charcoal. Plates and tiles will be hot while on the charcoal.

One other factor to consider is how you have structured your incense into your ritual. Some practitioners prefer to use single-aromatic incense rather than a blend, even if this would require five different aromatics for a single ritual. In some ways this is akin to "air mixing" (see chapter 6), and it allows you to add the different aromatics to the charcoal one by one as called for in your ritual. For example, if you wanted to call upon all four elements in your spell, you could call each individually and add the appropriate aromatic for that element.

Storing Incense Materials on Your Altar

If you plan to use non-combustible incense during a ritual, it is important that you have everything you need before you begin. Personally, I always run through a checklist of every item I will or could need during a ritual while preparing my altar. If you happen to forget to bring in charcoal, a tool to scrape the charcoal, plates, tiles, or a complete selection of required incense and aromatics, you will need to interrupt the ritual and open your circle to fetch them. That breaks your concentration and is really irritating, so I suggest that you have a complete review of materials before you ever begin work.

Many practitioners have a permanent altar or a portable altar (altar stand) that is used for every ritual. Those people will often store an assortment of incense and other ritual supplies in or under that altar. If this was the case and you forgot to bring in charcoal, it would be as easy as reaching under the altar and grabbing a brick. This is a great advantage to keep in mind. But those of us who do not currently have such a permanent setup can still enjoy this approach—we just have to prepare it for each ritual. My altars are almost always raised and covered with an altar cloth. That creates a perfect storage area below the altar for any supplies.

Another factor to consider is how your incense or aromatics are stored on top of your altar. I always keep a small amount of every type of incense and aromatic I will use during my ritual on the altar itself. You don't have to do this, but I like to see that everything is ready and easily available. I don't want to reach under my altar for supplies unless I absolutely have to. I store all such materials kept on my altar for any ritual in somewhat "formal" containers. You can certainly have plastic bags or other such containers on your altar if you wish, but I like everything on my altar to be as attractive as possible. After all, these are intended to be sources of power and offerings to greater powers. I wouldn't give anyone a gift in a cheap plastic bag, so I certainly would not do that for my patron god or goddess.

I have an assortment of wood, glass, stone, and metal containers that keep my incense neat and tidy while still looking very presentable. I try to match the container with the material it will store. This may mean a small wooden box for wood powder, for example. Most of these containers are dedicated to one type of incense or aromatic, although I keep a few more "generic" containers to store blends that may only be used one time. To further customize the containers to their contents, I will often paint or carve something onto the container to indicate the contents. My container for prosperity incense, for example, is a round soapstone dish with a lid. Since soapstone is so soft, I carved a prosperity symbol (in this case, a dollar sign) into the surface of the container. I will never use this container for anything else. If you are just starting to look for incense containers like these, you can find quite inexpensive small glass bowls at many discount stores. They work well, look nice, and make it easy for you to locate the exact incense you need at any given moment.

Rituals

I have gathered here rituals for the three types of non-combustible incense: loose, powder, and moist incense. As with all of my rituals, it is my most sincere hope that you will modify these rituals for use in your own practice. I always write my rituals or spells in such a way as to be somewhat "generic" so that they will fit with any path or tradition. Customizing the rituals for your own path will give you greater ownership of the ritual and should increase your personal comfort level as well.

You can also modify the vast majority of rituals throughout this book for use with forms of incense other than the ones called for as written. A ritual designed for use with stick incense could be modified for use with moist incense. A few of the rituals are pretty specific about the form of incense and how it is incorporated into the ritual, but most would be easy to modify.

Rituals for Loose Incense

As the oldest form of incense, many rituals incorporate loose incense without even mentioning the type. There are many traditions that use no other form, so why even mention the form in the ritual? I truly love loose incense in spite of its drawbacks, and I like rituals that are specifically tailored for it.

Cleansing

This is perhaps one of the most fundamental rituals that any of us perform. Although in the past I did all of my magickal work from inside a cast circle, this was one of the first ones that I started doing without a circle—at least a lot of the time. It is certainly a process that lends itself well to loose incense.

You can use any cleansing aromatics you would like for this ritual. I like a medium-coarse blend of bay leaf (laurel), frankincense, and rosemary

(3 parts bay leaf, 1 part frankincense, 1 part rosemary). Prepare your censer before casting your circle. I prefer to light my charcoal several minutes before casting my circle and then finalize the censer preparation after the circle is cast and deities have been called. I opt for such final preparation for this ritual especially because the preparation (including building the "volcano," explained in chapter 9) is a time for me to quiet my mind and focus on the work at hand.

Cleansing is the process of removing unwanted energies from an object. Typically, cleansing is used to remove all intrusive energy from an object, good or bad, and it takes a skilled and practiced mage to remove only selected energies. If you are familiar with cleansing selected energies, you can use this same ritual for that purpose, but I will assume that most readers will use cleansing to create a "blank slate" and purge all non-inherent energies. This is particularly beneficial for newly acquired magickal tools. I cleanse the majority of all of the tools I acquire. (There are times when an object has strong, desirable energies that I don't want to risk losing; in those cases, I will either do selective cleansing or leave the item exactly as I received it.)

I prefer to do cleansings as one of the first things I do in circle. Since I have brought the items I intend to cleanse into my circle, I want to banish any unwanted or unanticipated energies before I do other work—those energies could potentially interfere with the other work I have planned for that circle.

When you are ready to begin, hold the object to be cleansed in your hands. Feel its weight and the texture of its surface. This is to help you connect yourself to the object. If possible, move the item to one hand and with the other add a pinch of your cleansing incense to the charcoal or plate in your censer. Hold the object over the censer, in the smoke from the incense. Focus your concentration on the item. You may use an incantation if you would like:

Sacred smoke, cleanse this [name the item]
that it may be free of the energies of others that
it has acquired over time. Purify it as I accept
it into my life as a sacred object to be used
for my magickal workings.

If you are doing this work in a group setting, or if the tool is to be used by multiple people, you should reword the incantation to reflect that. I urge everyone to customize the words to fit with their own practices and circumstances. The best magick comes from your own heart rather than words written by a stranger. Of course, I also hope you think of me as more than just another stranger by now.

If you have multiple objects to cleanse, it is easiest to do them all in one sitting. I add a new pinch of incense for each object. As you hold the object in the smoke, visualize the smoke scrubbing the object clean. Where it once had a dull or dirty surface, the smoke turns it clean and shiny. Once clean, you will be able to touch and clearly visualize the inherent energy from the object. More powerful objects may even appear to glow during this process.

Once cleansed, the object is ready to receive your own energy impression. Designate the tool's purpose(s) in your work and concentrate on aligning its energies to your own. At this point you can physically mark the object as well as "branding" it energetically. This will mark the tool as yours (or your coven's, etc.) and leave it ready for its first use. Cleansed objects can be immediately employed in other work you plan to do.

Incense Divination

The working title of my first book was *Goddess in the Smoke* and incense divination was the meaning behind that title. Although it wasn't really a descriptive enough title for readers to know the subject matter of the book at a glance, it is a valuable working that I encourage everyone to try.

Divination is the art of seeing the unseen. It can refer to glimpsing the future, but it can also refer to the past or the present. The term "divination" is appropriate any time you attempt to gain knowledge or understanding purely through the use of magick. Incense is an excellent tool for divination. Although you can certainly use any type or scent of incense for divination, I like a blend of mugwort, white willow, and wild lettuce for this type of work. Divination works best for me when I have a very specific question in mind. You can do a "general" divination with no question selected, but interpreting the images can be far more difficult without a direction in which to go.

This work can be done inside your circle or out as you prefer. After adding a pinch of incense to your charcoal, sit comfortably where you can see the smoke easily. A single candle adjacent to your censer is a great way to highlight the smoke, but I suggest keeping the censer between you and that candle. That will provide backlighting to the smoke, which makes it easier to see. Some forms of divination require a lot of skill or experience: Tarot cards have to be understood and interpreted in a specific way, and scrying with water or a mirror can take years of practice. Incense divination can be used by anyone with minimal experience or expertise.

The process is very simple. Sit comfortably, watch the smoke, and add more incense as needed. That's it. It is somewhat akin to watching clouds in the sky. Watch the drifting smoke and look for images within it. The human mind seeks out patterns in everything we see, so your mind will search for patterns in the smoke. Much like dream interpretation, the results are quite personal to the practitioner. Two people watching the same smoke stream may see very different things or interpret things in very different ways. That's normal and natural. Just look for patterns that will answer your question.

Observing the divination is the simple part. Understanding the images and how they impact the question you have asked may require a lot of thought and reflection. When I do incense divination, I will often spend ten minutes observing and several days interpreting what I saw. If you ask about the future of your job and see an eagle in the smoke, that could have a very different meaning for you than it would for me. It might mean you are about to get a check from the government, or it could mean that you are about to soar away from your old job to something new. I often see images of deities during divination, and I try to understand what that deity has to do with the question I have asked. If you ask about a relationship and see Kali in the smoke, that might well mean that a big change is coming between you and that other person. If you see Loki, then perhaps one of the two of you are playing tricks on the other. Trust your instincts and practice this skill. It gets easier the more frequently you do it. I've found incense divination to be the easiest form for someone new to the art.

Summer Solstice Circle

This isn't a ritual but rather a circle casting. This casting can be modified for use outdoors but, as with most incense rituals, it was written for indoor use. Typically when I offer incense as part of a circle casting, I will place censers in all four quarters. This casting is a nice exception to that pattern and offers a more elaborate circle casting than many solitary practitioners use. It is easily modified for group use. It can also be modified for any type of circle. The summer solstice is used here merely as an example.

Using a hanging censer (thurible) or a censer with a handle that allows you to move the censer while in use will enhance this casting. Place one aromatic or incense blend in a container on your altar for each quarter. A single "quarter blend" could be used for all of the quarters, but I really like making a special offering to each (use aromatics that your tradition associates with each quarter, or you can consult the correspondence charts in the appendix at the end of this book). You will also need a bit of paper or cardstock (3x5 inches is perfect). Prepare your censer and complete your normal circle-casting preparations.

When you begin to cast your circle (typically in the eastern quarter) use this invocation:

> *Great Powers of Air*
> *I call to you at this moment when*
> *Earth tips closest to the sun*
> *I ask you to come into this circle*
> *and bring your gentle breezes*
> *As the promise of the colder days that are to come*
> *Bring with them your power and knowledge*
> *That I/we may be blessed with your presence.*

After completing the invocation and calling the quarter, sprinkle a pinch of the incense for that quarter onto your charcoal (or plate). If you have a censer that can be safely moved while in use, lift the censer and carry it around your altar for three complete circles. If your censer can't be safely handled while in use, simply circle the altar yourself. As you walk around your circle, feel the powers of air draw into the circle behind you. Like a wake, the energy will enter through the eastern quarter and stream in behind you. Circling the altar will mix that energy throughout your circle.

After circling three times, replace the censer on the altar and move to the next quarter (typically the southern quarter). Use an invocation similar to this one:

Great Powers of Fire
I call to you at this moment when you
are at your strongest point of the year
I ask you to bring your power and energy
into this circle on this day of honor to you
As a sign of your intensity of passion and victory
That I/we may be blessed by your presence.

Sprinkle the incense for the southern quarter onto your charcoal and circle the altar three times. As you circle the altar, see the power from the southern quarter flowing in behind you. Initially it is separate and distinct from the energy you previously pulled in, but as you continue to circle the altar, the two energies begin to blend.

Next move to the western quarter and repeat the process.

Great Powers of Water
I call to you at this moment
when you often stay hidden
I ask you to come forth on this special day
to join in this work I/we do today
As a sign of your purity and cunning
That I/we may be blessed by your presence.

Sprinkle the incense for the western quarter onto your charcoal and once again circle the altar three times. As you pull in the energy from the western quarter, you will again see the distinctive energy from the western quarter pull in as a separate energy at first. As you circle the altar, more energy will flow into your circle and begin to mix with the other energies you have already invoked.

Move to the northern quarter for the final invocation.

Great Powers of Earth
I call to you at this moment when you shine
brightly from the energy given by the sun
I ask you to join in this work I/we do today
Bring your wisdom and compassion into this circle
That I/we may be blessed by your presence

Complete three circles around the altar and end back at the eastern quarter where you began. Turn back to your altar and take a pinch of each of the four incense or aromatics you have used for your quarters. Sprinkle each onto the paper or cardstock you placed on your altar. Stir them together with your finger and then fold the card lengthwise down the center, creating a trough. Sprinkle some of this mixture onto the charcoal and complete one final circle of your altar. You now have circled your altar thirteen times and have an energy-filled circle ready for any work you choose to do.

Rituals for Powdered Incense

Powders behave a little differently than loose incense. They tend to burn more evenly and as a result may produce the desirable scent for a longer period of time. This also means that you need to control the amount you use carefully if you want the incense to burn only for a short time. It is easy to overdo incense when putting powder onto charcoal.

Prosperity

You can, of course, use any aromatic or incense blend you choose for this spell. I like a powdered blend of 1 part cinnamon, 2 parts allspice, 3 parts oak moss, and 1 part calamus. Make sure that whatever blend you choose is completely powdered. If you blend the ingredients yourself, it is a good idea to sift them through a screen to ensure there are no lumps or foreign materials.

You can begin this spell after casting your circle (if you use one) and invoking any other powers, or you can leave it for the end of your work. It's always best when you can limit a circle casting to one piece of magickal work, but we all know that sometimes there is a lot of work to be done and not much time. When you do have to combine several different workings into a single ritual, this prosperity ritual can be done at any point.

Although this is intended as a prosperity spell, you should decide on exactly what form of prosperity you need. While *prosperity* often means financial prosperity, even that can come in many forms. Magick works best when it is specific, so try to narrow your focus to the one aspect of prosperity that you need the most. If money is your need, then use the word *money*. Perhaps your real need is a better job, a way to relocate, replacement of a car, or one of hundreds of other needs that fall under this heading of prosperity. For my example, I will use the generic goal of money.

Clear your mind and then focus on your goal. Apply a pinch of the incense powder to the charcoal or plate and allow the smoke to waft up your body. As you feel the scent penetrate you, visualize the successful outcome of this work. In this example, I would imagine myself looking at my bank balance and seeing the amount I need, waiting to be used. Apply a second pinch of incense and "sweep" yourself with the smoke (see chapter 6). You can feel the negative energies you have accumulated, the energies that are preventing you from reaching your prosperity goal, being driven away from you by the powerful smoke.

Add a large pinch of incense to your charcoal and stand. If you use a wand, athame, staff, or sword during your magickal work, I would point it at your censer and slowly circle the altar chanting something like:

Money, money, come to me
It is my will
So mote it be.

I would circle the altar at least three times, but you can continue for as long as you feel it is necessary. If you feel more and more energy building then, by all means, continue to chant until you feel you have reached the limit of the power you can gather. Return to the front of your altar and repeat your chant one final time. As you say "So mote it be" the final time, raise your arms and release the gathered energies to the universe. That energy will move from you, now that you have been cleared of the negative energies, into the world to help create opportunities for you. Keep in mind that no amount of magick can help you change your life if you do nothing else to further your cause. Magick can open doors and create opportunities, but it is up to you to walk through those doors and take advantage of those opportunities.

Invoking the Power of Air

As I'm sure you can tell by now, I find a lot of value in communing with the elements and gaining a personal connection with each. That is the purpose behind this working. Its primary purpose is to create a conducive atmosphere to reflect upon air, the element of the east (in my tradition). It is easily incorporated into other spell or ritual work.

For this invocation, I like to use an even mixture of lemongrass and yellow sandalwood. I think that particular blend is light, like a gentle breeze. It is a fresh scent and, when used sparingly, will never overpower your space. Remember, to take care not to overdo it when using powders.

After casting your circle, if you use one, move into this work immediately. Meditations such as this one are not only beneficial for contemplation of a particular topic, but they also help to relax your body and open your mind to other work you have planned. This example is particularly effective before doing work that benefits from a large amount of elemental energy from air.

If you have a censer that can be handled while in use, carry your prepared censer to the eastern quarter along with a small container of your selected incense powder. Sit with your back to your altar, facing the eastern quarter. If your censer cannot be moved, sit before your altar with the censer between you and the eastern quarter, so you can look to that point on your circle while the censer is in your line of sight. Add a tiny pinch of incense to the charcoal. Control your breathing (I like to inhale for four seconds through my nose, hold for two seconds, and release my breath for four seconds through my mouth for most incense work, then wait another two seconds before beginning to inhale again). Allow the scent of the smoke to penetrate you on the inside, from your lungs outward. Also allow it to penetrate from the outside as the smoke swirls around your body.

As you immerse yourself in this enchanted air, open your mind to that element. Let the smoke take you where it wants you to go. Watch the swirling eddies and currents in the air and allow the energy to wash over and through you. As you do so, think about the powers of air. What messages have they for you? How does the element of air interact with the other elements to make your life complete? You can continue this exercise as long as it is productive. At some point, no matter how trained or experienced you may be, humans reach a point of overload. Stop as soon as you see this possibility approaching. The more often you do this invocation, the more insight and relaxation you will find in the process.

Rituals for Moist Incense

Unlike most forms of non-combusting incense, moist incense tends to smolder very slowly. As long as you keep the heat underneath the incense at a low level, one pellet of moist incense can smoke for ten minutes and leave its scent for more than an hour after it has gone out. As a result, I sometimes use a modified form of "air mixing" by placing two pellets adjacent to each other over the heat. The scents tend to blend as soon as they leave the censer, so it isn't the same experience as true air mixing. The work that I do with moist incense is generally focused on adding incense to the censer only once. If you use a source of strong heat (such as "self-lighting" charcoal), the pellets will burn away very quickly and you will need to scrape the charcoal and replenish the incense frequently.

Here is a recipe for one basic type of moist incense that I make myself. It is simple and you will be amazed at the results. Even the most novice incense maker can successfully make moist incense that will amaze all who happen to smell it. This recipe is reprinted from my first book, *Incense: Crafting and Use of Magickal Scents*. If you want to explore moist incense making in more depth or are interested in making many other forms of incense, I think you might enjoy reading that book. The charcoal used in this recipe is a step to significantly cut the curing time of the incense. You can leave the charcoal out (I would replace it with wood powder) but that will extend the curing time considerably. Traditionally, this type of incense would be rolled and then sealed in a container and buried for a year or more. You should only use low-scent charcoal for moist incense. Never use "self-lighting" charcoal for incense making.

2 tsp. red cedar powder

¾ tsp. clove powder

½ tsp. charcoal

¼ tsp. benzoin

½ tsp. oak moss

½ tsp. rosemary powder

(up to) 1½ tsp. honey

Grind all of the dry ingredients to a fine powder. You might find it easiest to add all of the dry ingredients into a large pestle and grind them to a blended powder with the mortar. Before adding the honey, you should sift all the dry ingredients through a fine mesh. Use only real honey and beware of "honey-flavored syrup" (which is just corn syrup and flavoring). Add the honey a tiny bit at a time. The listed amount of honey is a very loose suggestion. You should add just enough honey to bind the dry ingredients into a single ball of incense. After each drop of honey is added, knead the incense carefully to make certain the honey is evenly dispersed throughout the incense.

Ideall,y you will be able to gather the mixture into a smooth ball. If there is too much honey in the mixture, you might find it difficult to roll. Once you have rolled the incense (be aware, even perfectly proportioned uncured incense will be very sticky), place it into a plastic bag and seal it after pressing out all the air in the bag. If your mixture is too sticky to roll, you can still scrape it off your gloves into a bag. In some of the workshops I've done, we've even taken gloves covered in particularly sticky mixtures and just turned the gloves inside out. With the opening of the glove tied tightly, the mixture will cure normally.

If you included the charcoal in the recipe, it will be ready to open in four to seven days. If you make a blend without charcoal, I wouldn't consider burning a test sample of the incense until it had aged at least three weeks. You will see the texture of the incense change as it cures in the plastic. Once you can open the bag and easily handle the incense (it will have lost 90 percent of its stickiness), break it into pea-sized pieces and roll into a smooth ball. Put the individual pellets back into a sealed container for storage. Only remove the number of pellets that you plan to use at any one time and keep the rest sealed. If kept in an airtight container, the incense will continue to improve as it ages. The longer it cures, the more blended the scents will become.

Incense Meditation

This is the most general meditation included in this book. It is easily modified to fit any contemplation need, but I prefer it as an "open" meditation, as it is written here. This is not an elaborate ritual at all and is well suited for use outside a circle. This is a slightly modified version of a morning mediation I did for a very long time. Set aside ten minutes in your busy morning schedule and your whole day will often flow in pleasant and unexpected directions.

Take a few moments to prepare your censer. Sift the ash and use an unlit charcoal brick to make an impression in the ash that will hold the burning charcoal. Hold the charcoal with a pair of tongs and light it in the flame of a candle. Once the charcoal is glowing on all corners you can place it into the impression in the ash. If you have been using a mica plate or ceramic tile, you can place that atop the charcoal. For best results, bury the burning charcoal once the brick is glowing all over its surface. Use this time as the charcoal is being prepared to clear your mind. One good method to accomplish this is to focus on your breathing. Count the seconds and focus on nothing but putting your breathing into proper rhythm (see page 155 for a sample breathing pattern).

It is best to sit before adding the incense. Once your charcoal and optional plate or tile is in place, add one or two pellets of moist incense. You can use a single pellet, two of the same scent, or two different scents. I wouldn't use more than two scents for any one meditation.

Once you move your hand away from the censer, place both hands in your lap. If you are a highly visual person, you might benefit from watching the smoke, but I prefer to close my eyes and let the incense become the focus of my attention. Simply allow the smoke to enter through your nose as you practice controlled breathing. After a few sessions you will find yourself falling into the appropriate breathing without any conscious control on your part.

Use the focus of breathing to clear your mind of all other thoughts. Once you are able to let go of the conscious control of your breathing, you can set your mind free. This is the process I use to "listen" to incense and aromatics, and it is a wonderful way to start any day. If you have the kind of crazy mornings that so many families do, get up a few minutes early and use this meditation before anyone else is awake to disturb you. This type of regular meditation will reveal many surprising things to you once you learn to quiet your mind and listen to the energies around you. This is especially true if you learn to listen to your incense.

A Goddess Invocation (Bast)

Bast is the goddess of Upper Egypt. Although generally pictured as a delicate house cat, she also takes the form of a great cat prepared to defend her children. For this invocation, I like to use a moist incense containing catnip and palo santo wood, but any incense that you feel is appropriate will work just fine. If nothing else, the simplest moist incense made from honey and yellow sandalwood is a fine choice.

After casting a circle, if you choose to use one, and invoking all of the elements, you may call to Bast and ask for her help in the work that you plan to do. As she is my patron goddess, this is something that I do frequently. Occasionally I follow an invocation similar to this one and do nothing more than offer my thanks for all that is given to me. Sometimes that process can lead me to tasks I was not aware that I needed to complete.

Before adding the incense pellet(s) to your censer, call upon Bast to work with you:

Great Goddess Bast
Patron Goddess of cats and
fierce protector of her children
We/I invite you to this circle we/I cast this night
Please bring to us/me your wisdom, your
compassion, and your empathy
That we/I might be blessed with your energy
and guidance in all that we/I do here
Please accept this meager offering
to your mighty spirit.

Once the invocation and offering has been given, place the moist incense into your censer. Allow the scent to fill the space. To further raise energy and draw the power of Bast, you may wish to chant:

Join us/me Goddess, enter here tonight
Bring us/me your wisdom and power
If this is your will

You can continue to chant as long as you feel power raising. Be aware that this type of chanting can draw a great deal of energy and results in a very warm room when performed indoors. Once you feel the strong presence of Bast, move on to your other work. Be certain to thank the goddess any time you ask for her help or energy in any of the working that you do. When your work is done and you are releasing other powers, such as the elements, release Bast before any others. "Go if you must, stay if you will," is a traditional way to release any power.

Invoking Earth Power

I have always felt that moist incense, especially traditional Japanese nerikoh, is closely tied to earth powers. This invocation is very similar to the Invoking Air meditation given in the powdered incense section, and it is aimed at the same purpose: to draw powerful elemental energy into your circle while forming a stronger personal bond and understanding of that element.

Generally when one is working with elemental powers, it is common to work within a magick circle. If this is your choice, then perform this meditation when you invoke the northern quarter of your circle. If you prefer to do this as a stand-alone meditation, you need not draw upon the other elements. The former method is preferred when calling upon earth powers to aid in the work you are doing, while the latter is better as a meditation on the nature and relationship with earth.

Carry your censer to the northern quarter of your circle or, if you are doing this outside a circle, place it so that you can face north and the censer is between you and the northern horizon. Light your charcoal if you have not already done so. While it is always important to ground yourself anytime you are working magick, I think it is especially important when working with earth energies. With that in mind, carefully ground yourself and focus on your breathing for a few moments to quiet your mind.

Add a single moist incense pellet to the heat and focus on the censer. Try to position the censer so that you are sitting, facing north, looking down on the censer so that you can see both it and the ground upon which it rests.

I believe you can enhance this process even further if you use a stone or clay censer placed directly on the ground. Clear your mind and allow your eyes, and even your nose, to see the earth energies gathered at your censer. If you are using this meditation to draw energy into your circle, focus on the ground and visualize earth energy coming up around your censer and into the circle. If you are using this as a meditation, you can watch the energy gather and pool around you, absorbing into you. Earth energy is warm and heavy and is extremely comforting.

––––––––

Non-combustible incense has many uses in magick. It is the most popular way to incorporate incense into ritual magick. It offers scent, dancing smoke, and a level of control that is difficult to achieve with self-combusting incense. You do have a trade-off, naturally, as non-combustible incense requires an external heat source; is most subject to interference from breezes; and generally requires more paraphernalia. For the ease of preparation and more precise control it offers, non-combusting incense is the perfect choice in many situations.

9

Asian-Style
Incense Burning

Nowhere has the art of the censer and charcoal been brought to a higher level than in Asia. Whether in China, Korea, Vietnam, Japan, or other parts of the Far East, the preparation and use of the censer is an art form. The techniques and approaches used in Asian censers are easy to apply to Western practices as well. Censers for magick, ritual, or just for pleasure all benefit from the detail and traditions of the Far East.

I want to preface this section by acknowledging that I am no Japanese incense master. I have not been formally schooled in kodo (and yes, there are many formal schools for learning kodo, including at least two in the

United States), although I have been lucky enough to participate in several kodo ceremonies. What follows is my own interpretation of kodo and is definitely not the way that a Japanese master would teach the ceremony. Again, if you are interested in performing a true traditional kodo ceremony, there are several excellent books on the topic as well as videos and organizations that can give you traditional instruction.

In addition to the highly formal kodo ritual, there is also a wide assortment of incense games that have come from traditional Japanese sources. These games are easy to adapt to Western incense practices and you'll find Westernized versions of several of these games later in this chapter.

Critical Elements of Asian-Style Burning

This approach to incense use relies on the availability of appropriate materials and, to do it well, a great deal of practice. Fortunately, it's easy to translate many of the tools and techniques for any use from casual to high magick. There are three critical components to emulate the kodo-style of burning: ash, charcoal, and a mica plate.

It is also important to understand that traditional kodo is focused entirely on a single aromatic: aloeswood. Naturally, this implies a limitation that isn't actually present. When I first learned that kodo only used aloeswood (with the occasional inclusion of sandalwood), I felt that it would be quite limited. That belief grew from a lack of experience with aloeswood. As I gathered experience with this remarkable aromatic and came to understand that this was not a limitation, I also opened up my thinking with regards to *all* aromatics. Aloeswood and sandalwood in particular, but all aromatics to differing degrees, vary widely from plant to plant, valley to valley, region to region, and continent to continent. Learning to detect the subtle (and sometimes not so subtle) differences between different types and grades of aloeswood not only helps refine and improve one's incense palate but heightens awareness of the subtle differences in all aromatics.

David Oller once told me, in the midst of a heated discussion, that he could create at least a hundred different sandalwood combinations, each with a unique scent, out of his personal collection alone. I believed him then and I believe him now. Of course, we were debating the value of recipes for incense blends[1] and not the subtleties of scents in sandalwood, but no matter. His statement is still very accurate and important for any user (be it an incense "connoisseur" or a complete novice) to understand and always remember.

Ash

One of the keys to the Asian approach to censers is something I've mentioned before: ash. Ash is a key to all aspects of loose incense burning in Asia. The ash most commonly used, often called white ash due to its light color, is generally pure ash from bamboo. Because of this, the ash has virtually no scent even when heated. Ash used in rituals (such as the kodo ceremony) is generally of the highest quality and therefore produces the least scent. It is often sold in fancier containers and labeled "ceremonial ash." Even "ordinary" white ash is excellent for any censer.

Charcoal

A second important part of the Asian approach to loose incense is the charcoal. Unfortunately, we in the West have gotten used to low-quality "self-lighting" charcoal. The problems with this type of charcoal are many fold because self-lighting charcoal is loaded with potassium nitrate (also called saltpeter). This creates several problems. The potassium nitrate creates a foul odor. Even if the charcoal is allowed to sit and "vent," its smell is still horrid. Any aromatics you burn on such charcoal will blend their

---

1. My position was that recipes had definite value for incense makers; his position was that recipes have no place in the incense world and only sampling, testing, and consistency matter, and those traits are based solely on the skill level of the incense maker and the aromatics purchaser.

scents with that foul odor. This is always a problem for incense users, but it is particularly bad if you are trying to enjoy some very expensive aloeswood or sandalwood!

We know that self-lighting charcoal burns very hot, and this is the exact opposite of what incense users need, especially for kodo. High temperatures cause aromatics to burn very quickly. A sliver of aloeswood could cost $30 or more, which would be gone in a matter of seconds on self-lighting charcoal. It will burn so quickly that you might never be able to pick out the scent of the wood at all.

Self-lighting charcoal can even harm your ash. The scent from the saltpeter can permeate the ash and cause the ash itself to smell. Although the scent can be reduced through proper care, it is far better to keep the ash scent-free rather than trying to repair it after the fact. The ash from self-lighting charcoal smells almost as much as the burning charcoal does.

Rather than using this low-quality self-lighting charcoal, proper Asian charcoal is made from low-scent ingredients with no potassium nitrate. It is made from pure charcoal powder (usually bamboo, but sometimes other woods are used) and a binder so that it can be shaped into bricks. Low-scent charcoal generally burns just as long as self-lighting but at a much lower temperature. Beyond the lower temperature, Asian charcoal is also safe to bury below the surface of the ash in the censer. As mentioned in chapter 7, burying the charcoal is an excellent way to gain control over the temperature of the burning aromatics.

Mica Plate

A final key factor in Asian-style loose incense is a mica plate. This thin layer of mica (a mineral) is generally edged with silver (to make it easier and safer to handle) and placed atop the ash over the burning charcoal. This provides a flat surface to hold the aromatics. The plate also serves to heat the aromatics evenly, as the mica will heat to a consistent temperature over the whole plate.

The combination of ash, low-scent charcoal, and a mica plate give incense users nearly complete control over the temperature of the aromatics. As the next section will show, this ancient approach to incense burning is perhaps the best system ever devised short of modern electric incense heaters. Some of us think that the ancient approach is still superior to modern heaters.

Preparing the Censer

As with many other processes that have caught the Asian imagination, incense burning has been elevated to high art. The preparation of the censer has many rituals associated with it, but I will only touch on these lightly in their traditional role. As you will see, these traditions lend themselves well to magickal use. Although I will discuss and show several of these traditions, any readers who wish to learn more about Asian incense traditions will find several excellent books on the topic. Check this book's bibliography for the titles of the best-known books on the topic.

To prepare a censer in the kodo-style, you will need two round censers (a ceramic censer called a koro is traditional and its shape will produce the most satisfactory result), ash to fill the censers, two identical bricks of low-scent charcoal, tongs (small pliers will usually work), a toothpick or skewer, a pair of tweezers, and a mica plate (a small ceramic tile could be substituted).

Light the Charcoal

Never use self-lighting charcoal for this style of burning. Traditionally, the charcoal is held in metal tongs over a flame. Turn the charcoal regularly to allow all the edges to light. The charcoal is then placed in a separate censer just for allowing the charcoal to properly warm. This allows the charcoal to glow evenly and completely and to discharge any minor scent it might have. When the censer used for actual incense burning is prepared, the burning charcoal is transferred to the prepared censer.

Prepare the Primary Censer

Once the charcoal is lit and resting in a safe place, the primary censer can be prepared. Begin by filling the censer roughly two-thirds full of ash. Again, white ash is best, but any low-scent ash can be used. If you are recycling ash (which is an excellent idea) you might want to screen it first. The simplest way to accomplish that is to pour the ash through a wire mesh sifter. I don't recommend sifters that use an arm to force the ash through the screen (like many flour sifters have) as any resins or other soft materials can become trapped in the mesh and prove very difficult to remove. It is better to pour the ash into the sifter and gently shake it until all of the ash has passed through. This step also helps to trap additional air in the ash which will improve the burning characteristics of the charcoal buried beneath the ash.

You can sift the ash directly into your censer, but it is usually easier to sift it onto a sheet of paper and then pour the ash into the censer. Whichever way you choose to do it, once the ash is in the censer, lightly tap the censer on a solid surface to slightly compact the ash. Don't overdo it or you'll lose some of the benefits of sifting the ash. Once the ash is in the censer, level it out (most easily accomplished by gently shaking it side to side). Use an unlit charcoal brick the same size as the one you've lit to make an impression in the center of the ash. The impression should be as deep as the charcoal brick is tall. Carefully remove the charcoal brick (perhaps using tongs) and it will leave a perfect space for the burning charcoal.

Ash-filled censer with an impression for charcoal.

Place the Charcoal and Build the Volcano

Once the burning brick is completely glowing and the ash is prepared in
the primary censer, you can transfer the charcoal. Obviously, the charcoal
is hot and can easily burn you. Use tongs, pliers, or (more traditionally)
metal chopsticks to transfer the charcoal into the impression in the charcoal. Place it into the impression very carefully so that it is level with the
top of the ash or slightly below the level.

At this point comes the first truly delicate part of the process. Carefully begin to mound ash over the top of the charcoal. The goal with
this step is to create a "mountain" or "volcano" of ash over the top of the
charcoal. You want to create a tapered mound of ash that comes to a point
directly over the burning charcoal. This volcano should be roughly 1½
inches tall, although the height should be adjusted to fit the censer you
are using. The volcano should never extend beyond the top of your censer.

Ash "volcano."

Once the ash volcano has been formed, you can then create many different traditional and non-traditional shapes in the ash. Simple parallel lines or lines that are drawn in opposition to one another are often added. You can also draw magickal symbols or forms into the volcano if you desire, just make certain to draw quickly as the charcoal is burning away under the ash. Once you've drawn any desired symbols in the ash, a hole needs to be put through the center of the ash to the charcoal. Use a skewer or toothpick to penetrate the center of the volcano all the way down to the surface of the charcoal.

Piercing the volcano with a toothpick.

Place the Plate

Once the hole is pushed into the volcano, the mica plate can be placed on the top. The mica should be placed directly over the hole in the volcano. If no mica plate is available, a small ceramic tile or metal plate may be substituted. In a pinch, even a small square of aluminum foil could be used. The plate rests over the hole, which is directly above the charcoal. This means the heat will travel upward to the plate, creating indirect heat for your aromatics. Once all the elements are in place, you will have great control over the heat in your censer. If you find that the plate is not heating enough, you can gently push it down farther into the ash volcano. If you find that it is too hot, you can remove the plate, add a tiny bit of ash to the top of the volcano and replace the plate or, more simply, remove the plate and use your skewer to push the charcoal down a bit more into the ash, and then replace the plate. The farther apart the charcoal and the plate rest, the cooler the plate will be. The closer the two rest, the warmer the plate will become.

Using this approach for loose incense will allow you to get the most from every aromatic you burn. It gives you great control over the heat applied to the aromatics, keeps smoke to an absolute minimum and produces the purest scent possible short of creating joss sticks or cones. Although the technique seems elaborate, it is actually fairly simple once you become familiar with it.

Listening to Incense

What has been discussed so far is strictly part of the mechanical aspects of this Asian technique. This is, in fact, the least important factor when you examine the heart of kodo and kodo-inspired incense burning styles. The most important aspect of kodo, at least from some perspectives, is touching the power of the amazing aromatics. These incense materials are so revered that the experience transcends merely smelling the incense. The Japanese teach a tradition of "listening to" incense. While it may seem an odd way to look at things, with further thought and experience you will learn that there is a tremendous amount to be said for this approach to most areas of your incense use.

I have taught all of my students to use incense burning as an opportunity to learn and grow. I always reinforce the idea that no particular traditional association or practice will work for everyone, and if it does it may not work in the same way. I encourage everyone to begin building their "incense vocabulary" by taking time to sit with single ingredients and "listening" to what that aromatic has to say. If you still your mind and allow yourself to hear, aromatics will whisper their secrets to you. When I learned of the terminology used in kodo that described exactly what I had taught for years, I knew that this form of art had truly deep roots.

Deep Reverence for Incense

At the heart of kodo and related adaptations is the deepest respect for every part of the ritual and true reverence for the rare woods used in kodo. When the koro is passed in the kodo ceremony, some participants will turn their heads and place their ear to the mouth of the koro. This is a demonstration of reverence and is a physical action that reflects the spirit of the idea that they are listening to the incense. It is further proof that magick can flow in both directions with regards to the physical world: our physical actions can impact what we do on an energetic level, and magickal energies can shape actions in the physical dimensions.

All participants in kodo-style incense ceremonies are attentive and very respectful of one another and the process from beginning to end. The organizer is treated with impeccable manners and is likewise an extremely attentive host. Even in the far-less-formal "incense games," the level of decorum is far higher than is commonly found in kodo-inspired activities here in the West.

A Group Activity

Kodo, and most of the other activities kodo has inspired, are intended to be group activities. There are several reasons for this. An obvious one is the social nature of incense events. Not only does it allow one to host a very special (and expensive) party for the pleasure of friends, it serves as a way to display wealth in the materials used. It is also a way to show status based on those who attend your party and your access to special materials. At one time kodo was considered a necessary skill for any Japanese gentleman. Kodo gatherings, or even game nights, demonstrate your own skills to others.

On a more important level, the materials used in kodo and games are often expensive because high-quality aloeswood is quite rare. Not only is it a waste of money to hold these materials for only one person, it is also selfish. Eight people can enjoy a sampling of aloeswood just as easily as one person. It costs no more to share your incense with your friends, so why not allow them to enjoy this rare bit of beauty from nature? I think that all of those points are just as valid today as they ever were. I'm not suggesting that you never burn incense when you're alone, but any time you have a rare scent from the natural world, please share it with others. It is one way that Mother Earth speaks to her children. I hope you won't keep that message to yourself.

Study, Rituals, and Games

Kodo was once an essential part of Japanese life in the upper stratus of society. Incense use went far beyond kodo, but in some ways kodo is the ultimate elevation of incense celebration. Much like the Japanese Tea Ceremony, kodo is a precise ritual. It is studied as an art and a science, and its study survives into the twenty-first century.

Formal Incense Study

While the kodo schools are not nearly as large as they were in antiquity, many of them still exist. An avid student can spend years perfecting the techniques required to perform the kodo ceremony correctly. When I talk about kodo schools, I mean it in much the same way we would discuss martial arts schools. Some schools have their own variations on the ceremony or possibly the materials used. The essentials are the same, but the details may vary. If this is something that speaks to you, I suggest you read more about kodo and even look for one of the schools. They periodically hold in-person seminars and offer coaching in person or via electronic methods. Participating with these groups is also a great way to attend a formal kodo ritual.

Detailed Ritual

I have already offered one disclaimer, but I feel compelled to offer an additional one: I am no expert in kodo, and what I offer here is a reinterpretation of the kodo ceremony through the eyes of a Neopagan author. If you enjoy the kodo approach, as I do, you should seek proper training in the art if you want to perform an accurate ceremony. Fortunately for the rest of us, we can adapt techniques and philosophies to fit within our normal incense framework. I believe a great starting place would be Kiyoko Morita's excellent book *The Book of Incense* (Kodansha International, 1992).

Specialized Tools

To be a true practitioner of kodo, you need a proper set of tools. Those of us who aren't such precise practitioners substitute items for the traditional tools, but you should locate a set of the real thing in order to conduct a formal kodo ceremony. They aren't horribly expensive and are available from several different retailers in the United States. The traditional tools include a pair of wooden and a pair of metal chopsticks. The wooden ones are used for handling small pieces of aromatic wood, while the metals ones are used for handling charcoal and ash. Silver tweezers are used to handle mica plates, and an ash press is needed to shape the volcano. A tiny broom is required to keep the edge of your censer clean, and an incense spoon can be used to handle aromatics as well.

Kodo tool sets are sometimes given as gifts to kodo aficionados but they make a great gift for yourself as well. If you want to try some kodo techniques but would rather hold off on the expense of purchasing a tool set immediately, you can use some less-expensive substitutes. If you look around your home, you will likely find viable options to replace the traditional tools. Clearly you don't have to use silver tweezers since the ones in your medicine cabinet will serve the purpose. While pliers are one substitute for tongs, an inexpensive nutcracker (two rods of metal that are hinged together at the top) works pretty well too. Wooden chopsticks (even bone or plastic) are easily located, and very inexpensive ones can be found in many grocery stores. While not ideal for handling charcoal, a large pair of tweezers can also work. Any small, clean paint brush will serve to replace the feather brush, and many letter openers and butter knives (as suggested by Kiyoko Morita) will work as an ash press.

Censer Preparation

In addition to the "nuts and bolts" of censer preparation I discussed earlier in this chapter, there is also an aesthetic aspect to the preparation of a censer for kodo. Different formal traditions or schools mark the top of the prepared censer with a signature pattern drawn or pressed into the surface of the incense volcano. Specific books on kodo will give you the details of those patterns but, in informal use, you can create patterns in your volcano either as a personal signature or using an emblem that is important to you. Some covens have adapted this style into their own rituals and some of those use a unique pattern to denote their coven.

With the volcano being round, you can take advantage of this and use decorations on it just as you would a circle of symbols on paper or other mediums. Conversely, you could treat it as a reflection of a magick circle and mark the four quarters with appropriate symbols. Adapt this method to your own practices in whatever way you see fit. If you can imagine something, you can impress those thoughts into the surface of your volcano.

Many aspects of censer preparation, seating arrangements, and more are part of the ritual of kodo. A table is prepared so that all the participants can sit comfortably around it, near enough to pass the censer. Traditionally, the master of ceremonies will sit at the central position with an assistant beside her. The master will place a clean mica plate on the top of the volcano and add a single splinter of aloeswood to it. The censer (koro) is passed to the master's left. Each participant will hold the koro with the left hand under it and the right hand cupped over the top. The participant lifts his right hand slightly so that his nose can be placed at the top of the koro. The fragrance is inhaled and enjoyed. The most respectful participants will often turn their heads and momentarily place an ear above the koro to symbolize listening to incense. Once the koro has been passed to each participant, it is handed back to the master, who replaces the mica plate with a clean one. A new type of aloeswood is added and the koro is passed again.

Incense Games

Incense games in the kodo style (called numikoh) are often created with the idea that there is no competition involved and there are no "wrong" answers. Other games can be highly competitive affairs where each guest attempts to accurately identify different kinds of aloeswood (a difficult task for any nose that is not well practiced) or even write poems or stories based on what they smell. You can certainly play the traditional games, especially as the incense knowledge of you and your guests grows. For this section, I've adapted traditional incense games into forms that might be a bit more familiar to the magickal community.

Once you grasp the basic concepts of incense games, you will see how they can be easily adapted to use in your own practices. Incense games are a great way to bring people together into a common experience that has familiarity to it. It is also a great educational opportunity. Games can be adapted for use from total novices to the most experienced herbalists.

The two sample games that follow will give you the concept of these games. You can then modify them or use them to inspire completely different games. You will know best what level and style of game will work for any given audience you might have. The games test the scent memory and palettes of each guest, but most games also contain another aspect beyond the incense.

The typical arrangement for an incense game would be to have one master of ceremonies seated at a center seat at a table (sometimes an assistant will sit to the right), and the guests will sit around the table. Incense will be prepared in a censer and passed to the entire group (clockwise, or deosil). Each participant should have a pencil and sheet of paper to record his or her answers to the game's questions. The master of ceremonies does not play in the game but still needs pencil and paper to record information as the censer is passed. Although the master of ceremonies and any assistants do not play the game, they can still enjoy the scent of each passing of the censer. The purpose of this type of game is to grow closer to others and to have fun.

Journey Across America

This game uses incense to represent a journey from one coast to the other. Four aromatics are selected for the journey and the participants will get to sample three of the scents before the game begins. You will need Western cedar wood (you could substitute any other cedar but the Western is the most appropriate), piñon, sage, and rosemary. All of the aromatics should be powdered. Ceramic tiles or mica plates are not absolutely mandatory but they are very helpful. You will also need at least one censer with prepared charcoal (using multiple censers makes the game flow more quickly and smoothly). You need to select censers that can be passed when scentless charcoal is burned inside. Obviously a Japanese koro is an ideal choice as it has a perfect shape for holding to one's nose and "listening to the incense" while remaining cool enough to easily handle. Ideally you would use two koros with prepared charcoal, the seven packets of aromatics, and seven mica plates or small ceramic tiles plus pencils and paper for everyone.

The game represents a trip across the United States from the West Coast to the East. There is one stop in the Pacific Northwest (cedar), one stop in the desert (piñon), one where the Great Plains meet the desert (sage), and one near the fragrant gardens of the East Coast (rosemary). The master of ceremonies should have packets of the powders prepared before the game begins. There should be two packets each of cedar, sage, and piñon and one packet of rosemary powder. The packets should be subtly marked so that the master of ceremonies can identify them, but not in any way that a player could identify the scent by its markings.

The master of ceremonies should explain the four stops and the scents associated with each. Next a mica plate or tile will be placed over the charcoal in one of the censers. One packet of cedar should be added on top and the name of the aromatic should be announced to everyone at the table. Once it begins to release its scent (usually this only takes a moment or two with a properly prepared center), the master of ceremonies will hand the censer to the person to his or her left. After the cedar has been passed to every participant, it is returned to the master of ceremonies. The second censer should be sent around the circle with sage atop it. As the sage censer is passed, the master of ceremonies or the assistant can clear the first censer and add a clean mica plate or tile. Finally, the first censer is passed again with rosemary on it. The process of cleaning one censer while the other is passed will continue throughout the game until all seven scent packets have been emptied.

After the three announced scents have been identified and passed, the master of ceremonies should shuffle the four remaining packets. There are now three packets that the participants have sampled and one they have not. The idea is that players will not only have to identify the three introduced scents but also one that is unfamiliar. The players know that piñon represents the stop in the desert but haven't had the opportunity to sample that scent.

After the packets are shuffled, each scent will be passed. Only pass one censer at a time, and you should not put the next aromatic into the prepared censer until the first censer has been cleared. As the participants smell each aromatic, they should write down which one of the four stops the scent represents.

After the final scent has been passed, the participants should be given a moment to consider their answers, but players should not consult one another. When the final censer has been cleared, the master of ceremonies should announce the correct order of the scents that were passed. There are no winners or losers in this kind of a game. Everyone has some fun, enjoys some wonderful aromatics, and perhaps learns more about that aromatic. Each player can even create their own retelling of the journey based on their identification of the scents.

If you feel that these scent choices are too easy for your friends, substitute anything you'd like for the suggested aromatics. If, however, your group is made completely of novices, you could consider passing all four scents with names before passing them again and having people guess which scent is which.

Name that Sage

As with the previous game, you can modify this game to suit the participants and materials available to you. For this game you will need two packets each of desert sage (sagebrush), garden sage, and white sage. As in the previous game, the master of ceremonies will announce the three aromatics and pass them one by one so that all of the participants will have the chance to sample them. The master of ceremonies will then shuffle the remaining three packets and pass each scent around the table. Each participant should try to correctly identify which type of sage has been passed. Once the final scent has been passed and the participants are satisfied with their answers, the master of ceremonies can then give the correct order.

Participants who correctly identify all three sages should be declared a "sage mage." Those who correctly identified two scents are "sage coaches." Those who identify one scent correctly are "sage bunnies." Those who miss all three scents are "missing the sage." If you play the game as written, nobody will ever guess just two correctly; for more excitement, the master of ceremonies can use more than one packet of each scent. Two packets of each scent could be available and the master of ceremonies could draw three packets randomly. That would make it possible for one scent to be used twice. This can make the game a lot more challenging and fun.

Adapting to Western Magick

The approaches in technique that I have offered here have a lot of application in Western magick. I am the first to admit that my overviews of Asian approaches in general, and kodo specifically, have been very broad. I am certainly not an expert in this aspect of incense use. However I hope that you share my excitement when you read about these things and see how you can employ them for your own needs.

Censer Preparation

Certainly one important aspect that can be easily adapted to Western practices is the care and thought that goes into the preparation of the censer. A well-prepared censer can not only ensure a pitfall-free incense experience, but it is also a great way to alter your mindset and work toward your purpose within sympathetic magick. Also, a censer prepared in the kodo style will provide superior performance from the censer itself. Heat is easier to control and you can use the minimum amount of materials to accomplish your task. This means truer scents, longer-lasting incense, and maximum control. Even cleanup is easier.

The ability to utilize your censer as yet another tool for focusing your energy and intent is a tremendous benefit that requires no additional materials. Simply devoting your time to the preparation of your censer makes it a tool that is utilized to its fullest potential without the need for any further expenditure. Drawing or making impressions within your censer helps to focus the energy released from your incense. This will help to focus your thoughts as well. Since magick is, in its simplest definition, creating change purely through the force of will, finding ways to bring even greater focus into your circle is always desirable. Incense is one way to help practitioners to focus their will and their energy, but adding yet another layer of focus and direction is not only beneficial but, in this case, acts as a passive magick tool. Once you have prepared your censer, it will contribute to your work without any additional energy or attention.

Use During Ritual

The techniques that have been discussed in this chapter can be used for meditation, the mundane scenting of a room, or for the highest of rituals. I urge you to explore this wonderful world in any way that you please. Perhaps you can utilize incense games to teach others about aromatics and how to listen to them. You might discover that using ash to control the temperature of your incense will open up new understanding of aromatics that you've used for years. Above all else, I hope these techniques will bring you closer to Nature and allow you to harness her boundless energies to accomplish all of your goals in life. The best way to do this is by using the techniques right on your altar.

Applying these Asian techniques to your own practices might open your eyes as it did mine. It is so easy to sideline incense as just part of a complex tableau on your altar. When we realize how important your censer and your incense are to your success and enjoyment of magick, it can lead us to re-examine all of our practices. It is natural for humans to gravitate toward repetition without considering the impact of each aspect of our actions. In fact, part of the benefit of performing the same ritual multiple times (be it in one week or over the span of decades) is that the familiar symbols and approaches allow us to easily slip into the appropriate mental state. It is, in fact, something that I advocate. The burning of the same incense every time you perform healing work will turn that incense into a trigger for your mind.

On the other hand, the exploration of new techniques (well, new to us in the West—the practices are certainly *not* new) brings a renewed excitement to what can grow into tired routine. Adding new approaches breathes fresh life into what is a truly beautiful path. Spending a lot of time and giving care to your censer can bring back some of the excitement you felt when you were first touched by those mystic energies. I also hope that the excitement that new incense burning and censer techniques brings can extend into every aspect of your spiritual work. Re-examining something like incense, considered to be a mere footnote to magickal work by some, may help you to revisit everything that you do to find new excitement in well-established practices.

I will also mention that this type of incense preparation, the right tools, and the right techniques, may give you freedoms in groups that you have never experienced or have forgotten. Using the kodo approach, you can prepare censers that can be safely passed from person to person within your circle. You can each "listen" to the incense in turn and pass the censer without fear of burns from an overheated burner and with a very controlled way to share the magick inherent within all aromatics.

––––––––

The adoption and modification of Asian approaches to enjoying and utilizing incense is a mind-enhancing experience. Perhaps this very elementary explanation will inspire you to seek out experts on kodo and explore that path as it has been traditionally practiced. Many of us adapt and modify practices of other cultures into our own practices regularly, but there is also much to be said for following traditions that have been formalized over centuries. Whether you modify these techniques widely or adapt them in their traditional forms, it is time that the West tapped into centuries of research in the East. Japan has taken incense to its greatest stage of evolution so far, and looking into that past is almost certainly where we will find the future of incense and its application to magickal practices.

Part Three

Combustible Incense

10

Overview of Combustible Incense

Combustible incense adds a whole new dimension to the incense experience. Nearly everyone has burned a stick or two of incense, but combustible incense comes in a wide variety of forms beyond the masala-style incense stick.

Advantages

Combustible incense is much newer in the incense world than loose or other non-combustible incense forms. But thanks to talented incense makers around the world, it is easy to locate high-quality combustible incense. Even all-natural combustible incense can now be located with little effort. If you can't find any in your town, try the Internet for a huge variety of retailers of natural, combustible incense.

The most obvious benefit to using combustible incense is that you don't need any outside heat sources. That makes it easier to transport and easier to use for both mundane and magickal purposes. Combustible incense can be found in virtually any town or city, which is also very convenient. In general, combustible incense is less messy and less susceptible to the effects of wind and weather. Most combustible incense (with the exception of powdered forms) requires minimal equipment to use. Beautiful censers are a real boon to combustible incense, but they are rarely required. A cone burned atop a coin still allows the users to enjoy the richness of the scent.

If purchased from a consistent maker (be it from a large corporation or a local incense crafter), combustible incense can be depended upon to burn under most conditions. Wind and moisture can easily disrupt the use of charcoal or candles, but most combustible incense will remain lit despite adverse conditions. Combustible incense is still subject to changes due to humidity. There might be some variation in burning time under different moisture conditions, but the incense should still burn completely.

Disadvantages

The primary disadvantage to combustible incense won't impact most incense users: combustible incense is more difficult to make than noncombustible forms. It requires more precise control of portions of ingredients, the correct amount of binder so the incense is strong but not so hard that it can't burn, and many other factors to create a reliable stick or cone. Luckily, there are many incense makers in the world. From master Japanese incense makers who faithfully reproduce scents first created hundreds of years ago to the local incense maker selling her wares at area Pagan festivals, you can find a wide variety of quality incense that is ready for use.

I would never discourage anyone from exploring the world of incense making. It's a very fun craft with many rewards. It's an activity that I've personally taught to thousands of eager learners. It's true that combustible incense is harder to make than non-combustible, but I think the rewards dramatically offset that drawback.

Another disadvantage to combustible incense is that a great deal of it is fragile. Joss sticks, coils, and other thin or extruded incense can break very easily. It requires transportation in a rigid container to keep it safe from damage in transit. This is actually the primary reason that cones were developed. If you need to toss a little incense in your pocket for use on a trip, a cone or large cylinder will usually survive, while a joss stick won't.

Forms

Incense comes in a practically endless variety of forms. Even as I write these words, I know there must be at least a dozen forms of incense I've yet to see. I don't want anyone to think that this is an exhaustive list of forms for combustible incense. As recently as the late 1990s, major incense manufacturers were introducing new forms, so I'm confident that there are more we'll get to explore in the future. The one thing that all these different forms share is that they create their own heat. There is no need for charcoal or flame to use combustible incense, but that's where the similarities end.

Masala Stick Incense

This is the form of incense that most Americans are familiar with. During the 1970s, this type of incense took domination over the incense market. This domination continues to this day. Masala (a Hindi word meaning "spice") incense is the familiar form of incense material rolled onto a long, thin wooden stick. Most frequently sold alongside "boat" style incense burners, low-quality versions of masala sticks can be found in grocery stores, discount houses, "head shops," and New Age stores across North America. Unfortunately, the bulk of this style of incense is low-quality, synthetic incense. It's really unlikely that you'll find natural incense in the local discount store.

That doesn't mean that all masala incense is low quality. A lot of it is, but a number of companies sell natural masala-style incense. One advantage to using this form of incense grows from the fact that it is such a popular product. There is an incredible assortment of burners designed specifically for this form. Masala sticks can also be used in many outdoor situations with ease. If the stick in the center is sturdy, it can be pushed into the ground. Just remind everyone of the location of the burning incense—bumping into a burning incense stick can cause painful burns.

Joss Stick

This is the form of incense most familiar to Europeans. Unlike masala incense, joss sticks have no wooden rod. Joss sticks are a solid stick of incense material. Omitting the wooden stick has several advantages. First, that wooden stick can be difficult to burn. It is used to make the incense sturdier, but it can also make it less reliable. Second, the scent is also more pure with joss sticks. With masala incense, the wooden stick contributes significantly to the overall scent produced. With joss sticks, you smell only what the incense maker meant for you to smell.

Of course, joss sticks have an obvious drawback: without the strength from the wooden rod, joss sticks are much more fragile. You can't drop a joss stick, even a thick Tibetan-style joss stick, into your pocket and hope it will survive. When joss sticks are tightly tied in thick bundles they are more durable, but joss sticks are best kept in a rigid container for safe transportation.

Cone

The incense cone is another familiar form of incense. Unlike the long and thin stick, cones are squat and wide (although they are made from the same incense materials that comprise sticks). The shape of cones dramatically affects its burning habits. Cones will usually light easily but, if made improperly, they will go out as they burn closer to the wide base. That's why I always teach people to make cones that are tall and thin rather than short and squat. If the cone is well made, it will not go out under most conditions.

The benefit of the cone shape is its durability. Cones were created so that incense could safely be shipped from Asia to the West. Under the roughest shipping conditions, cones might have their thin tips broken off, but the cone is still basically intact. I've carried incense cones in my shirt pocket on backpacking trips and can vouch for their hardiness.

Cylinder

Cylinders are something of a cross between cones and joss sticks. Cylinders, which look a bit like miniature incense logs, are extremely thick joss sticks. You could alternately view them as cones that do not taper. This shape has several advantages. First, cylinders are easier to make than cones, so incense makers like them. Second, cylinders are much stronger than their thin cousins. Their durability in a bundle is unrivaled.

Of course, this is balanced by drawbacks as well. Cylinders are more difficult to light than sticks or cones. It can take much longer to properly light a large cylinder than any other form of incense. Having many of the properties of the cone, it shares a drawback as well. If the incense is not properly made, the cylinder will be difficult to light and difficult to keep lit. At least with cones, the thin end tends to burn. With a cylinder, burning might be difficult from start to finish.

Dhoop

Dhoop is an Indian form of incense that is similar in shape and size to cylinders, only it is a softer material. This is a result of the binder used in dhoops. Functionally, a dhoop works just like a cylinder, except it is usually easier to light. Like so many other things, the dhoop's strength can be its weakness as well. Since dhoops are softer, they are more easily damaged in transit. On the other hand, dhoops can sometimes be pressed back together or back into a proper shape. That's something that you can't do with the other forms I've discussed.

Coil

Incense coils are essentially spiral-shaped joss sticks. A very long joss stick, while still wet, is coiled around and around so that it takes up very little space. Coils are great because they will give you a long burning time while occupying very little space. They are, not surprisingly, fragile and therefore not particularly well suited for travel. But they can survive long journeys if carefully packed in a rigid container. Coils of amazing proportions are produced in Asia. Some coils will burn for a week or more—even as long as a month. If you wish to maintain a constant scent for a long period, coils are an excellent choice. Since coils of incense burn in a spiral shape, they can have special meaning to Pagans and Heathens.

Powder

Unlike the other forms of combustible incense, combustible powder shares many traits with non-combustible powder incense. The only difference between combustible and non-combustible powders is the need for a heat source, but this is an important difference. As you will see in chapter 11, the ability of combustible powder to burn on its own is the heart of "incense trails" and "incense seals." Unlike any other form of incense, you can use combustible powder to create incense in any size and shape you wish. From simple circles to elaborate words or magick symbols, the flex-ibility of powder incense is tempered a bit by the amount of paraphernalia that is required. Powder incense allows those who don't make their own incense to create the shapes and forms that they desire, empowering their magick in new and exciting ways.

The most suitable form of combustible incense depends on many things, including when and where it will be used, its magickal purpose (if any), and the materials that you possess. Each form has its own strengths and weaknesses. The form of incense you use on your indoor altar is very likely to differ from the incense you would take to an outdoor ritual. Of course, the form you select will also depend on what's available in your area. If you can't locate the form of incense you want locally, you can turn to the Internet and find any form of incense described in this book.

Self-combusting incense is convenient and nearly as flexible as non-combusting forms. It comes in a huge variety of shapes and composition from large and rigid to small and pliable. While it is not difficult to make your own self-combusting incense, it can be found in a wide enough as-sortment of scents and forms from commercial producers that even if you never make your own incense you can enjoy new incense on a regular basis for your entire life.

11

Using
Combustible Incense

Combustible incense offers flexibility, in most cases, that can't be found in the world of non-combustibles. The ability to take incense (ready for use) with you just by grabbing a cone or stick is a technological advancement beyond the paraphernalia and materials needed for many types of non-combustible incense. Combustible incense is the choice of the modern Pagan on the go!

Smudging

The oldest form of combustible incense is also the simplest. "Smudging" refers to the use of smoldering bundles of dried herbs to scent both spaces and objects. Smudging is a tradition among numerous indigenous people in North America and is becoming more common every year within many Pagan circles. Bundles of sweet grass are often braided together to make large "smudge sticks." Dried bundles of white sage are also commonly used.

Smudging is a way to use the pure power of fragrant smoke to cleanse and purify. Smudging bundles are sometimes held in the hand or, more frequently, the smoldering herbs are held in a special bowl or shell. This is an advantageous approach since bundles of herbs can come apart during use and scatter burning material. As with any kind of incense burner or censer, you need to handle the bowl or shell with care. Although smudging bundles tend to burn with less heat than charcoal tablets or large incense cones, the bowl can still get hot enough to burn you. If you choose to hold the bundle in your hand, still keep a bowl or shell handy to catch ashes. It's also handy if you unexpectedly need to put the smudging bundle aside momentarily.

Smudging is often carried out with the aid of a feather as well. A large feather is a great tool for moving smoke to a specific place. Since one of the primary goals of smudging is cleansing, the smoke may need some help to reach every place it needs to go. Gently fanning or drawing the smoke with a feather will allow the smoke to reach every nook and cranny (a process called "incense sweeping," which is discussed in chapter 6). Smoke can be similarly moved with your hands, although feathers are more adept at the process since they were created to direct the flow of air.

In addition to cleansing people and open spaces, smudging herbs are also used to cleanse doorways and windows by moving the herbs around the entire outline of the opening. For example, to smudge a doorway you might begin with the bowl at the bottom of the doorway and then raise the bowl to trace the entire outline of the door, ending where you began.

People can be smudged in a very similar way if the need for cleansing is great. Beginning at the feet, moving to the head, and then back to the feet on the other side of the body is very effective. More commonly, the bowl is offered to a person who uses the smoke much like water. As the person doing the smudging (the "smudger" as we sometimes laughingly say) holds the bowl or moves it around the head of the person, she can reach into the smoke and draw it off with a feather or her hands. The smoke can be drawn towards the top of the head and down the length of the body. This process is not only an external one. The person being smudged is also offered the smoke as a way of shifting into a more magickal state of mind as well as releasing accumulated negative energies.

In many traditions, smudging goes beyond simply touching the smoke to the face and head or even feet. Some call for smoke to be drawn to the mouth, eyes, and ears to purify the entire self. The smoke draws away negative energies—not merely external negative energies that have been accumulated but also the negative energies from our own thoughts and the words that have come through our mouths. Personally, I see this as a symbolic gesture, much like holding an incense burner to your ear in order to "listen" to the incense. Smudging your ears and mouth is a symbolic release of the undesirable things you've heard or said. You are magickally washing your mouth out with soap is, I suppose, one way to look at it.

Entire rooms or even buildings can be smudged as well, although that can be a very time-consuming process. A room that is regularly smudged can be cleansed in just a few moments by carrying the smoldering herbs around the room. A room in serious need of cleansing will require much more work. The smoke needs to reach both the floor and the ceiling, along with every corner and turn in the room. As you might guess, it could take an hour or more to smudge a room with a large amount of negative energy (such as a place where you had repeated arguments or where an act of violence took place). Smudging an entire building might require multiple sessions to thoroughly cleanse each room and entry.

Smudging is often done as a first cleansing step before ritual magick. Like all incense, smudging is an excellent first step in separating sacred space from the ordinary world. Not only does smudging help to remove the negative energies and shift the mindset of those participating, it can also serve as a sort of magickal "announcement" that the space is about to be enchanted. Smudging doesn't have to mean that, but it often does. The fragrant smoke tells all beings, both physical and spiritual, that a change has been made. It is a sort of preliminary invitation to deities and other beings beyond the physical plane. I like to think of it as turning on a "magickal porch light," letting the world know that I am here and welcome to visitors.

Many different plants can be used in smudging, but sage and sweet grass are the most commonly used. In many Native American traditions, smudging with sage is seen as a process of cleansing and purification. This may be followed with smudging using sweet grass, which is sometimes seen as a plant that will draw positive energy. Other Native traditions see both sage and sweet grass as purifying plants.

Many different companies offer smudging bundles, but you can also make your own very easily. Although sweet grass and white sage are the most traditional, a wide range of herbs can be used. A bundle of dried rosemary is a powerfully fragrant way to smudge. Any herb that dries well on the stem might be a candidate for smudging. Flowers aren't always the best choice, but the foliage from the same plant might be. Lavender flowers, for example, are pretty thin on their stems and you would need heaps of them to make a bundle. On the other hand, a bundle of lavender stems covered with leaves can work well. You can also mix stems with leaves and stems with flowers. You don't need to limit yourself to a single kind of herb in a bundle either.

If you have several good candidates, try braiding them together. The herbs should be gathered while fresh and green, then bundled or braided before drying. You may need to tie the bundles with string at both the top and bottom. Many herbs are wrapped with string from top to bottom to keep them tightly bound while in use. The string will burn as the herbs smolder, so it's a good way to help your herbs stay together throughout the process. Harvest McCampbell, the author of *The Sacred Smoke*, recommends using only 100 percent cotton string to avoid possible toxins released from synthetic string. I completely agree with her. McCampbell also recommends that you allow material gathered for smudging to wilt for a few hours before bundling, but make certain to tie up the bundles before the material dries or becomes brittle.

Rituals

Rituals using smudging techniques are surely as old as the first shamans in the earliest days of humanity—perhaps even earlier than that. While it is true that all ritual connects the modern practitioner to the ancient ones, smudging rituals (much like the use of a bale fire) seem to bring that connection into sharper focus. For many, smudging is simply a part of every ritual performed.

Home Cleansing

Even the happiest magickal household can accumulate negative energies. Much like a clean floor gathers dirt from the shoes of those who walk across it, any home can suffer from a buildup of negative energy simply from the forces of daily living and the various visitors that enter. This ritual is an excellent way to purge those energies with the cleansing power of incense. You can use it as often as you'd like, but I'd recommend it (or a similar ritual) at least once a year as a sort of magickal "spring cleaning." If you live in a multi-family dwelling (like a duplex or apartment building), you should limit the ritual to the areas that are yours alone unless your neighbors consent to it. You don't want any group forcing their beliefs on you, so it's important to offer that respect to the non-magickal community.

For this ritual, you will need a large smudging bundle or braid and a large shell, dish, or censer (preferably with a handle). If nothing else is available, an old skillet might be a good choice. For best results, try to perform the ritual at a time of pleasant weather. If possible, open as many windows and doors in the home before you begin.

Start the ritual outdoors if at all possible. Carefully light the smudging bundle and place it in your shell or censer. Some bundles will smolder in the censer without a problem, but if you notice the bundle going out, you can lift it from the non-burning end and turn it or hold it for a few moments and it will likely resume burning. If the bundle ever goes out, it can be easily re-lit; just remember to keep matches or a lighter handy during the ritual.

Begin with an invocation of the powers or deities of your path. You can modify this rather generic phrasing to suite your own path or beliefs:

> *Great Goddess, Mother of us all,*
> *Cleanse and purify my/our home.*
> *Great God, Father and guardian,*
> *Dispel all the unwanted energies*
> *that dwell within.*

If the building is not too large, circle it entirely while holding the shell or censer. You can use the invocation as a chant if you wish, or simply state it once before you begin. After completing the circle around the outside, enter the home through the main entrance. Before you pass through the doorway, smudge the entire opening.

How much time and effort you put into this smudging depends on how badly the home needs cleansing and how much time you have to devote. If the home is in need of deep cleansing, you should smudge every doorway and window, including closets and small bathroom windows. Every corner of each room and the length of each wall is also suggested for particularly needful rooms.

As you smudge each location, you can use a spoken invocation (such as "negative forces be gone") in conjunction with visualization, or you can silently use visualization alone. First, visualize the energies in the home. As you focus, you will be able to "see" in your mind's eye the energies in the building. Some will be energies that you've worked hard to accumulate (such as energies of blessing, luck, or others that benefit you and the people in your home). Other energies will be undesirable, such as those of doubt, despair, and anger. Cleansing can often clear out both the desirable and undesirable energies indiscriminately, but careful control of the process through visualization can help keep the energy you want and purge the rest.

As you move through the home with your censer, watch the path of the smoke. As the smoke nears energy, good or ill, the energy will move away. For undesirable energy, that's perfect. For energy you want to keep, either avoid smudging that area or, better yet, control the cleansing through visualization. As smoke nears a positive energy, use your own will to create an opening in the smoke that allows it to bypass the energy. In this way, you can keep what you want and dispel the rest.

As you smudge doorways and windows, you can use the smoke to create a magickal barrier to at least temporarily block any outside energies from coming through. This is a good step as you smudge each area. By "sealing" the door in this way, you can stop the dispelled energies from escaping back to any area you've already cleansed. Because of this, it's a good idea to leave one window or doorway until the rest of the room is cleansed. That gives an easy exit for the energies that you force out. Sometimes, this isn't an option (such as in windowless rooms), but you can still use tiny exits such as sink drains and holes for electrical outlets. The layout of some homes might leave you no choice but to go to the most closed room first and force the energies out one room at a time. For this same reason, if you choose to smudge closets you may want to make them the first stop in each room so that the undesired energy can be "flushed out" into the main room and not trapped beyond the smudged closet door.

Once every room and space has been smudged, the ritual can be completed by circling the outside one final time. A simple chant, such as "Bless this home," can be added to help create a temporary barrier against outside energies. Naturally, such a simple cleansing ritual can't serve in the place of a proper protection spell, but at least it can give you a clean slate. Negative energies will still accumulate, but periodic smudgings can help keep your space free of significant unwanted energies.

Personal Purification

The daily acts of living can cause us to accumulate negative energies, just as objects can accumulate them. Simply walking in a crowd, dealing with an angry person, or performing an unpleasant task can bring us into contact with undesired energies. It is highly refreshing to "wash" these residual energies away through a personal smudging. This ritual can be performed with any style of incense, but I most commonly use it with a smudging bundle. This quick ritual is also a great addition to the conclusion of ritual bathing. If you do this, remember to dry off completely to ensure you don't drip any water that might extinguish the incense or smudging bundle.

Begin with your dish or censer on the floor. The censer should either have a handle or be placed on a ceramic plate or similar fireproof material. It needs to be easily handled with material burning inside. Light the bundle and place it in the dish, then stand in front of it with your back to it. This ritual is best performed skyclad; if you do choose to wear clothes, make certain there is no fabric that hangs low. If the material comes in contact with the smudging bundle, it could ignite. Stand still for a few moments while the smoke meanders up your back. Look down at your feet and carefully step backward over the censer. Take care not to touch or bump the censer.

Take a second step back and kneel down. By this point, the bundle might have gone out, so you may need to relight it. With the bundle burning, lift the censer in both hands. Raise it to eye level and then carefully pass it above your head, completing the circle of smoke around your body. Finally, hold the censer in front of you and slowly turn a complete clockwise circle. Place the censer on a table (or some other safe surface away from you) and allow the smoke around you to carry away the negative energies you have collected. As the smoke dissipates, visualize it carrying away the undesired energies that pollute your life. Not only does this little ritual cleanse negative energies, it also has the added benefit of scenting you or your clothes. This is my favorite way to end a ritual bath (after drying off, of course) in preparation for ritual.

Sticks

A more modern technique for making incense involves using gums and barks as "binders" to "glue" powdered herbs together. This style of incense is not only self-burning, but the binder allows incense to be formed into many shapes, some practical and others that are purely artistic. Although a bit more skill is required to create these types of incense, they are generally much more convenient to carry and to use.

Joss Stick

"Joss stick" is a generic term referring to any solid stick of incense. To me, joss sticks represent the purest form of incense since they are self-contained and composed of nothing but pure incense materials. Burning a joss stick that is inserted into a censer will usually result in a "nub" of unburned incense in the burner or fill material. If you wish to burn the entire joss stick and waste nothing, try this amazing trick. Burn the stick on an ash bed rather than sand or other materials. Ceremonial Japanese white ash is the best choice, but any non-fragrant ash will work fine. Tap the censer lightly to slightly compact the ash. Light a joss stick and lay it flat on the surface of the ash. On any other material, the stick would quickly go out, but on a bed of ash it will burn completely and leave no "stub" behind.

Another advantage of the joss stick over most other forms of incense is the control they offer over the amount of smoke given off. A typical joss stick is quite thin, so it produces a thin stream of smoke. The amount of smoke given off by any self-burning incense is primarily determined by its composition and diameter. Fat incense gives off a lot of smoke compared to the same formula in a thin stick. There are times when greater amounts of smoke are called for, but that can be achieved, and better controlled, through the use of multiple thin joss sticks rather than one fat stick or a cone.

Joss sticks work well in many rituals. For a shorter burn time, simply break a stick to the desired length. They can be empowered just like any other form and are available in scents you won't find in any other form. This is because a joss stick is thin and has an enormous surface area. The result is that incense makers can create blends that will burn in the joss stick form that would be difficult or impossible in another style. Thinner sticks always burn better than thicker ones made from the same recipe.

There is less material to ignite and superior oxygen flow, so even difficult aromatics (like parsley) can be considered practical ingredients.

Masala Stick

Magically speaking, masala sticks are nearly identical to joss sticks. The only physical difference between them is the wooden rod in the center. That rod should be accounted for both physically (by the incense maker) and magickally. It has to be physically considered when the incense is formulated to ensure that it will burn properly in spite of the wooden rod. I have read in some books that the rod is there to help the incense burn more evenly but from a physical perspective, it is only there to provide support to the incense.

Accounting for it magickally means accounting for the wood type's magickal energy. Using pine, for example, in a ritual of banishment may bring in undesired or wasted energies. If the rod in your masala stick is made of pine, then it might not be the best choice. I feel that as long as a material doesn't run *counter* to your magickal purposes, then it is unlikely to result in any ill effects. You are, however, releasing energy that serves little or no purpose in your ritual, which is somewhat wasteful. I see charcoal as a neutral component unless it contains saltpeter. Wood, however, is never neutral.

Some masala sticks are very well served by the wooden rod. Companies like Juniper Ridge in California focus on many wood-based incense and the inclusion of a wooden rod seems very appropriate to those scents. While not all woods are complementary, they will generally work in harmony with one another.

Timing

In ancient times, before the advent of reliable mechanical clocks, incense was employed as a time-keeping device. It still serves very well in that role in magick. Although you can use many different forms of incense as magickal timekeepers, joss sticks and combustible powders are good choices for most people. The joss stick in particular can be a fairly reliable timer.

Still, incense clocks have some obvious drawbacks. The speed the incense burns can be greatly affected by air currents, temperature, humidity and the composition of the incense itself. If you choose to use incense in this role, you need consistency if timing is critical to you. Choose one scent for timing and use nothing else. The best way to find the needed consistency is to use incense with a solid history. There are numerous Japanese incense companies, for example, who have been making incense for hundreds of years. If you use the same scent from that company exclusively, you should have a fairly consistent result. On the other hand, if you make your own incense, I would recommend the use of an extruder (essentially a metal tube that functions like a pastry bag to squeeze incense dough through a specially designed tip) to make joss sticks of identical thickness. Make as large a batch of incense as you can manage. That way your entire "stock" will have the exact same composition of ingredients and thus the same burning properties. A change as simple as switching sources of sandalwood could radically impact the burning times of your incense.

When you select a scent to use for timing, choose a scent that you like and that can serve as an all-purpose scent. A cleansing scent, such as sandalwood, is a great choice. A scent that is seen as power-drawing is also a good choice. Dragon's blood or aloeswood are excellent choices. If you study their properties closely, you could even use multiple scents for timing. (This, however, would require calculating the burning times of each type.)

To determine the burning time of a joss stick, break off a 1-inch piece of the stick. Light and lay it flat on a bed of lightly compacted ash. Use a stopwatch to time how long the stick burns and record the time in seconds. The more times you do this test, the more accurate your results will become. You should do this at least three times (which you can do simultaneously if you observe each stick carefully). After you've conducted the test, find the average by adding together the seconds from each test and dividing the result by the number of tests you conducted (average = total seconds/number of tests). That will allow you to calculate a "seconds per inch" burn time on that particular scent. If you know it takes 150 seconds for a scent to burn 1 inch and you want to time part of a ritual to be 10 minutes long, you can calculate that you need a joss stick 4 inches long (10 minutes = 600 seconds, 600 seconds/150 seconds per inch = 4 inches). For even more accuracy, conduct the same test with 3- or 5-inch sections of joss stick.

If you're like me, that kind of precise timing isn't needed in your rituals. I prefer to use what I sometimes call "natural incense" timing. J may use several different scents for timing in a ritual, but I select a length of stick that "feels right." I know from experience roughly how long the stick will burn, but I don't try to determine it to the second. This supports more of a philosophy of allowing fate to choose the precise length. It makes each ritual unique in timing and can even be a form of divination or introspection. I know roughly how long a stick is likely to burn, but with random lengths of incense, a particular part of a ritual might move faster or slower than expected. If the time is short, I generally take that as a sign that the energies I need are already present or my question (during divination) is of no concern. If a section takes longer than expected, I will dwell on that part of the ritual and see if there is some important information I'm not seeing clearly.

For example, if I was doing a ritual for friends who needed energy, I might light a different joss stick for each person in turn. If one stick burned longer than I anticipated, I will devote extra time to sending energy to that person. I would also be likely to investigate the person's situation more closely to see if I could do more to help or if their need was greater than previously known.

Rituals

The ritual use of incense sticks is practically unlimited. There are a few circumstances where masala sticks might be a better choice than joss sticks. Even so, I feel that if you only use one form of incense, the joss stick is a great choice. In any event, the two types are essentially interchangeable for many ritual uses. As with all the rituals that I write, please modify the following to suit your own path and needs.

Reflections

This ritual is intended as a meditation or reflective ritual. You will need at least one stick of incense (joss or masala, it does not matter) and an appropriate censer. Although it is ideal to focus your mind on a single topic, this could be a useful ritual for dealing with multiple issues that concern you. Select scents based on your personal associations with the scents. Select one scent for each topic of concern or interest that you plan for this meditation. As was discussed earlier in this book, your personal associations with scent "trump" all traditional uses or any "magickal association" listed in any book (including this one). Scent is very personal in how it impacts our minds and our bodies, so select scents that you feel are appropriate. Only if you have not formed any associations with the topic(s) for your reflection should you look to outside sources for appropriate associations.

For example, if you are reflecting on your family, you would want a scent that brings family to mind. You can use unpleasant scents, but I find the process far smoother if you use pleasant scents. If your family spends a lot of time camping, perhaps pine or another woodsy scent would be a good choice. If your family is like mine, you may have strong associations between family and the kitchen. Cinnamon, basil, or another cooking herb incense could work best. (This ritual is not well suited to the use of loose herbs, but with a carefully prepared censer, a skilled incense user could perform this ritual that way.)

If your reasons for reflection have no scent associated with them, select one scent for each topic you plan to reflect upon. Incense with a high aloeswood content is a good choice. Aloeswood has been used as a part of mediation for generations. Although not a formal study, David Oller has done preliminary research that indicates that aloeswood helps to create a deeper meditative state. There are a variety of Japanese incense companies that produce excellent aloeswood incense. Buddhist monks have used this type of incense to create very deep meditative states, so it is a great choice for those new to meditation or reflection.

Take a moment or two to clear your mind. That is the real purpose of meditation, so if you plan to use the time strictly for meditation, the entire process will be spent "silencing the mind." If you plan to use the ritual for reflection, these few quiet moments will help you prepare for the work to come. As with most rituals, it is best to select a time when you can be alone in relative peace. Close the door, turn off your phone, and create the most peaceful atmosphere possible.

If you normally work within a magick circle, you can begin by casting your circle as you normally do. After completing any other magickal work that you may have to do, you can begin. First, sit before your altar in a comfortable position. Although most people sit on the floor or ground, you can use a chair if you'd like. It is important to be comfortable to minimize the amount of distraction caused by your body. Just make certain that you do not get so comfortable that you lose focus or fall asleep!

Place your censer or ash catcher in the center of the altar. Lay out each stick of incense you have chosen for the ritual. If you are using only a single stick, lay it near the center of your altar in front of the censer. If you plan to use more than one incense stick, a censer filled with ash or sand might be the best choice. It is best to use a censer that will accommodate all of your incense sticks, but if you are using a single stick holder you can exchange the incense sticks when the new one is lit.

Hold the first stick of incense in both hands for a moment. As you look at it, bring the topic of your first reflection to the forefront of your mind. Light the stick and gently insert it into the censer. If you have lighted candles present on your altar, you can light the incense from an appropriate candle, otherwise you can light it any way you prefer. I personally do not like to use matches to light incense (because of the sulfur smell they create), but if you are comfortable using a match, feel free to do so. Once the flame is out and the incense has begun to glow, take a slow, deep breath and close your eyes. Focus your mind on the topic for your reflection. Even when I have specific areas I want to consider for the topic, I find it is best to first just let the topic hang in your mind. If you are reflecting on taking care of your debts, for example, I would begin by simply reflecting on money in general. Something as simple as picturing your wallet or a $100 bill can be a good focal point.

From there, allow your mind to turn from the simple to the more complex as you allow your mind to "run free" when considering your debt. Open your eyes and use the glowing tip of the incense as a focal point for your eyes. You do not need to stare at it (although that might be a good starting place). Let your eyes fall on it and then relax your body. Allow your eyes to do the same. You might retain your focus or even let the focus go. This gaze is simply a way to give your eyes a point in space. Generally I pay little to no attention to the visual input I receive from my eyes when I am in a reflective state. That is one of the uses for the incense.

Vision is relaxed, but the sense of smell is often the new physical focal point.

Continue your reflection until the incense goes out. Not only might the disappearance of the glowing tip of incense register in your mind, the sudden loss of the strong scent from the incense smoke will also help to bring your mind back to this plane. If you have another topic for your reflection ritual, hold the next stick of incense in your hands and concentrate on the new topic. Then place it into the censer and repeat the process for each topic. This is a rudimentary way to use incense both for timing and as a signal to transition to the next stage of the ritual.

Once the final incense stick has burned out, take a deep breath and rise from your seat. Spread your arms as wide as you can and slowly bring them together in front of you, symbolically gathering all of your thoughts. Raise your head and look straight up, then slowly release your breath. As you do so, visualize all of the thoughts from your reflection and contemplation coalescing into a single white cloud between your hands and then moving into your body. Release your magick circle, if one was cast, and clean your altar.

Spring Equinox

Quarter days (summer and winter solstices plus the spring and autumn equinoxes) are important in most Pagan traditions. The spring equinox is symbolic of rebirth and growth. It is the emergence from the cold days of winter into the warmth of spring. In Japanese traditions, incense is often named for the thoughts and feelings it brings to a user. Therefore you will find a lot of Japanese incense that would be appropriate for this ritual, although any incense you feel is appropriate will work fine. Select one stick for the primary ritual. You can also select several smaller sticks of incense that represent different aspects of spring *to you*. For example, dogwood, lavender, and dandelion are all often associated with spring and growth.

Select a medium to large censer filled with ash, sand, gravel, or other fireproof materials. If your censer is bowl shaped, you can use as little as 1 inch of material in the bottom. If your censer is shaped more like a cup (such as a Japanese koro), you will need to fill it nearly to the top. Set the censer on a solid surface and very gently shake it by moving it side to side with the bottom firm on the solid surface. This shaking will level the surface with a minimum amount of compaction. Place the censer in the center of your altar with the incense stick before it. You can even use multiple sticks of incense in this ritual. If you choose to do that, place all the sticks in front of the censer. I would suggest choosing a primary stick for the ritual and making it considerably longer than any of the others. A stick of 4 to 5 inches is a good choice. The smaller sticks should only be about 1 or 2 inches long.

If you normally work within a magick circle, begin by casting the circle and calling upon any deities or other powers as prescribed by your path or tradition. Light the incense stick you have selected (if you selected more than one, light the "primary" stick you chose). Insert the stick into your censer and begin to circle the altar clockwise. As you circle, you may wish to chant:

> *Sky churn, incense burn,*
> *as the wheel again does turn.*

As you circle your altar, focus on the most important aspects of spring arising from winter. This will depend, naturally, on your own perceptions and ideas about the seasons so—as with all good rituals—your own personality and views of life will figure heavily in the process. As you circle the altar and chant, open yourself to the spirits of spring. Feel the life within Nature awakening. Feel the growing length of day warming the soil and the winds stirring the dormant trees back to bud. See the clouds releasing life-giving rains. Circle your altar three times. At the end of the third time around, stop where you began and face your altar.

If you have selected more than one stick of incense for this ritual, light the second stick and lay it flat in the censer (but only lay it flat if you are using ash as your fill material). If you have broken the smaller sticks into 1-inch size, light the second stick carefully from a candle on your altar to avoid burning your fingers and quickly place it in the censer. If you are using a dedicated stick censer (such as an "incense boat"), you will want to have at least two censers: one for the primary stick and another for each of the secondary sticks. Think about the relationship between that blend and the rising of spring. For example, if you choose a small stick of lavender incense, think about how lavender is affected by the coming of spring. Visualize the greening of the foliage and the tiny purple flowers emerging on the stems. As the scent of the lavender penetrates the room and your clothing, feel the presence of the lavender as if it were already in full bloom upon your altar.

After circling your altar once, stop and simply revel in the scent until the second stick of incense has finished burning. Continue this process until all of your small sticks have finished burning. If the large stick is still burning, resume chanting until it has burned completely. When all of the incense is completely burned, stand before your altar and welcome spring. You can do this with silent meditation or, as I prefer to do, with a booming vocal welcome:

> *Welcome, Springtime!*
> *Your warming winds and longer days*
> *will bring joy to the whole Earth.*

You can then continue with any other ritual or meditative work you would like to do, or you can open your circle (if one was cast). After the ritual is complete, clean your censer carefully. If you used masala-style incense sticks, you may wish to store the sticks that were pushed below the surface of your censer. Those sticks can be used later in a campfire or within your cauldron when you need to kindle a small fire. If you used joss sticks, there may be unburned ends below the surface of your censer. You can also save those for later use in a fire, or you could grind them to powder. This type of saved incense powder can be used in many other rituals, and it will be especially potent because of its previous ritual use.

Cones, Cylinders, and Dhoops

As was explained earlier, cones and cylinders share similar burning characteristics and limitations. Although cylinders are more akin to joss sticks in shape, their thickness gives them burning characteristics more like cones. Dhoops are most often made in one of those two forms. One of the problems with these forms is the tendency to go out or to be difficult to light. Normally this is a result of the thickness of the incense. Thinner incense is always easier to burn, but properly made cones and cylinders will work for virtually any purpose.

Burning on Ash

Although the thickness of cones and cylinders can pose a challenge, there are a few strategies that will improve the reliability of these forms of incense. The first is burning on ash. A properly prepared ash bed will trap air that will help these forms of incense burn. Cones and cylinders can be burned upright, but even some of the best-created incense can have trouble burning completely to the end. They tend to leave an eighth of an inch or a little less of unburned incense. Burning on ash will generally allow the incense to burn completely. The tiny bit of air trapped in the ash below the incense makes the difference.

Ash also allows you to burn cones and cylinders lying on their sides. This increases the odds of the incense burning completely. While burning on the side is not mandatory in all cases, if you encounter a blend or brand of cone or cylinder that tends to go out before burning completely, side burning could resolve the problem.

Burning Upside Down

One final strategy to deal with cones that will not burn completely, although it does not apply to cylinders, is to burn the cone upside down. There are two approaches to doing this. One approach is to use a cone holder that will hold the cone upside down. There are commercial holders made of wire that will hold the cone upside down while it burns, but it is easy to make one yourself with stiff wire. It is important to put the wire inside a fireproof censer. Once the cone burns beyond the last loop of wire that holds it in place, the burning incense may drop out of the holder. As long as the wire is mounted inside a fireproof censer, this will not present a hazard.

A second way to burn a cone upside down is to literally flip the cone over and light the wide base. The thin tip of the cone can then be inserted into sand or, better yet, ash. If inserted into sand or another medium, the thin tip of the cone may not burn, but at least the bulk of the cone will burn. If inserted into ash, even the thin tip of the incense may burn.

Rituals

Cones, cylinders, and dhoops can all be used for rituals just as any other form of incense. And just like other forms, they offer their own strengths and weaknesses. Cones, unless they are very large, have a fairly limited burning duration. Cylinders come in many sizes, so the burn duration is a direct relation to both the thickness and length of the cylinder, although the length is what primarily determines how long it burns (width = amount of smoke, length = burning time). Dhoops often have a shorter burn time than other forms of the same size.

Raising Power

This basic process isn't truly a ritual on its own but rather an important precursor that can be added to most rituals. This is the basis for the Summer Solstice Circle ritual found on page 149. As you know, burning incense releases energy. The energy from all of the aromatics and base materials in your incense are storehouses for natural, magickal energy. This is also a great opportunity to try air mixing (see chapter 6).

Begin by selecting a variety of cones or cylinders. Select one scent for each quarter and then use a fifth scent on your altar. This ritual should be performed in an area with good ventilation. *A point of caution*: I have talked before about the potential mishaps that incense can cause with smoke detectors and that is particularly true with this ritual. I suggest an open window in the room or an open door to allow for an exchange of air. Smoke detectors in the room where your circle is cast are particularly susceptible, but any in your home could be triggered if you don't keep the air in motion and at least a minimal amount of ventilation.

Place censers and your incense at all four quarters and on your altar before casting your circle. As you call the quarters, light the incense at that quarter. When you invoke that quarter, make a clear statement that this is an offering for that element (e.g., "Powers of Air, I make this offering to you"). When the circle is complete, light the incense on your altar. Before you begin any other planned ritual work, draw the energy from the incense and hold it within the circle. The easiest way to accomplish that is by walking around your altar and chanting.

I call all of the elements one by one. I would start with the eastern quarter (air) and make one complete circle around the altar calling that element:

Great Powers of Air, bring your energy
into this circle that it may be released
for the work at hand this night.

Depending on how you practice and the time available for your ritual, you should consider actually doing this three times for each element. Continue to chant as you circle the altar. Your chanting not only helps to raise additional energy, but it is also another way to align the energies from the incense with your planned work. Keep your mind focused at all times on the element you are calling and the goal you hope to achieve.

Once the circle is cast, invoke whatever other powers you plan to call and proceed as you normally would. One thing you may notice, as I have on many occasions, is that the smoke from so many cones of incense will swirl and dance through the room as you circle your altar. Especially as the smoke moves over a lighted candle, I sometimes see gossamer shapes dancing around the flame.

Winter Solstice

While not a true ritual, this practice can be added to any ritual that you do on or around Yule. The beginning of winter is an important event for those of us who celebrate the turning of the wheel. You can draw even more impact from your incense whether you are indoors or out. For this ritual you will need incense cylinders of an appropriate scent. If you are not an incense maker willing to create your own cylinders for this occasion, you can still find commercial incense that will fit the need. There is at least one incense producer (and likely more) that makes incense cylinders that look very much like tiny logs (about 1 inch in diameter). They are made in different "forest" scents and would work well. If you are unable to find large cylinders like this, you can bundle smaller cylinders or even sticks. Tie them tightly with thread. Rather than using one long thread, tie it with multiple threads spaced out slightly. That way the bundle will still remain intact when one thread burns through.

In place of your typical stick of incense on your altar, use one of these "mini logs" as a representation of the traditional Yule log. Burning a large cylinder on a bed of ash is a wonderful symbol of that ancient tradition. If you are holding your Yule ritual outdoors but you are not planning to go through the involved process of creating and burning a Yule log, or if you just don't have enough time, bring the same miniature Yule logs with you. They can be added to hot coals to create a burst of winter scent or can even be thrown into a lit fire. Hot coals work best, but if you are unable to have any kind of a fire at all then simply bring a rugged censer with you, with a lid or cover if there is wind blowing, and burn your miniature Yule logs within the censer. Even with a lid, the stiffer the breeze, the faster your logs will burn. You may go through quite a few of them in an hour if there is any significant amount of wind. To avoid the need to repeatedly light logs in the wind you can use incense chaining as described in chapter 12.

Powder

Powdered incense is perhaps the most versatile form of incense. It might seem confusing to have powder incense listed twice in this book, but keep in mind that it can be made both as non-combustible and self-burning formulas, which require different treatment. Powdered incense gives you the ability to draw or stencil with incense—no other form can boast that capability. Although it is subject to blowing away in breezes or drafts, and thus is essentially only suited for indoor use, powdered incense can be used in almost any situation with maximum visual as well as scent results.

Preparing Combustible Powder

Unlike loose incense, powdered incense must be properly ground to a fine consistency. Beyond that, combustible powder must be reliably self-burning. Any incense powder can be burned on charcoal, but the style of powdered incense needed for the following techniques needs to burn without an outside heat source. All of the materials you use in the powder must be finely ground and sifted through a screen mesh to ensure there are no large particles in the mixture.

This type of powder needs to follow the same rules of composition as any cone or stick of self-combustible incense. As a general guideline, start with 80 percent base material and 20 percent aromatic material. Wood powder is the most common base material. Any wood is a good candidate as a base if it has good burning properties and either very little scent or a scent that complements your blend. It is also critical to keep the magickal properties of the wood powder in mind to ensure they align with the goals for that blend. The only aspect of making other forms of self-combusting incense is that you omit is the binder. The ash in your censer will act as a substitute for binding the incense.

Specialty Burners

In the incense market in the United States there are small incense companies that sell powdered incense and special burners for them. The burners have a single, long channel cut into them in an assortment of designs. The powder is lit at one end and burns its way through the tray. I personally haven't found one that works well with natural powdered incense. I would guess that it's the lack of oxygen to the bottom of the incense trail that's causing the incense to burn poorly. I have often wondered, however, if the makers of this style of incense realize that they are making a tool that can be used in the creation of impressive incense trails and seals. For incense seals, you can fill the burner with your own powdered blend and cover it with a heat-proof material (such as a ceramic tile or sheet of metal). Invert the burner and carefully lift it to create a perfect incense seal. Conversely, you can invert the empty burner and gently press it into a bed of prepared ash. When you lift the burner it will have created an incense trail for you to fill with powder.

Incense Seals

Incense seals could be viewed as an incense trail without the ash. Drawing or writing is made with incense powder and it is burned much like one of the specialty burners does, only a line of powder is spread onto a non-flammable surface. One way to make this type of incense trail is with the use of a seal, which is a kind of stencil for powdered incense.

Seals would typically be used on a smooth, flat-surfaced censer dedicated to the purpose; however, any surface that meets the requirements could be used. A stone or ceramic tile is a good choice. Even a fairly flat rock could be used. The incense seal is held near the top of the burning surface and the powder is scattered through the cutout areas in the stencil. It takes practice and a steady hand to use an incense seal, but the results can be very interesting. I'm not aware of any incense seals commercially available in the United States at this time, but you can definitely make your own. Simple designs can be made with paper notecards, while more intricate designs can be made from wood or metal.

To make an incense seal, use a piece of corrugated cardboard or other thick cardboard. If none is available, you can make an acceptable seal using a stack of thinner cardboard glued together. The thicker, the better, up to ¼ inch. The seal won't be able to hold up to the weight of the incense powder and will bend if a piece of the cardboard is too thin. Draw or trace a design on the surface of the cardboard. Keep in mind that you will get the best results if your design is a single wide line. It can wind and curve into any shape you wish, but the line should never cross itself. (That is a technique you can use with incense trails but is more difficult with seals.) If any part of your design is physically disconnected from the rest (for example, if you wanted to make a seal that made the letter "O" where the center of the letter would be disconnected), the part that you cut would need to be put back onto the seal using thin wire to allow the disconnected piece to almost appear to float. The wires are strong enough to hold the disconnected piece but thin enough that your incense powder will flow past the wires with virtually no change to the final look of the incense seal.

Cut out your drawing. You need to make the cutout line from ⅛ inch to ¼ inch wide. The entire design can be as large as you like as long as it will fit on your burning surface. When it comes to cardboard seals, you are more limited in design by the material. Lines need to be fairly simple, and the line should never get too close to touching another section of line. If you have used corrugated cardboard, it is a good idea to cover the cut edges of the design. That way, when you sprinkle incense powder through the seal, none of it will get lost in the pockets inside the cardboard. Tape can cover the edges very easily. If you used a thick piece of solid cardboard or thin pieces glued together, you still might want to use this step to ensure the design has a very smooth edge.

Once you've created your stencil and prepared your powder and burning surface, you are ready. Lay the seal on the burning surface and sprinkle the powder through the openings in your stencil. Carefully lift the seal from the burning surface and it is ready. Light one end of the trail and enjoy. You do need a powder with very good burning properties, since this technique doesn't have the advantage of oxygen-rich ash beneath it. Pure sandalwood powder is a good choice for incense seals.

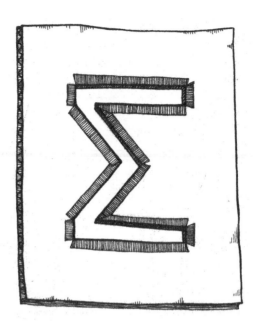

An incense seal made from cardboard—notice the tape along the edges.

Incense Trails in Ash

I've talked about using ash as a fill material in censers, and trails in ash is the ultimate advantage that ash has over all other mediums. You can take the art of incense to a whole new level visually as well as use a variety of mixtures in the trail for surprising scent changes as the burn progresses. For example, put a sandalwood blend for the first half of the trail and a frankincense blend for the second half. You can change scent every few inches if you choose to.

The concept of the trail is simple, but that gives it the flexibility to create a virtually endless variety of designs. You need to begin by "fluffing" the ash in your censer. This means you should stir it or sift it to capture more air and to give you a more flexible surface with which to work. After fluffing the ash, lightly tap the censer on a flat surface to slightly compact and level it. You can then make impressions in the surface of the ash and fill those impressions with incense powder. Just as with incense seals, the incense will slowly burn along the "trail" you have created.

Drawing in Ash

This is the fastest and easiest way to make trails in ash. Toothpicks, chopsticks, skewers, feather quills, and even capped ink pens can be used to draw the trail. Depending on the size of your censer, you can write words and even phrases, draw elaborate scenes, or any geometric shape. Just remember that it is best to not allow your line to cross or touch itself. If the "burning line" of incense were to touch incense at any other point, it will ignite. If, for example, you drew the letter "K" in your ash as a trail to be lit at the bottom left tip of the letter. The burning line would move up the left leg of the "K" until it reached the point where the left leg joined with the two diagonal lines. At that point the burning line would continue moving up the left leg, but it would also ignite both of the diagonal lines.

Drawing an incense trail in ash.

This can be used to great effect to set off secondary burn lines, but at the same time you can create an overwhelming amount of smoke. If you are drawing a very thin trail, such as with a toothpick, this is less of a problem than when you are making deep and wide trails. For your first trails, I wouldn't suggest trying anything complex. Why not start with a spiral? Without lifting your drawing instrument, continue to draw more and more layers of the spiral, taking care that it is composed of only one line. Don't put the spiral arms too close together. I would suggest that you keep at least one trail width between sections of the line.

Once you have the trail made in the ash, you can add the powdered incense. (Just as a reminder, use only self-combusting incense powder. Don't use incense powder designed for scattering on charcoal.) To place the powder with some amount of precision, I use a 3x5-inch notecard folded in half along the longer edge. This creates a long trough in the center. Place a few teaspoons at one end of the card and fold the two halves together at the other end. Spread the two edges just far enough apart to allow a small amount of powder to slip over the edge of the card.

Place the notecard, with the folded end closest to the ash, an inch or so above the trail. By holding the card with one hand and gently tapping the side of the card with your free hand, you can cause controlled amounts of powder to slide off the card and into the trail. Don't worry if your first few attempts seem shaky or don't come out as clearly as you would like. With practice, you will quickly master this aspect of trail making. Move the card along above the entire trail and fill the trail with powder. Fill the trail until it is even with the top of the ash. Ideally, you want the top of the incense exactly level with the top of the ash. You can slightly compact the ash and incense combination after pouring for more reliable burning, but this tends to distort the shape.

Filling a trail with incense powder.

All that's left to do is light the trail. There are several ways to accomplish this. Perhaps the purest is by lighting a joss stick and inserting the burning end into your trail. Don't insert it deeply or the trail may not light. You can also lay a burning match on the end of the trail or hold a butane lighter to the tip of the trail. It is not always easy to light a trail with a lighter, so prepare for the lighter to get hot. Don't burn your fingers! A fireplace lighter will keep your fingers safe.

Stamps

This is another option for making incense trails. Rather than drawing in the ash freehand, you can use a stamp to create the trail for you. This has several advantages over drawing in the ash. You can make your own stamps and re-create even complex trails perfectly every time. The depth of the trail will be consistent, which improves its burning characteristics. Stamps can also be purchased. However, finding commercial stamps that are appropriate for magickal incense trails is difficult. The most useful commercial stamp I've found is letter stamps.

I have a set of block stamps of the alphabet that I have used frequently for trails. I will level the surface of the ash and then press in each letter individually. I leave a moderate gap between each letter. Once all of the lettering is complete I will use a skewer to draw single connecting lines between each adjacent letter. Once a letter gets to the end it will light the connecting line, which will burn and then light the next letter.

Besides actual stamps, there is one other type of commercial product that is very useful for making trails. You may remember that I mentioned earlier in this chapter that there are burners designed for commercial incense powder, and some of them are in attractive designs. Smooth the ash, turn the empty burner upside down, and gently press it into the surface of the ash. Carefully remove the burner from the ash and it will have made a reversed yet perfect image in the ash. Fill the trail with powder and enjoy those clever designs with natural incense powder.

If you want to make your own stamp, the process can be as simple or complex as you'd like. The key is to mount the stamp on a flat surface and make the design deep enough to leave a clear impression. You can make very deep or very shallow stamps, but they must be deep enough to leave a proper trail. I have a pentagram stamp that I made years ago with rectangular strips of bass wood mounted on a small unfinished wooden plaque. The bass wood is about ¼ inch square and sold in long lengths. I created an image of the design on my computer and used a software program to reverse it. More simply, print your image on thin paper and turn the sheet over to create your design.

With the printed design taped to my desk, I cut the bass wood into pieces that were the exact size of the arms of the star in my printout. As I cut each, I laid it in place atop the printout to ensure all the pieces fit. Once all the bass wood arms were cut, I glued them together according to my design onto the surface of the wooden plaque. With the addition of a wooden knob on the reverse side of the plaque, the stamp was complete. Once it was dry I was able to press it into the surface of an ash-filled censer. When the stamp was lifted away I had a perfect incense trail that I could re-create as many times as I wanted.

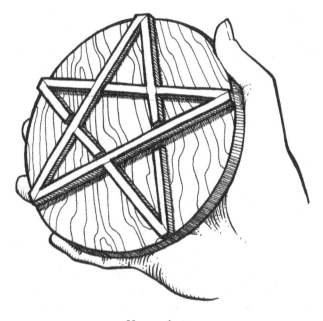

Homemade stamp.

The pentagram stamp I made has a fairly complex burning pattern. You can make a far simpler stamp than that. A triangle or circular stamp would be easy to make. Any shape that can be drawn with one continuous line could be a good candidate for a stamp.

Other Tools

There are other tools you can experiment with while making trails. I have a small wooden tool for working clay that is fantastic at straightening out joss sticks that I make. It is also a great tool for both drawing in ash and going back over the initial drawing to make certain there is a clean, firm side to the trail.

Another useful tool for making trails is the common cookie cutter. You can find them in virtually any shape imaginable and you might be surprised at how many can be adapted to use in ash. Begin with a smooth surface just as you would with any other trail. Carefully insert the cookie cutter and push it below the surface of the ash evenly. You want the entire cookie cutter to push the same depth into the ash. Once inserted, gently move the cutter in a circular motion. Don't move it around very much, of course, but enough to triple the width of the cut from the cookie cutter. You can then remove the cookie cutter and you will have a very "clean" trail to fill with powder. If the trail is going to follow a circular pattern (so that it will not burn in two different directions from the lighting point) you can use a toothpick to push ash to create a break across the trail, forcing the incense to burn only in the chosen direction.

I often use a homemade ash press. It is just a disk of plastic with a handle. The disc is perforated so you can press it against the open top of a tuna fish can and drain the liquid without spilling any of the fish. I covered the surface with a little aluminum foil (to block the perforations) and made a very functional press for less than $2. I use it to level and sometimes compact the ash before creating a trail. You can find all sorts of incense trail tools around the house or the garage. Even kitchen sifters are excellent for sifting your ash. I like fine-meshed nylon the best.

Writing in Ash

This is one of my favorite things to do with incense. You can write anything for which your censer has space. Although you can use a toothpick as your writing instrument, I recommend something a bit wider than that. A wooden chopstick is a great choice. A wooden pencil also makes a good choice, as does the quill of a large bird feather. The key is for the writing to be clear and the trail to be smooth on the sides. For the best results, you should compact the ash in your censer a bit more firmly than you would otherwise. You want a very flat, even surface.

Insert your writing implement of choice and move very steadily through the writing. Ideally, you would write in cursive with each letter connected by a single stroke. Of course you can print, draw shapes rather than letters, or anything else you can imagine to create the trails. Then fill the impressions just as you normally would. You can fill different letters or shapes with different incense blends if you choose. This is a particularly good idea if you are using your trail for more than one working. If, for instance, you wanted to perform prosperity and health spells in the same circle, then you could draw one symbol representing the core purpose of each spell (perhaps a dollar sign for prosperity and a smiling face for health). Draw a trail connecting the two symbols. When the first symbol finishes burning and you smell the second scent begin, you will know it is time to move on to the second spell.

This type of incense use is not at all new and is one more example of what modern incense users can learn from ancient ones. Using multiple incense in trails is a modern application of the incense clock. The changing of scent can also function in other ways. Rather than using it as a time-keeping device, it can be a tool to change your attention. If you were, for example, doing a meditation on the four quarters of the circle, each change of scent could reflect that it was time to move on to the next element.

Hidden Trails

This is an amazing twist on incense trails. I'm certain that some ancient users had to have done this, but I've never found a reference to it in any literature. Since we know that incense charcoal burns just fine beneath a bed of ash, I wondered if other incense would burn below the surface.

It was easy to confirm that they do. However, testing this idea with an incense trail was going to be a little tricky. You can't simply push an incense trail below the surface as you can with most other forms of incense. So I decided to scatter ash over the top of my trail until it could no longer be seen. I left one tiny bit of trail visible so that I would know where to light it.

When I burned this first "hidden" trail I was struck by its potential for magick, art, and entertainment. The trail burned as planned, but it was almost as if an invisible hand was writing in the ash with a burning finger. The clean, white ash darkens quickly when the trail burns beneath it, leaving a dark drawing. And with clean ash, it smells just as it would if burned uncovered. I suggest covering the entire surface of your censer with a small amount of clean, white ash. If you only cover the trail itself, the form might be obvious even though the incense itself is covered.

For magickal work you can create an appropriate trail and then cover it. The others in your circle will have never seen the design, so they will have a natural attraction to the trail as it is revealed. This extra focus and attention can strengthen the alignment of the energies that are raised in the circle. The most surprising part for me is that even if I create the trail and know exactly how it should look as it burns, I still find myself rapt by the slowly revealed symbol or word.

Covering a hidden trail with ash.

This technique has non-magickal applications as well. Sadly, I am not an artist. I can draw interesting shapes and letters, but beyond that I fear I am incompetent. But I can envision someone with actual drawing talent using this medium. Can you imagine a gallery showing of incense art where the visitors are part of the process as they watch the art reveal itself slowly? Scents can be paired with hidden trails as appropriate. As different parts of the incense art is revealed, the scent can change to complement it. If a tree is appearing, then a nice cedar might be appropriate, while drawing a meal or food image might use an oregano blend. I'm sure a real artist could employ this medium far more effectively than the way I've described it here.

This technique can also just be for fun. You could have your own incense night when everyone makes their own hidden trails and lights them at the same time. Doing something like this would best be done with one censer in each room to allow the scents to stand on their own. With small censers you could use several in one room. As the trails reveal themselves, the guests can try to guess what shape or scene will be revealed. Just watching even the most mundane shape appear in the incense is fascinating. I still enjoy it after many years and can't imagine ever growing bored with hidden trails.

Rituals

Incorporating incense trails into your rituals is only limited by your imagination. Many of us have gotten used to making the incense component of our rituals nothing more than lighting a stick of incense and forgetting about it. Incense trails are the exact opposite approach. They require time, either before or during your ritual, and lots of care. An incense trail can move incense from having a peripheral presence to being a point of focus in your ritual.

Circle Meditation

For those of us who aren't artists, this is an excellent ritual use of incense trails. Prepare your censer for drawing in the ash. Make a circular impression in the ash. You will find many suitable stamps around your home, including water glasses. The size will only be limited by the size of your censer and the amount of ash filling it. If you are using a small censer then make the circle as large as you can within your censer. If you are using a larger censer (I have a large ceramic mixing bowl filled with ash for making large trails), the size of circle you use should be determined by the amount of time you want the incense to burn. The wider and longer the trail, the longer it will burn.

Use the open end of a drinking glass to make a small circle. An up-ended bowl will make a larger circle. Slightly move whatever stamp you choose to use to create an impression ¼ inch wide and ½ inch deep. When you fill the trail with incense powder, you have a couple of options.

You could fill the entire circle with one scent, or you could use a different scent for each quarter. If you choose to use four scents, try to keep them all balanced in length. Try to fill exactly a quarter of the circle with each scent. You can also mark each quarter of the circle.

Select a starting place where you will light the trail. You should then make a break in the circle at that starting point by pushing a bit of ash into the trail. (If you don't put a break in the trail then the incense will burn around the circle in both directions. That can be a good effect, but only if it is anticipated.) If you want the incense to burn clockwise (deosil), light the trail on the left side of the break you made in the circle. If you want it to burn counterclockwise (widdershens), light it on the right side of the break.

As the incense burns around the circle, spend your time in contemplation about the element represented by that quarter. As the circle burns through the eastern quarter, think about the power of air (or whichever element is associated with that direction in your tradition). Consider air in its many aspects and how it contributes to the magickal work that you do. As the incense burns into the southern quarter, contemplate the power of fire. At the end of the circle you will have spent equal time contemplating all four elements. When the incense is extinguished you can enjoy the blending of the four different scents and contemplate how the elements work together.

A Spell of Parting/Joining

The time comes in everyone's life where they must part from someone or something that has been important to them. This could be from the end of a relationship, a death, or loss of a home or job. Any time a person needs to be separated from someone or something important, this is a great ritual to ease the transition.

Prepare your censer while you are preparing your altar for the ritual. Stir the ash in your censer and level it, packing it lightly. Draw an inverted capital "Y" with the single line facing away from you. Fill the trail with incense powder. If you wish to take the ritual to another level, you can make each of the legs with different scents. A single scent burns down the single line then two new scents begin after the line splits.

First complete any preliminary work you need to do (cleansing, casting of a circle, calling of deities, or any other preparation your tradition follows). When you are ready to begin the spell of parting, light the top, single leg of the trail and say:

> *Paths cross and separate again. Our time together*
> *has ended and now we must each return to the*
> *path to which we are drawn. I bid peace to you*
> *and yours, but from this time forth,*
> *you have no control over me, nor I of you.*

You can repeat this if you wish or simply contemplate the relationship or situation that is ending. Remember the good times and the bad. Remember why this person or thing came into your life and why it is leaving. Though the mechanics are the same, the ritual you would do for someone who has passed away would clearly be different from a ritual for the end of a romantic relationship. Always try and see things as they truly are. You had this person in your life for a reason and the person has left for a reason. Face that reason, whatever it may be, and consider it as the incense trail breaks off into two different paths.

As the two new paths burn, think about your future and how you want it to look now that this change has taken place. Where are you going and what do you hope to find? You can enhance this ritual even further with the use of a hidden trail. You can cover the entire trail before lighting it or, if you prefer, you can cover just two or even one of the branches. Covering the trail can represent the unknown, which is what we all face at the end of a relationship or situation.

You can also reverse this spell and use it for a joining instead. What a wonderful thing to have in your censer at a handfasting or other event of unification! Simply turn the form over into a right-side-up capital "Y." Light each of the two top arms at the same time. As they burn down to the single trail toward you, the two paths become one.

A Magickal Surprise

This is one of my very favorite uses for hidden trails. It's a lot of fun and a way to share your incense creativity with your friends. Create a hidden incense trail and then present the censer to someone else. Mark the place where the trail should be lighted and then allow the other person to enjoy your surprise message. Likewise, a hidden trail could be prepared by a host for a gathering. The censer could be displayed and the guests could enjoy the surprises that are hidden beneath the ash.

12

Chaining
Combustible Incense

When using an ash base in a censer, you have some amazing options for incense burning. One of the most versatile and useful techniques is "chaining" incense. Just as a chain of dominoes can be knocked down by tipping a single tile, multiple pieces of incense can be burned by lighting a single piece. This ability has many obvious applications for both fun and, more importantly, magickal purposes.

There are a few techniques that can be performed without using an ash base, but most chaining techniques will require an ash bed to work properly. Chaining uses one burning piece of incense that, properly positioned, can be used to light many others with ease. An ash bed ensures the incense will burn completely and will properly light any incense touching it. Since incense will burn underneath a properly prepared bed of ash, some incense may even be burned below the surface.

Naturally, the first step for most chain burning is to prepare the ash bed. This can be done just as you would prepare ash for charcoal. The simplest approach is to stir the ash to fluff it and then lightly tap the censer a few times to level and slightly compact it. The ash needs to remain fairly loose but compacted slightly so incense placed on the surface won't sink too deeply.

Joss Stick to Joss Stick

Any form of self-burning incense can be chained, but the easiest is the joss stick. Most commercial (and even homemade) joss sticks work great for this technique. Keep in mind that all incense used in chaining must be small enough to fit inside your censer. For instance, if you plan to chain three joss sticks, all three must be able to fit in your censer simultaneously. The only exception would be incense used to light the chain, which could stick up above or out of the censer.

Admittedly, some joss sticks will work better than others. I've found that most commercial joss sticks can chain easily, but occasionally I'll find a scent that isn't completely reliable. Homemade incense is more likely to have problems, although most of what I've tested has worked. To test a joss stick's suitability, make a simple chain with it.

Begin by breaking the stick into two pieces small enough to lay comfortably together in your censer. Lay one piece of the stick on the surface of the ash. (Don't forget to lightly pack the ash first or the stick might immediately sink below the surface.) Place the second piece at a 90-degree angle to the first so that *only the tip* of it overlaps the first piece. Don't allow the second piece to hang over the edge of the first—only its tip should be on top of the first piece. You can place the second piece anywhere along the length of the first piece, but for best testing results, overlap the second stick at least 1 inch away from the end you light.

With the two pieces overlapped, you are ready for testing. I'll talk more about lighting chains later, but for now just use a butane lighter to ignite the end of the first stick. You can simply apply the flame directly to the end of the joss stick as it lay on the ash bed. Remember, the first stick is the bottom one, below the overlapping second one. You may have to keep the flame in contact with the end of the stick for several seconds longer than normal since it is lying flat. Usually a piece lit this way won't flame, but simply start to glow. If yours does flame, remember *not* to blow it out. After all, it is atop a bed of ash that can be easily blown. If the stick flames for more than a few seconds, fan it lightly with a card or small paper to gently blow out the flame. Better yet, you might briefly cover the censer to extinguish the flame. The censer's lid is the best choice for this, although any flat, non-flammable item (like a ceramic tile) will also work. For obvious reasons, avoid placing paper or cardboard over the censer to extinguish flaming incense, and definitely don't use your hand.

When you light incense in this way, you may notice that where the flame touches it, the ash might change colors. This is especially true with older, heavily used ash. That's to be expected and is actually a cleaning technique for soiled ash (see the Ash section of chapter 5). It is also normal for ash to change colors where burning incense touches it. Oils deposited from the incense smoke often cause this. The heat may also change the color of used ash, as can incense with a large amount of resins since some tiny particles may not burn completely.

Overlapping joss sticks to create a chain
(the overlapping is exaggerated for illustration).

Once the first stick is burning, watch as it burns down to the point where the second stick overlaps it. At first glance, the incense may appear to go out, but don't fear. Even if the second stick fails to ignite, the first will nearly always continue to burn, although the second stick might obscure the glowing point for a minute or two. In most cases, just as the glowing point emerges from beneath the second stick, both sticks begin to glow and burn normally. As long as that happens, the incense is well-suited to chain burning. If the second stick fails to light, you might try the experiment a second time to be certain. The vast majority of incense I've tested this way (including samples from every major Japanese manufacturer) works just fine. Once you've confirmed that your joss sticks will burn in a chain, you can begin to experiment and have fun. Just remember that the burning stick should always rest *below* the stick you wish to chain.

Masala to Masala

You can use the same technique for sticks with a wooden rod in the center. Naturally, it's a good idea to test any particular brand or scent first to make certain it will burn while lying flat. If it will, then it stands a good chance of chaining also. In many cases, masala sticks can use the same techniques as joss sticks. It may be necessary to break off the part of the wooden rod that extends beyond the incense material.

You can also take advantage of the wooden rod in masala sticks to create "crossed sword" chain burning. While you can do this with joss sticks, it usually results in part of the incense left unburned, so I prefer the technique only for masala-style sticks. This technique will also work using many kinds of censers, so an ash-filled censer is not mandatory for "crossed sword" burning. Begin with one stick set in a censer at an angle. A normal incense boat can be used for this, but a censer filled with ash, sand, or other materials will also work very well.

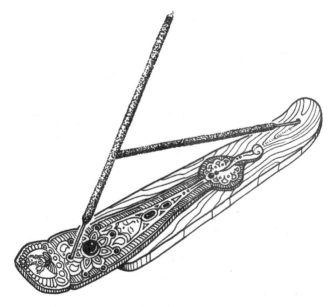

"Crossed swords" incense chain.

Place a second incense stick so that it crosses the first stick much like two crossed swords. It is usually best to have the second stick have the least amount of overlap as possible, so you may want the second tip set very close to the first stick rather than overlapping in the middle, as crossed swords are normally seen. The reason is that when the first stick burns down to the point of overlap, the second stick will ignite and burn in both directions. If you overlap the two sticks in the middle, the second stick will ignite, burn into two pieces, and the top part of the stick will fall, posing a fire hazard.

Cone to Cone

This is a more difficult process, but it can still be done with a proper ash bed. There are several different configurations that will work for cone to cone burning. The easiest method is to lay both cones on their sides. Place the second cone so that its narrow tip is in direct contact with the bottom of the first cone. Light the first cone at the narrow tip and once it burns down to the wide base, it will ignite the narrow end of the second cone fairly easily.

Alternately, the cones can be placed on their sides so that the wide bases are touching as completely as possible. This may pose a bit more of a challenge since the wide base of the second cone will be more difficult to ignite; if the second cone has extremely good burning properties, it should work for you. This method will also produce a bell curve of smoke. It will begin with a thin stream of smoke that builds into a larger and larger stream. When the second cone is ignited there will be a considerable amount of smoke coming from the pair. As the first cone burns out and the second cone burns toward its narrow end, the amount of smoke will continue to decrease. This technique can be effective for chanting or other ritual work that begins slowly, builds to a crescendo, and then reduces slowly to a low volume or speed.

Another technique for chaining one cone to another is to place the second cone on the ash lying on its side. Place the first cone upright with the wide base on top of the narrow end of the second cone. This will cause the second cone to be pressed into the ash a bit, but that should not be a problem. Light the narrow end of the first cone. As it burns down to the wide base the second cone's tip will ignite. The second cone will then burn on its side. This second cone can also then be chained using one of the other cone-to-cone techniques, creating a chain of three, four, or more cones to suit longer rituals.

Combinations

The most fun and exciting form of chain burning is combining these various techniques. The basic concept is simple: one piece of burning incense can ignite another. Once you have experimented a little with that simple idea, your only limit is your own imagination. I hope by this point in reading you already have many applications for these techniques in your own incense burning practices and rituals. What follows is merely a few suggestions on how you can combine these techniques. I have been using these methods for years, so most of these ideas are based on my own experimentation.

When combining various techniques, keep a few basic principles in mind. First, it is easiest to use a large burning area to ignite a small one. For example, it is much easier to ignite a joss stick from the base of a cone than to ignite a wide cone from a joss stick. Both can be done, but the large surface area of the burning base of a cone makes igniting other incense fairly simple.

Next, keep in mind that it is easier to light incense at the end rather than in the center. Thin incense (be it joss stick, masala stick, or even an incense trail) can be lit at any point on its length, but large incense cylinders, dhoops, and cones are far less likely to ignite in the middle. The reason is that heat has to penetrate the entire thickness of the incense in order to light. When you light incense at its end, the heat can easily reach the entire thickness of the incense, but lighting it along its length means all of the heat must penetrate from one side.

Not all incense burns at the same temperature. Different incense ingredients burn at different temperatures. Incense that contains clove or saltpeter, for example, will burn hotter (and therefore faster) than incense without those ingredients. Thus it is easier to ignite other incense from hot-burning types than from cooler-burning types. If you are using incense that burns very slowly, it may not be a good choice to ignite other incense. You might want to put it at the end of your chain rather than at the start or the middle.

Incense will usually burn when buried under ash, but it is harder to smell. The deeper the incense is buried, the less the scent will reach the air. Sometimes this is advantageous since you might use a small piece of joss stick buried deep under ash to connect two sections of an incense chain. The incense will burn, but it will not give off scent or discolor the ash above it if placed deep enough in the ash. That can be used to great effect, as your chain will appear to be finished burning only to then, seemingly without any intervention, ignite a new chain or a new section of the first chain. This can be a wonderful sleight of hand.

Keeping these simple tips in mind, you can create seemingly complex trails. The only real complicating factors, of course, are the length of the chain and the number of difficult transitions (such as igniting a cone from a masala stick). One combination that I really like to use is a chain of joss stick (set out as described earlier) ignited by an upright cone. The joss sticks can be overlapped as desired on an ash bed, then a cone is inserted into the ash so that it either overlaps or is firmly pressed against the end of the first stick. The advantage to this approach is that an upright cone is very easy to light in place, whereas a joss stick on its side can be a little tricky to get started. The cone generates a lot of heat and will ignite a joss stick easily. This type of arrangement is great to use if you want to set up your chain well in advance of its use. If you wanted to create a chain for a ritual that is to take place hours later, this arrangement will sit patiently waiting to be lit and will generally work flawlessly when called upon.

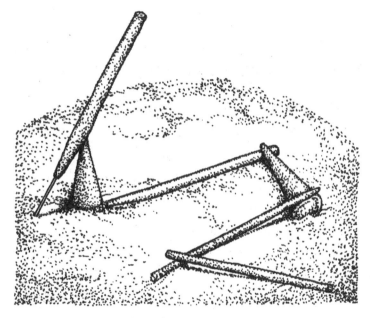

A sample combination chain.

Another great combination for an incense chain is to use an upright cone to ignite an incense trail. That trail can then be used to ignite a variety of joss sticks placed along its path. I like to think of the cone as a volcano, the trail as a river, and the joss sticks as streams. Never forget that burning too many pieces of incense at once can cause a scent overload as well as plumes of smoke, so plan these chains carefully. Place each item far enough down the trail from the previous item that you won't have multiple "streams" burning at once.

Chaining Rituals

Using chain burning for rituals adds a whole new dimension to spells, celebrations, and even just to chanting. As with all incense, chains can be used for timing as well as for scent and the creation of a magickal atmosphere. As with all of my rituals, what follows are merely my general suggestions and approaches to certain rituals. Please modify them to fit with your specific path or tradition and personalize them to make them your very own.

Fall Equinox

The autumnal equinox, sometimes referred to as Mabon, is an important time for many Pagans and followers of Earth-based religions. An equinox is a time when Earth is in perfect balance between night and day. It also marks the transition from summer to autumn. This is a widely celebrated holiday and a perfect time to use your newfound skills in making incense chains. This simple ritual uses a very basic incense chain, so it is a great choice for anyone to incorporate into a personal or group ritual to celebrate this change of seasons.

Select two incense blends. I always prefer to use the same form for both blends. You can choose self-burning powder, sticks (joss or masala), or cones. Powder or joss sticks work best, but any of these forms are acceptable. You could even use dhoop or incense cylinders, but I would strongly recommend making them the first scent or using the same form for both scents. It is easy to light a joss stick from a cone or cylinder but much tougher to reverse them.

Select one incense blend that represents summer and a second that represents fall. You should really make the selection based on your own concepts of what constitutes a summer or fall incense blend, but you can also consult the correspondence charts near the end of this book or a variety of other sources if you need some suggestions. Once you have made your selections, lay out the chain in your censer.

Place the summer blend in the censer first. If using self-burning powder, create a channel in the ash to hold the powder. You can create any
shape you wish, but try to make a clear mid-point in the shape. I like to
make a "V" shape for this ritual. Fill the first half of the shape with the
summer powder and the second half with the fall powder. If using other
forms, place the summer incense in the censer first. If you use cones, place
the cone on its side on the bed of ash.

Next, place the fall incense in the censer. If using sticks, dhoops, or
cylinders, overlap the incense so that one end of the fall incense is on top
of one end of the summer incense. If you use cones, place the Fall incense
so that the thin end of the cone firmly touches the wide end of the summer incense. If you use a combination of forms, make sure that you place
the incense so that the summer blend will ignite the fall blend.

Cast your magick circle if you normally work within one. Perform
any invocations you prefer before beginning this ritual. Since this is such
a simple ritual, you may want to incorporate it into a larger or more
elaborate ritual. Although there are times when a simple ritual is the best.

After casting your circle or doing any other ritual work, you can light
the incense. Light the summer blend on the end that does not touch the
fall blend. As you light the incense, say the following:

> *Summer's heat and Summer's sun*
> *will Autumn's season now become.*
> *Turn the circle, turn the wheel,*
> *As harvest winds we soon shall feel.*

As the summer blend burns, reflect on the summer just passed. Think
of the changes in your life and the joys you experienced. You may wish to
chant as the incense burns. Here is a nice, simple chant:

Summer sun no longer burns,
once again the wheel turns.

When the summer blend ignites the fall blend, it is symbolic of the moment of Mabon. At that moment, I like to shout or cheer to celebrate the change of seasons. After the fall blend begins to burn, you can change your chant:

Now does pass the Summer's heat,
prepare we will for harvest sweet.

When the fall blend has finished burning, you should stir the ash to return all of the incense into one collection of ash, saying:

The wheel has turned, so mote it be.

You can then open your circle or perform any other magick or rituals you have planned.

Quarters Meditation (Chain Incense Version)

This is one of my very favorite rituals of contemplation. While not a true meditation in the sense of attempting to disconnect the self, it is very useful for centering as well as for focusing your mind in preparation of other magickal or ritual work. Although I would typically perform this meditation within a magick circle, that is not a requirement.

I use a large, round censer filled with ash for this meditation. I personally use a very large censer—a ceramic bowl that is about 8 inches in diameter. I realize that you may not have a censer that large or have enough ash to fill it, so you may want to use a round ceramic plate instead. Use a shallow plate, as you only need about ½ inch of ash. Even a single packet of Japanese white ash should be enough to cover a plate of this size with a thin layer. A thicker layer of ash makes the process easier, but it is not mandatory.

Sift your ash if you have not done so recently. If using a plate, carefully sprinkle the ash to create an even, level surface of ash. This usually means using more ash in the center where the plate is the deepest. Begin your chain by creating an incense trail around the outside diameter of your censer. Keep the trail 1 or 2 inches from the side of the censer, but try to make the circle as wide as possible. If your ash is thick enough, use a feather, skewer, pen tip, or toothpick to create a channel in the ash. You can then fill that channel with sandalwood, makko (a type of wood binder that it is also an excellent base material for incense), or other incense powder. If you are using a thin layer of ash, do not create a channel. Instead, create the circle with the incense powder on the surface of the ash. In either case, make the circle thin (no more than ⅛ inch wide), but ensure that it is solid with no breaks. Any breaks will cause the chain to go out before it completes burning.

Leave the circle open about 1 inch. If you create a closed circle, it will burn in both directions at the same time. That can be a useful effect, but not for this ritual. Where you choose to leave the circle open is up to you, but I usually leave the gap on the right-hand side just above the two o'clock position.

With your trail in place, select combustible incense to represent each of the four elements and, if you wish, a fifth type to represent yourself or Spirit. You can use joss sticks, cones, masala sticks, or even incense powder to represent the elements and yourself. You will find that joss sticks are the easiest to use, but any of those forms can be included. You could use dhoops or cylinders, but I do not recommend them since they will be difficult to ignite from a thin trail. You could use a thicker trail and then include dhoops or cylinders, but only in very well-ventilated locations (thicker trails = lots of smoke).

When selecting the incense to represent the elements, consider what each element represents to you. That will help you determine which incense to select. You may keep different blends made specifically for each element, and those are an obvious choice for this meditation. If not, you may want to consult the correspondence charts near the end of this book or consult other sources to help you decide which scents would be the most appropriate. Finally, select a scent to represent yourself. Choose a scent that you find exceptionally pleasing and relaxing.

Once you have selected incense for all four elements and yourself (if you choose to include that part of the ritual), carefully connect the incense to the trail. If you are using stick incense to represent any of the elements, break off a section of stick 2 or 3 inches long. If you are using a masala-style stick, also break off any uncoated part of the wooden rod. You can adjust the length of the stick if you feel that the element it represents requires more or less of your attention than the other elements. You can adjust the length of that element's trail if you choose to use powdered incense, but this is not practical with cones.

Begin with the incense for the element of air. Connect the incense you have selected to the trail at the three o'clock position. You should place the stick or cone so that it connects to the inside of your circular trail and extends directly toward the center of your censer. If you are using stick incense, overlap the stick on the top of the trail so that only the tiniest bit of trail can be seen. Do not completely cover the trail unless you were successful in making an exceptionally thin trail. Do the same if you are using a cone, but be certain to place the cone on its side and connect the thin end of the cone to the trail. Lightly press the stick or cone into the ash, but be careful not to break the trail.

If you choose to use an incense trail to represent any elements, create the trail just as if you were laying down an incense stick. Make a straight trail that connects from the circular trail and extends towards the center

of the censer. As you fill the trail, overlap the incense representing the element over the circular trail. Just as with an incense stick, the trail should
be 2 or 3 inches long. This length also depends on the size of your censer.
If you are using a small censer, you may need to make the sticks or trails
even shorter. In no case should any of the incense in the center of the
censer overlap any other incense except the incense representing self. The
only place two blends should touch is on the outer circular incense trail.

After connecting the incense that represents air, do the same with the
incense for fire. Connect this incense to the circular trail at the six o'clock
position, also extending toward the center of the censer. Connect the incense representing water at the nine o'clock position and the incense for
earth at the twelve o'clock position. Finally, connect the incense that represents you (assuming you include that in this meditation) to the very end
of the trail near the break above the three o'clock position. If you choose
to only use incense for the four elements and not for yourself, then just
leave that area of the censer empty.

With the incense laid out, take a few moments to quiet your mind. If
you normally enjoy a ritual bath before working magick or meditating,
take the time to do that. Once you feel quieted and prepared, you may
cast your magick circle if you choose to do so. When all of your normal
casting procedures are complete, light your incense. As this meditation will
last for thirty minutes (or more, depending on the size of your censer), it
is best to sit down in a comfortable position, but in a place where you can
see the censer. Remember that scent will travel on the air, so if your censer
is set higher than your nose you might never smell the incense. You may
get the best results from placing your censer on the floor.

Light the circular incense trail on the right side of the break you made
in the circular incense trail, so that the chain will burn in a clockwise
direction. As the chain initially burns, simply focus on the energy of the
burning circle. Enjoy its presence around you. As the outer circle burns to

the first overlapping incense (at the three o'clock position), the incense you have selected to represent the element of air will ignite and begin burning toward the center of your censer. Once that incense ignites, begin to focus on the element of air. Feel the air where you are sitting. Watch the smoke from the incense drifting around you. Think about this important element as you slowly breathe in and out.

Air is life. We can only live for a few minutes without breathing. Air is also energy—you can feel its power as it moves in and out of your body. Think about all of the ways this element impacts your life and your magick. Continue to focus on the element of air until the incense you have selected to represent it has burned out. As mentioned earlier, you can adjust the amount of time you will focus on any element by shortening or lengthening the incense you select to represent it.

While the incense representing air is burning, the outer circular trail will continue to burn as well. After the incense for air has completed burning, the outer circle will continue to burn clockwise and will ignite the incense selected to represent the element of fire. While you wait for the burning circle to come around and light the incense for fire, simply enjoy, once again, the power of the incense in your circle. Once the circle reaches and ignites the fire incense, focus on the element of fire and its meaning in your life and in your magick.

Fire is seen in your censer. Especially in a dimly lit area, you should be able to clearly see both the outer circle of incense and the incense representing fire burning. That thin glowing line that crawls along the length of the incense is a good focal point. Fire is life. The warmth of your body, the heat of the light of the glowing sun, and the fire that cooks our food are all critical to our survival. Think about how fire not only benefits us in practical ways but its importance in your magickal life as well. Fire represents spirit. The fire that burns within you is your drive and your passion. Fire is also energy—without it there would be no life and no magick. Continue to focus on the element of fire until the incense you have selected to represent it has completed burning.

While the incense representing the element of fire burns, the outer circle of incense will continue to burn as well. After the incense representing fire has completed burning, resume simply enjoying the energy of that circle until it ignites the incense you selected to represent water.

When fire meets water, magick is always present. As the incense for water ignites, reflect upon the element of water and its importance to you. Water is life. Without water we cannot live. Just as you cannot live without water, neither can plants, animals, or the world itself. Your body is primarily made of water and you can easily feel it within you. Even in the driest environments, you can close your eyes and imagine rain coming down from the clouds. We can smell water on the wind as storms approach. Also consider how water impacts you spiritually. It is the element of birth and rebirth. Water washes away unwanted energies and cleanses the mind and soul as well as the body. Water nourishes the energy that makes us magickal beings.

Continue to focus on the importance and meaning of water until the incense you have selected to represent it has completed burning. Again enjoy your presence in the circular energy until the outer circle of incense ignites the blend you have chosen to represent the element of earth.

Once the earth incense ignites, focus on that element. Earth is life. Our bodies are formed from the materials of earth. Every plant that grows digs its roots in the ground to draw nutrients. Earth provides our footing in both a literal, physical sense but also in a spiritual and magickal sense. When we need to release unused or unwanted energies, we often "ground" those energies by sending them to the earth. Earth is the foundation upon which all of our creations are built. Many wondrous gifts are hidden within the ground and the planet herself is often called "Mother." The materials of earth flow in our blood and without them we could not live.

If you have included the fifth element in this meditation, the incense you have selected to represent yourself will be ignited when the outer circle of incense reaches its end. Optionally, you could place the fifth element incense where it would be ignited by the earth incense when it reaches its end. This will avoid the possibility that it will begin to burn before the earth incense was finished. Once the incense representing self has ignited, begin to focus on how you personally interact with the four elements. Also consider what those elements mean to you, not only magickally and physically, but in personal and intimate ways. This is an opportunity to focus on your place within the larger scheme of the elements and the universe as a whole.

Once the last of the incense has burned completely, stir the ash to erase all traces of the incense you have used. You are returning your magick circle and all of the elements back into part of the greater whole. Take a moment to center yourself and ground. You can then complete any other magickal workings you had planned and open your circle, if one was cast. End by thanking the elements for their guidance and inspiration.

Conclusion

The joy of incense can be experienced in so many different ways for so many different purposes. From mundane to magickal, incense can be part of your daily life. It enhances virtually all that we do while bringing us closer to Nature. I don't expect everyone to run out, buy all the incense materials they can find, and turn into an incense fanatic like me, but I do hope you will allow this very special magick to occupy a new place in your heart and in your home. The magickal uses of incense are virtually unlimited—I hope this book has given you insight into how you can more effectively, and enjoyably, enhance all of the work that you do.

It is unfortunate that I couldn't include samples of all the many wonderful things I've discussed in these pages. For me, this book, although a very long time in the making, was a wonderful trip through familiar realms as seen through fresh eyes. I appreciate you letting me into your life to share this joy with you. I hope that you will do the same for others.

The Tremendous Power of Scent

Scent is the only sense that is connected to our brains in two completely different ways. Science has yet to determine how all of it works, but those who experience incense daily know that scent impacts more than just the smell of the room. Scent impacts our mood, our perceptions, and our connection with the natural world. Incense is one of the best tools we have to control the scents in our lives.

Try burning some incense in a pitch-black room. Shut off all the phones, music, television, and computers to eliminate the sound and light they produce. Sit in the dark in a quiet room where the only light is from the glowing tip of a joss stick. That is the surest way I know to demonstrate the power of scent in all of our lives. With all the other senses muted, scent becomes an almost visual experience. I hope you won't let foul odors overwhelm you any longer and you will allow you mind, spirit, and body to swim in the oceans of pleasant scents that incense offers us.

The Magick Power of Botanicals

The use of incense in magick and ritual predates written history. It may even predate humans. We have no way to know what our pre-human ancestors did in the incense realm, but there have been moments when I have listened to incense and I could have sworn I heard voices stretching back into the deepest depths of time echoing my experience.

Botanicals—be they herbs, woods, or resins—have incredible power. They are the embodiment of the elements and are in essence (yes, another incense pun) magickal batteries. They store energy, sometimes in enormous quantities, until we release it and put it to use. Roots stretch into the earth, air and water are used for growth, and fire (in the form of sunlight) provides the engine to make it all work.

All cultures have recognized the power of botanicals. Even in our modern lives of speedy computers, Internet, fast food, and instant entertainment, we still haven't lost sight of this as a culture. Walk into any drug store in the United States and you will find many plant extracts and even some whole herbs and herbal blends waiting on the shelf for eager customers. Those botanicals might be in the form of capsules, liquids, teas, or pills, but they are still evidence that we recognize the power of botanicals.

Industry is aware of this power as well. The pharmaceutical industry still researches the natural world, looking for new compounds that can be concentrated or synthesized into new medications. Although it took the advent of chemistry to unleash the pharmaceutical trade, drug makers still rely on Nature to show them where to go and what to do.

The Honored Place of Incense in History

The incense trade helped to build the Roman Empire. Virtually unassisted, incense built several African empires of the ancient world. Although it is often called the Silk Road, the ancient trade routes that brought different peoples together and built and destroyed empires is more accurately called the Incense Road. In the East and the West, incense was revered throughout much of history.

I find it very ironic that the story of the birth of Jesus Christ features the importance of incense in the ancient world, yet it was Christianity that derailed the evolution of incense in the West. The association of incense with the Pagans of the Roman Empire nearly removed the word *incense* from Western lexicons. In yet another twist of irony, it was the limited use of incense in the Christian church that kept the only surviving Roman incense traditions alive.

Now that the West is rediscovering incense, this fragrant companion is once again regaining its place of honor in our traditions. And you, dear reader, are an important link in that chain. I am thrilled that incense is once again considered valuable enough that publishers are willing to print books like this one to bring traditional and modern approaches to incense use to everyone. The body of work on incense in the West is still minute compared to what exists in the East. Slowly, some of those Eastern documents and traditions are being translated and made available to us. At the same time, incense enthusiasts from around the world are now able to exchange not only information but even actual incense! As the body of incense knowledge continues to grow, so will our appreciation for Mother Earth and what she offers us every day.

The Value of Incense in Your Life

There are so many abstract and philosophical ideas presented in the incense world that it is easy to lose sight of how incense impacts you. After all, what does any of this matter if incense has no relevance for you? How incense enhances your life is really up to you. I spend a lot of time talking to other incense enthusiasts, so it still shocks me when I hear people speak about incense as if it were an obligation or an undesirable part of ritual. I know that there are some people with genuine health issues when it comes to incense, but for the most part everyone can enjoy natural incense. Synthetic incense, in my experience, is much more of a health problem and it saddens me that most people think that synthetic incense is the only kind there is. "I am allergic to incense" is very rarely an accurate statement, but it is one I've heard hundreds of times. For those who really can't enjoy incense, I feel true sympathy.

Incense certainly doesn't have to dominate your life, but it can easily become a part of daily living. From meditation to fumigation to magick to romance and even sleep, incense can make virtually every aspect of our lives more enjoyable. I encourage you to experiment on your own. Use this book as a starting place if incense is not already a part of your life, but make it just that: a starting place. Discover for yourself how incense can improve your life and your magickal work.

For those of you who already understand how amazing incense is and how it can enhance many aspects of life, I thank you and salute you. I hope that you found new excitement about incense in these pages and that you will contribute to our body of knowledge as time marches on. Don't keep the power of incense to yourself. Incense is an experience to be shared.

Incense is not simply a part of magick. Incense *is* magick. May all of your lives be filled with magickal scents!

I want to leave you with a bit of an incense mystery. The following is a wonderful poem by my best friend. Hidden within it is an incense puzzle for you to sort out during the coming hours of meditation with your amazing new incense skills. My thanks to her for giving me permission to include it in this book. Even if you never uncover its mystery, I hope it has meaning for your life and incense journey.

Mine Own Eye
By Michelle Hawkins

Do you know me, I a wretched stranger? Alas, I know you.
I have touched thee.
I have caressed thy soul
I have made thee mine
We are never far apart
My beloved, we shall meet again.

....

How dost thou long for my touch?
Dost thou call to mind, images of our meeting

And smile knowingly
Or dost thou tremble in sweet recollection?

....

Ah! thy eyes betray thee; thy memory is sound
Those ghostly voices are but memoirs of the past
They entice thee with a story
Listen my beloved, listen to their tale, for they do
    not deceive
Listen to their whispers.

....

Yes, gentle stranger, I have heard the voices of
    which ye speak
And I have seen the shadows, for they disturb me
    in my reverie
Would'st thou have me believe my visions are
    not unfounded?
Be ye sincere, I pray thee
For I find such spirits a comfort in my ails.

....

They allow me to see, yet without my own eyes,
The exquisite beauty of a soul that surely does not exist
Yet in hushed tones they murmur and quiet me and tell me
    that I always was
That he too, will always be.
I take comfort in these fanciful visions
Please, I beg of thee, do not take these from me!

....

Tell me, beloved, what do thy specters say to thee?
Do they speak of your protector, who merely exists
    to aid and comfort thee?
Do they speak of a man who has long roamed this
    lifetime seeking his lover?
Perhaps they tell you of his longing for your
    recognition alone.
Surely thou knowst thy savior?

....

Come!
Take my hand and I shall lead thee gently among
    the honeysuckle
Though the nettle flourishes and may pierce thee
I shall cast it aside and heal thy wounds
I will lead thee true
For thou art secure in this life
And those many lives yet to come.

Appendix of
Correspondences

Personally, I have always felt that correspondence charts written by others have limited usefulness. Although authors can cite traditional associations or their personal associations based on their own studies, I still believe that the best way to understand how and when to use any particular aromatic or blend is to listen to the aromatic yourself. Sit in a quiet space and enjoy the scent. Then open yourself to the aromatic and listen to what it tells you. If you listen, you might find that you need to use an aromatic in a way that directly contradicts what is written here. I encourage you to listen to your aromatics and don't let any book—even this one—dictate how you choose to use your incense.

That being said, some people are new to the path and need a starting place. It is also useful to hear opinions of others, so I offer my own correspondence charts. Even I have used many aromatics in ways different than what I list here. This is a combination of traditional correspondences and those from my own practices that I hope will be useful to the novice;

still, I strongly encourage you to "listen" to aromatics and create your own correspondence chart if you feel you need one.

Elements

Air: acacia, anise, benzoin, gum arabic, horehound, hops, lavender, lemongrass, marjoram, mastic, oak moss, palo santo, parsley, pine, sage, sandalwood (red), star anise

Fire: allspice, bay leaf (laurel), cedar, cinnamon, clove, copal, damiana, dragon's blood, frankincense, galangal, ginger, golden seal, guar gum, hyssop, juniper, pennyroyal, rosemary, saffron, tarragon, turmeric, woodruff

Water: calamus, camphor, cardamom, catnip, chamomile, coltsfoot, costus, eucalyptus, hibiscus, irish moss, myrrh, myrtle, sandalwood (yellow), spikenard, thyme, tonka bean, tragacanth gum, valerian, white willow

Earth: aloeswood, amber, makko (tabu noki), mugwort, patchouli, red cedar, vetiver, wild lettuce, yohimbe

Seasons

Spring: anise, chamomile, damiana, gum arabic, guar gum, hibiscus, hyssop, lemongrass, marjoram, myrtle, palo santo, pennyroyal, rosemary, spikenard, star anise, wild lettuce

Summer: acacia, allspice, bay leaf (laurel), camphor, catnip, cinnamon, clove, copal, dragon's blood, galangal, ginger, horehound, hops, lavender, makko (tabu noki), patchouli, sage, tragacanth gum, turmeric

Autumn: aloeswood, benzoin, coltsfoot, goldenseal, irish moss, mastic, myrrh, oak moss, red cedar, saffron, sandalwood (yellow), tarragon, thyme, tonka bean, white willow

Winter: amber, calamus, cardan⬛⬛⬛ ⬛⬛in-cense, juniper, mugwort, pi⬛⬛⬛ ⬛⬛an, vetiver, woodruff, yohimbe

Spec⬛⬛⬛poses

Cleansing: aloeswood, anise, ⬛⬛ ⬛af (laurel), benzoin, chamomile, copal, frankincense, lavender, palo santo, parsley, rosemary, sage, sandalwood (red), vetiver

Divination: aloeswood, camphor, coltsfoot, damiana, hibiscus, hops, mugwort, sage, sandalwood (red), white willow, wild lettuce

Healing: amber, bay leaf (laurel), calamus, camphor, cedar, cinnamon, eucalyptus, galangal, goldenseal, horehound, juniper, marjoram, mugwort, myrrh, pine, rosemary, sandalwood (yellow), spikenard, thyme, white willow

Love: cardamom, catnip, chamomile, clove, coltsfoot, copal, costus, damiana, dragon's blood, ginger, hibiscus, lavender, marjoram, myrtle, patchouli, saffron, vetiver, white willow, yohimbe

Luck: calamus, irish moss, oak moss, palo santo, star anise

Protection: acacia, amber, bay leaf (laurel), cedar, cinnamon, clove, dragon's blood, eucalyptus, frankincense, galangal, gum arabic, horehound, hyssop, juniper, lavender, myrrh, parsley, pine, woodruff

Prosperity: allspice, benzoin, calamus, galangal, goldenseal, irish moss, oak moss, patchouli

Purification: acacia, cedar, hyssop, sage, turmeric

Sleep: chamomile, hops, lavender, rosemary, thyme, valerian

Strength: cinnamon, dragon's blood, ginger, mugwort, palo santo, pennyroyal, red cedar, saffron, tarragon

Success: cinnamon, ginger

Chart

Common Name	...	...mental	Season	Purposes
Acacia	*Acacia sene...*		Summer	protection, purification
Allspice	*Eugenia pementa*		Summer	money, prosperity, wisdom
Aloeswood	*Lignum aquilariae*		Autumn	cleansing, meditation, divination
Amber	*n/a*	Earth	Winter	healing, protection
Anise (seed)	*Pimpinella anisum*	Air	Spring	cleansing, youth
Bay leaf (laurel)	*Laurus nobilis*	Fire	Summer	protection, healing, cleansing
Benzoin Gum	*Styrax benzoin*	Air	Autumn	cleansing, prosperity
Calamus (root)	*Acorus calamus*	Water	Winter	luck, healing, money, protection
Camphor	*Cinnamomum camphora, et.al.*	Water	Summer	healing, divination
Cardamom	*Ellettaria cardamomum*	Water	Winter	love, care
Catnip	*Nepeta cataria*	Water	Summer	felines, love, beauty, happiness
Cedar	*Cedrus spp.*	Fire	Winter	healing, purification, protection
Chamomile	*Matricaria chamomilla*	Water	Spring	sleep, love, cleansing
Cinnamon (cassia)	*Cinnamomum cassia*	Fire	Summer	success, healing, power, protection
Clove	*Caryophyllus aromaticus*	Fire	Summer	protection, exorcism, love
Coltsfoot	*Tussilago farfara*	Water	Autumn	visions, love
Copal	*Buresera microphylla*	Fire	Summer	love, cleansing
Costus (root)	*Saussurea lappa*	Water	Winter	love, rejuvenation
Damiana	*Turnera aphrodisiaca*	Fire	Spring	love, visions
Dragon's Blood	*Calamus draco*	Fire	Summer	love, protection, exorcism, potency
Eucalyptus	*Eucalyptus globules*	Water	Winter	healing, protection
Frankincense	*Boswellia spp.*	Fire	Winter	protection, summoning, cleansing

Aromatic Chart

Common Name	Latin Name	Elemental	Season	Purposes
Galangal (root)	*Alpina officinalis*	Fire	Summer	protection, health, money, hex-breaking
Ginger (root)	*Zingiber officinale*	Fire	Summer	love, success, power
Goldenseal (root)	*Hydrastis canadensis*	Fire	Autumn	money, healing
Gum Arabic	*Acacia Senegal*	Air	Spring	protection
Guar gum	*Cyamopsis tetragonolobus*	Fire	Spring	devotion
Hibiscus	*Hibiscus rosa-sinensis*	Water	Spring	love, lust, divination
Horehound	*Marrubium vulgare*	Air	Summer	protection, mental powers, healing
Hops (flower)	*Humulus lupulus*	Air	Summer	sleep, visions
Hyssop	*Hyssopus officinalis*	Fire	Spring	purification, protection, sanctification
Irish moss	*Chrondus crispus*	Water	Autumn	money, luck
Juniper	*Juniperus spp.*	Fire	Winter	protection, health, sanctification
Lavender (flowers)	*Lavandula officinalis*	Air	Summer	love, protection, sleep, cleansing
Lemongrass	*Cymbopogon citratus*	Air	Spring	separation, purity
Makko (tabu)	*Machilus thunbergii*	Earth	Summer	cleansing, truth
Marjoram	*Origanum majorana*	Air	Spring	love, happiness, protection
Mastic	*Pistacia lenticus*	Air	Autumn	transformation, visions
Mugwort	*Artemisia vulgaris*	Earth	Winter	strength, divination, healing
Myrrh	*Commiphora molmol*	Water	Autumn	protection, healing, spirituality
Myrtle (leaf)	*Myrtus communis*	Water	Spring	fertility, love, long life
Oak moss	*Evernia prunastri*	Air	Autumn	luck, money
Palo Santo	*Bursera graveolens*	Air	Spring	cleansing, luck, strength
Parsley (leaf)	*Petroselinum sativum*	Air	Spring	protection, cleansing, fertility

Aromatic Chart

Common Name	Latin Name	Elemental	Season	Purposes
Patchouli (leaf)	*Pogostemon patchouli*	Earth	Summer	money, fertility, lust
Pennyroyal	*Mentha pulegium*	Fire	Spring	strength, protection, peace
Pine	*Pinus spp.*	Air	Winter	healing, fertility, protection
Red cedar	*Juniperus virginiana*	Earth	Autumn	strength, honor, honesty
Rosemary	*Rosmarinus officinalis*	Fire	Spring	sleep, healing, cleansing
Saffron	*Crocus sativus linnaeus*	Fire	Autumn	love, strength, happiness
Sage (leaf)	*Salvia officinalis*	Air	Spring	immortality, longevity, wishes
Sage (white)	*Salvia apiana*	Air	Spring	divination, cleansing, purification
Sandalwood (yellow)	*Santalum album*	Water	Autumn	wishes, healing, spirituality
Sandalwood (red)	*Pterocarpus santalinus*	Air	Winter	cleansing, revelation
Spikenard	*Aralia racemosa*	Water	Spring	health, fidelity
Star Anise	*Illicium anisatum*	Air	Spring	luck, power
Tarragon (leaf)	*Artemisia dracunculus*	Fire	Autumn	strength, courage
Thyme (leaf)	*Thymus vulgaris*	Water	Autumn	health, sleep, courage
Tonka (bean)	*Dipteryx odorato*	Water	Autumn	courage, wishes, love
Tragacanth gum	*Astragalus tragacantha*	Water	Summer	binding
Turmeric	*Cucurma longa*	Fire	Summer	purification
Valerian (root)	*Valeriana officinalis*	Water	Winter	sleep, cleansing, love
Vetiver (root)	*Vetiveria zizanioides*	Earth	Winter	luck, money, hex-breaking
White willow	*Salix alba*	Water	Autumn	love, divination, healing
Wild lettuce	*Lactuca virosa*	Earth	Spring	divination, visions, revelation
Woodruff	*Asperula odorata*	Fire	Winter	victory, protection
Yohimbe (root)	*Pausinystalia yohimbe*	Earth	Winter	love, lust, desire

Bibliography

Alexander, Jane. *The Smudging and Blessings Book*. New York: Sterling Publishing, 2001.

Bedini, Silvio A. *The Trail of Time = Shih-Chien Ti Tsu-Chi: Time Measurement with Incense in East Asia*. New York: Cambridge University Press, 1994.

Bird, Stephanie Rose. *Sticks, Stones, Roots & Bones: Hoodoo, Mojo & Conjuring with Herbs*. St. Paul, MN: Llewellyn Publications, 2004.

Boyd, Andrew. *Spirit of Air: A Complete Book of Incense*. Np: Lulu.com/ self-published, 2005.

Bremness, Lesley. *The Complete Book of Herbs*. New York: Viking Studio Books, 1988.

Buckland, Raymond. *The Witch Book: The Encyclopedia of Witchcraft, Wicca, and Neo-paganism*. Detroit: Visible Ink Press, 2002.

Clapp, Nicholas. *The Road to Ubar: Finding the Atlantis of the Sands*. Boston: Houghton Mifflin, 1998.

de Claremont, Lewis. *The Ancient Book of Formulas*. St. Helena, CA: Antiquity Press, 2006.

Crowley, Aleister. *The Book of Lies*. Boston: Weiser Books, 2001.

Crow, W. B. *The Occult Properties of Herbs & Plants*. Wellingborough, Northamptonshire, UK: The Aquarian Press, 1980.

Cunningham, Scott. *The Complete Book of Incense, Oils & Brews*. St. Paul, MN: Llewellyn Publications, 1989.

————. *Cunningham's Encyclopedia of Magical Herbs*. St. Paul, MN: Llewellyn Publications, 1985.

————. *Magical Herbalism: The Secret Craft of the Wise*. St. Paul, MN: Llewellyn Publications, 1986.

Damian, Peter, and Kate Damian. *Aromatherapy: Scent and Psyche*. Rochester, VT: Healing Arts Press, 1995.

Fettner, Ann Tucker. *Potpourri, Incense and Other Fragrant Concoctions*. New York: Workman Publishing Company, 1977.

Fischer-Rizzi, Susanne. *The Complete Incense Book*. New York: Sterling Publishing, 1998.

Friedman, John Block, and Kristen Mossler Figg, eds. *Trade, Travel, and Exploration in the Middle Ages: An Encyclopedia*. New York: Garland Publishing, 2000.

Galadriel, Lady. *The Magick of Incense and Oils*. Oxford: Twin Serpents, 2006.

Gardner, Amanda. "Long-term Exposure to Incense Raises Cancer Risk" in *US News*; available from http://health.usnews.com/health-news/family-health/cancer/articles/2008/08/25/long-term-exposure-to-incense-raises-cancer-risk: Internet; accessed March 20, 2011.

Groom, Nigel. *Frankincense and Myrrh: A Study of the Arabian Incense Trade*. London: Longman, 1981.

Heger, Paul. *The Development of Incense Cult in Israel*. New York: Walter de Gruyter, 1997.

Le Guérer, Annick. *Scent: The Mysterious and Essential Powers of Smell*. Trans. Richard Miller. New York: Turtle Bay Books, 1992.

Gunter, Ann C. *Caravan Kingdoms: Yemen and the Ancient Incense Trade*. Washington, D.C.: Smithsonian Institute, 2005.

Hyams, Gina. *Incense: Rituals, Mystery, Lore*. San Francisco: Chronicle Books, 2004.

Junemann, Monika. *Enchanting Scents: The Secrets of Aroma Therapy, Fragrant Essences that Stimulate, Activate and Inspire Body, Mind and Spirit*. Durach-Bechen, Germany: Lotus Press, 1988.

Kinkele, Thomas. *Incense and Incense Rituals*. Trans. Christine M. Grimm. Twin Lakes, WI: Lotus Press, 2004.

Langenheim, Jean H. *Plant Resins: Chemistry, Evolution, Ecology, and Ethnobotany*. Portland, OR: Timber Press, 2003.

McCampbell, Harvest. *Sacred Smoke: The Ancient Art of Smudging for Modern Times*. Summertown, TN: Native Voices, 2002.

Malbrough, Ray. *Charms, Spells & Formulas*. Woodbury, MN: Llewellyn Publications, 1998.

Miller, Richard Alan. *The Magical and Ritual Use of Herbs*. Rochester, VT: Destiny Books, 1993.

Moldenke, Harold N., and Alma L. Moldenke. *Plants of the Bible*. London: Kegan Paul, 2002.

Morgan, Keith. *Making Magickal Incense & Ritual Perfumes*. London: Pentacle Enterprises, 1993.

Morita, Kiyoko. *The Book of Incense: Enjoying the Traditional Art of Japanese Scents.* Tokyo: Kodansha International, 1992.

Mulryan, Lenore Hoag. *Ceramic Trees of Life: Popular Art from Mexico.* Los Angeles: UCLA Fowler Museum Of Cultural History, 2003.

Neal, Carl F. *Incense: Crafting & Use of Magickal Scents.* St. Paul, MN: Llewellyn Publications, 2003.

"Occupational safety and health guideline for dipropylene glycol methyl ether" in Occupational Safety and Health Administration (OSHA) Health Guidelines database [database online]; available from http://www.osha-slc.gov/SLTC/ healthguidelines/dipropyleneglycolmethyl ether/recognition.html; Internet; accessed June 28, 2002.

Oller, David. *Kodo: The Japanese Incense Ceremony.* Albuquerque, NM: Esoterics LLC, 2002.

———— "Yes! We Have No Bananas" available from http://www.oller .net/incense/yeswe.htm: Internet; accessed December 31, 2006.

Pybus, David, and Charles Sell. *The Chemistry of Fragrances.* Cambridge: Royal Society of Chemistry, 2004.

Quinlan, Ginger. *Scents of the Soul.* Findhorn, Forres, Scotland: Findhorn Press, 2009.

Ronngren, Diane. *Sage & Smudge: The Ultimate Guide.* Reno, NV: ETC Publishing, 2003.

Rouby, Catherine, et al, eds. *Olfaction, Taste, and Cognition.* Cambridge: Cambridge University Press, 2002.

Schafer, Edward H. *The Golden Peaches of Samarkand: A Study of T'ang Exotics.* Berkley, CA: University of California Press, 1963.

Smith, Steven R. *Wylundt's Book of Incense.* York Beach, ME: Weiser, 1989.

Stoddart, D. Michael. *The Scented Ape: The Biology and Culture of Human Odour.* Cambridge: Cambridge University Press, 1990.

Turin, Luca. *The Secret of Scent.* New York: Ecco, 2006.

Unknown. "Propylele Glycols" available from http://dow.com/propylene glycol/app/foodflav.html: Internet; accessed December 2, 2006.

Unknown. "TRP Agarwood Project Information and Conference Web Site" available from http://www.therainforestproject.net/page7.htm: Internet; accessed December 7, 2010.

Vinci, Leo. *Incense: Its Ritual Significance, Use and Preparation.* Wellingborough, Northamptonshire, UK: Red Wheel Weiser, 1980.

Watt, Martin, and Wanda Sellar. *Frankincense & Myrrh.* Saffron Walden, Essex, UK: C. W. Daniel, 1996.

Wildwood, Chrissie. *The Bloomsbury Encyclopedia of Aromatherapy.* London: Bloomsbury, 1996.

Index